AT THE FRONT LINE

AT THE FRONT LINE

Experiences of Australian Soldiers in World War II

MARK JOHNSTON

CAMBRIDGE
UNIVERSITY PRESS

Published by the Press Syndicate of the University of Cambridge
The Pitt Building, Trumpington Street, Cambridge CB2 1RP, UK
40 West 20th Street, New York, NY 10011–4211, USA
10 Stamford Road, Oakleigh, Melbourne 3166, Australia

Printed in Australia by Australian Print Group

National Library of Australia cataloguing-in-publication data

Johnston, Mark Robert, 1960–
At the front line: experiences of Australian soldiers in
World War II.
Bibliography.
Includes index.
1. World War, 1939–1945 – Personal narratives, Australian.
2. World War, 1939–1945 – Australia I. Title.
940.541294

Library of Congress cataloguing-in-publication data

Johnston, Mark, 1960–
At the front line: experiences of Australian soldiers in World
War II/Mark Johnston.
p.   cm.
Includes bibliographical references (p.   ) and index.
1. World War, 1939–45 – Personal narratives, Australian.
2. World War, 1939–1945 – Campaigns. 3. Soldiers – Australia –
Biography. 4. Australia. Australian Army – Biography. I. Title.
D767.8.J62 1966
940.54′8194–dc20   96–6066

A catalogue record for this book is available from the British Libarary.

ISBN 0 521 56037 3 Hardback

Contents

vi   CONTENTS

Plates

Unless otherwise stated, all pictures are courtesy of the Australian War Memorial, Canberra.

Jacket
Strained but triumphant mates of the 2/12th Battalion, photographed after helping to capture a Japanese mountain gun on Mt Prothero, New Guinea, in January 1944.

Facing page 50
An Australian writes home from front-line Tobruk in August 1941.

Exhausted and strained Australian troops rest after the charge that captured Gona, in December 1942.

In January 1945, men of the 9th Battalion move past temporary graves of Australians killed in recent fighting on Bougainville.

At Sattelberg in New Guinea, November 1943. Infantrymen are tensed to go 'over the top'.

In December 1943, two privates wait pensively for the order to advance on Shaggy Ridge in New Guinea.

Happy Australian infantrymen, some of them wounded, have disembarked at Alexandria after leaving Tobruk in September 1941.

A forward observation post in the Sanananda area, January 1943.

Australian infantrymen on Bougainville in January 1945 await a possible Japanese raid in their water-filled dugout.

This private has just been wounded by a Japanese grenade on Shaggy Ridge in December 1943.

Tired but proud victors of Bardia, where the Second A.I.F. tradition was founded in January 1941.

Facing page 122
An Australian looks reverently at the Tobruk grave of Corporal John Edmondson, V.C.

Soldiers working together in the perilous conditions of Buna, December 1942.

Two Australians carry a wounded mate to medical help in appalling conditions near Lae, in September 1943.

Soldiers sleep on the bench seats of the grandstand at the Adelaide Oval in 1942.

Tobruk, 1941. Captured Italian anti-aircraft guns in use against bombardment by German aircraft.

An infantryman's comment on the migration of front-line soldiers to base units.

In a front-line position in New Guinea under enemy bombardment, tired but cheerful infantrymen receive mail.

Militiamen of the 61st Battalion patrolling at Milne Bay, in September 1942.

September 1942. Militiamen of the 3rd Battalion prepare to go on patrol.

In February 1945 an Australian infantryman carries a cross to a forward position on Bougainville, where it will mark the burial place of a comrade killed in action.

Tables

ix

Acknowledgements

This book has taken the best part of ten years to produce. Its origins lay in a PhD thesis begun at the University of Melbourne in 1988 and completed in 1991. I am grateful for the help offered by the three supervisors of that project: Dr Lloyd Robson, who advised me in 1988; during the compilation of evidence Dr D. E. Kennedy, who oversaw the main part of the work through 1989 and 1990; and Dr John Lack, who saw the thesis through its final stages in 1991. Dr Barbara Falk also read the work and offered invaluable advice on style. In the process of turning the thesis into a book, I was given valuable criticism and advice by Dr E. M. Andrews, Dr Bill Gammage, Dr Jeffrey Grey and Associate Professor John McCarthy. I am very grateful for the editorial support of Cambridge University Press, in particular Phillipa McGuinness and Jane Farago, and my copy editor Janet Bunny.

My thanks also to the staffs of the Australian War Memorial in Canberra (notably Ron Gilchrist, Jane West and Andrew Jack), the Australian Archives (Victoria) at Brighton (especially Tim Bryant), the Central Army Records Office (notably Tony Roe, Kevin Canny and Claudio Cominotto) and the La Trobe Library in Melbourne, the Mortlock Library in Adelaide and the Mitchell Library in Sydney. Dr John Barrett, of La Trobe University, generously gave me access to the archive he created for *We Were There*, his indispensable survey of Australian soldiers in World War II. This enabled me to get in touch with several veterans who lent me useful documents. My mother, Jan Johnston, located an important archival document in Tasmania.

This project has depended very largely on materials lent to me by private donors, and I have many debts of gratitude in this regard. My apologies go to the many people who lent or offered material that I have been unable to use here. Those whose documents I have used are listed in the bibliography.

My particular thanks go to those who offered information or assistance beyond the diaries or letters they sent. Prominent among these people are: Grace Butler; Mrs E. Currie; Ron Eaton; Cec Greenwood; Lola Jones; Mrs E. McKean; Ern MacLeod, M.B.E.; Don Mearns; Thomas Neeman, M.M.; Mavis Parks; and H. C. and R. Sunley. Thanks are also due to the secretaries or presidents of various battalion associations: especially Max Herron (2/1st Pioneer Battalion), Charlie Crouch (2/8th Battalion), Frank Gillen (2/6th Battalion), F.G. Yoxon (2/23rd Battalion) and Jack Marotte, Tom Gilchrist and Laurie Catchlove (2/43rd Battalion, in Victoria and South Australia).

Several veterans made a substantial contribution to the text through their answers to questions about diaries, namely Bob Anson (who helped the project in many ways), Jack Craig, Reg Dove, Winston Fairbrother, John May, M.B.E., Les Murphy, Phil O'Brien, Claude O'Dea, Mick Paget and Bill Phillips.

A special word of appreciation goes to four veterans who read large parts or all of the draft chapters of the original thesis. John Lovegrove offered advice on the combat chapters. Clive Edwards, whose wartime writings have been invaluable, read all the chapters. Gordon Combe, C.M.G., M.C., whose memoirs have been a superb source of quotation and reference, offered detailed criticism of chapters in two drafts of the work. Allan Jones contributed enormously to the project with original documents, his memoirs, comments on the drafts, and answers to numerous questions. The assistance of these former front-line soldiers has made an immeasurable contribution not only to the accuracy of the work but also to the morale of its author. Of course, the responsibility for any errors of fact or interpretation is entirely my own.

The extracts on pages 46, 47, 49, 53, 80 and 81 © Copyright *The Medical Journal of Australia* and on page 86 Copyright Melway Publishing Pty. Ltd. are reproduced with permission.

Without the encouragement of my wife, Deborah, this project would not have been commenced. Without her love and patience, it would not have been completed.

Conventions and Abbreviations

The most detailed information about sources appears in the bibliography.

On the first occasion that each soldier-writer is referred to in a chapter, the reference in the endnotes is presented as follows: the rank of the soldier at the time he wrote the relevant comment; his initial and surname; his unit at the time of writing; the written document (usually a letter or diary); and the date of writing. As the following typical note shows, most of this information is presented in abbreviated form:

Tpr B. Love, 2/7 Cav. Regt, D23/12/42.

By referring to the key below, the reader can decipher this example as showing that the reference is to the diary entry written by Trooper B. Love of the 2/7th Cavalry Regiment on 23 December 1942. More detailed information about B. Love and his writings can be found in the bibliography, but subsequent references within the same chapter as the above will be less detailed. Unless the next reference to him concerns a comment made when his rank and/or unit was other than in the first reference, only his surname and/or details of the diary entry will appear, thus:

Love, D19/1/43.

If his rank and/or unit had changed, this information would be included, in the order shown above, thus:

Sgt Love, 2/12 Bn, D20/12/43.

Any second or subsequent reference to a soldier will not include information about rank or unit unless at the time he wrote the pertinent comment these biographical details were other than in the preceding reference (not necessarily the first).

If I am in doubt about any of the biographical or bibliographical details – often the case with dates – a question mark appears next to the uncertain information.

Even with these abbreviations, the notes are lengthy, and so the subtitles of published works, which in unit histories tend to be very long, have generally been presented only in the Bibliography. In many cases, more references than I have given are available for the notes.

Key to Abbreviations Used for Repositories, Ranks, Units and Sources

Repositories

A.A.V.	Australian Archives (Victoria)
A.A.T.	Australian Archives (Tasmania)
A.W.M.	Australian War Memorial
M.L.	Mitchell Library
MS	La Trobe Library
PRG	Mortlock Library

Ranks

A/–	Acting/(usually A/Cpl or A/Sgt)
Bdr	Bombardier
Brig.	Brigadier
Capt.	Captain
Cpl	Corporal
Gnr	Gunner
L/–	Lance/ (usually L/Cpl or L/Sgt)
Lt	Lieutenant
Lt-Col	Lieutenant-Colonel
Maj.	Major
Maj.-Gen.	Major-General
Pte	Private
R.S.M.	Regimental Sergeant Major

S/	Staff (usually S/Sgt)
Sgt	Sergeant
Sigmn	Signalman
Spr	Sapper
Tpr	Trooper
W.O.II	Warrant Officer Class II

Unit titles

A.A.M.C.	Australian Army Medical Corps
A.A.R.D.	Australian Advanced Reinforcement Depot
A.A.S.C.	Australian Army Service Corps
A.G.H.	Australian General Hospital
A.I.F.	Australian Imperial Force
Amb.	Ambulance
Amn	Ammunition
A-Tk	Anti-tank
Bde	Brigade
Bn	Battalion
Bty	Battery
Cav.	Cavalry
Cdo	Commando
C.M.F.	Citizen Military Forces
Con.	Convalescent
Coy	Company
Div.	Division
Fd	Field
Fd Coy	Field company (basic unit of engineers)
Fd Regt	Field regiment (basic unit of artillery)
G.B.D.	General base depot
H.Q.	Headquarters
Indep. Coy	Independent Company
I.T.B.	Infantry training battalion
M.G.	Machine gun
O.C.T.U.	Officer cadet training unit
Ord.	Ordnance
Pnr	Pioneer
Pro.	Provost
Regt	Regiment
Reinft or Rft	Reinforcement

Rlwy Constr.	Railway construction
Sigs	Signals
Svy	Survey

Note: the type of unit most often referred to in the footnotes is the battalion. Where 'Bn' is immediately preceded by a number in a note, it always refers to an infantry battalion. Where that number has the prefix '2/', as in 2/24 Bn, it refers to an original Second A.I.F. battalion; where it has a prefix higher than 2, or no prefix at all, it refers to an original C.M.F. battalion, as in 29/46 Bn, 24 Bn. The same system applied to most units other than battalions, although the brigades with numbers from 16 to 27 (without prefixes) and divisions numbered 6 to 9 (without prefixes) were original Second A.I.F. formations.

Codes for sources

D	Diary
DR	Diary with additional postwar comments or reconstruction
LB	Letter to business or other institution (for example, school)
LC	Letter to writer's child
LF	Letter to female friend or acquaintance (not necessarily romantic)
LK	Letter to relative outside immediate family (kin)
LM	Letter to male friend
LP	Letter to parent or family
LS	Letter to sibling
LU	Letter to unidentified recipient
LW	Letter to wife
MS	Manuscript

Introduction

Two days into his second New Guinea campaign, Private Arthur Wallin recommenced the task of keeping a daily record of his thoughts and experiences. He was not very optimistic about the project, for after noting that his equipment weighed about 40 pounds he reflected: 'I dont know how long I will persist with this descriptive effort. Most likely end up by throwing pen and ink, paper also, away as the going gets harder.'[1] He chose to continue his daily reflections for the remaining eight months of the campaign, and the result is fascinating in the detail it gives of the life of Australian infantrymen at the front, and especially of the way he and his comrades responded to the extraordinary stresses under which they were serving.

Fortunately, hundreds of other Australian front-line soldiers kept diaries and wrote letters in which they told of their responses to their new and unnatural lives, and their accounts make a revealing study of Australian front-line soldiers' reactions to their ordeal in World War II. The main components of that ordeal were the physical and mental stresses imposed by service within firing range of the enemy, as well as the more general strains that membership of the army entailed. Whereas soldiers throughout the army could feel burdens such as inefficiency, boredom and inequality, the additional stresses of the front line gave a different dimension to the experience of the combat soldier.

The heart of the work is an archive of wartime testimonies written by more than 300 soldiers. The letters and diaries that comprise almost all of this archive were produced by a very diverse group, including soldiers from nearly every battalion and regiment that saw action, and who served in every major campaign in which Australian troops fought. Some of these sources are diaries written by men in German or Japanese captivity, but the tribulations of prisoners of war are a huge topic in themselves, and so only those parts of the diaries that refer to the period between enlistment and capture have been used here. Commando-type activities have also had to be excluded because of limitations of space.

The writings of more than half the individuals represented are to be found in public archives and libraries, where they have been collected since the war. However, the single greatest source of my material has been private donors.

Wartime army documents, official and regimental histories, published and unpublished memoirs and other writings are cited here in order to supplement and substantiate the conclusions drawn from the letters and diaries. When supplementary evidence has not been available, I have had to speculate upon what seems probable. In so doing, I have sought where possible the advice of war veterans and tried to make comparisons with other armies, although a systematic set of such comparisons falls outside the scope of this work. My speculations are thus informed, but necessarily inconclusive. Wherever the terms 'most', 'some', 'many' or 'a few' occur, they must be taken, unless stated otherwise, not as statistically established but as interpretations based on the material available. In this I am following the precedent of Bill Gammage's *The Broken Years*, which concerns Australian soldiers in World War I.[2] Like him I have also provided, in Appendix B, a statistical comparison of my sample and the population from which they came. Readers who wish to look further into the claims made in this book are invited to look at the much more detailed and academic evidence in my original thesis, which can be found in the Baillieu Library at the University of Melbourne.

At the Front Line is less a study of specific individuals than of the messages their writings convey about the nature of the ordeal they and their fellow-soldiers endured.

Although the Australian army was more literate than armies in the past, its men made so many errors of spelling, grammar and especially punctuation in their writing, that as a matter of good style, '*sic*' has been omitted after errors in the quotations made in this text.

In their communications Australian front-line troops were generally men of few words. It would, for instance, be difficult to imagine a more laconic or prosaic description of traumatic happenings than this diary entry concerning an action near Alamein: 'Arrived in area, and started attack at about 5 oclock, had to go 3,000 yards. Have had 4 casualties in section this morning, only 4 of us left.'[3] Or this account of the Australian assault on Tobruk: 'The day of the attack we put over a heavy barrage and when the infantry advanced the Italians surrendered.'[4]

On the other hand, many soldiers wrote long as well as short letters and diary entries. This suggests that the following comment, by a normally reticent writer, was fairly representative: 'no doubt you will be surprised at my long-windedness, but I felt in the mood to write and my mind was clear about it all'.[5]

One should not overstate the literary limitations of the soldiers' writings. In fact, in many cases their words have enormous emotional power. They remind the reader of the American wartime censor's comment on the G.I.s' letters: 'I read some of the greatest prose in the English language, written by kids who couldn't spell. It didn't matter. It was the feeling.'[6] For example, most Australians would find something touching about the few, apparently unremarkable words penned by a soldier on hearing of the death of one of his best friends elsewhere on the Alamein battlefield: ' . . . heard that Baron died, rotten bloody news'.[7] In the chapters that follow, it should become clear that Australians' wartime writings contain much that is touching, shocking and even amusing. They move the emotions not so much through inspired or even very expressive language — although neither is entirely absent — as through the direct, matter-of-fact simplicity with which men described and responded to the dreadful realities of war.

Wartime censorship was to some extent a limiting factor in communication. All mail was subject to random censorship at base. The letters of the man in the ranks had also to be read, or 'franked', by an officer in his unit. The only exception to this rule was that letters sent in special, hard-to-obtain green envelopes could bypass the unit censorship stage. Each officer censored his own mail until June 1945, when, on the grounds that there was too much criticism of strategy, unit censorship was also introduced for those below the rank of command-ing officer of a unit.

Sometimes the regulations were very strict, as in New Guinea campaigns where troops were prohibited from mentioning their location or operations, even though radio and newspapers were already disseminating that information. However, restrictions usually seem to have relaxed during or soon after campaigns.

Even when censors did not interfere, soldiers often felt constrained in what they could write, and there were complaints that the knowledge that a third party would read one's missives cramped one's style. The only constraint that worried some was on their ability to express romantic feelings, but others felt inhibited, and with good reason, about writing of matters more germane to this book.

In particular, little could be said about forthcoming actions, which of course had to remain secret. Officers, who were generally in a pos-ition to write with less personal restraint than the other ranks, were likely to be most careful with security: this is typified by a passage in a lieutenant's letter from Tobruk, which concludes suddenly with a hole in the page, followed by the words, 'Sorry – decided I said too much.'[8]

However, as in World War I, by far the most important sources of censorship infringement and excision were references to location and destination, and the inclusion or exclusion of those matters in the let-ters has little or no bearing on the subject-matter of this book. One indication of the fact that places, rather than attitudes or activities, were the censors' main concern is that the strictest censorship generally seems to have applied on troopships taking men overseas.

The vast majority of letters fared well under the eye of the censor. Official figures for the 18 months between December 1943 and May 1945 suggest that a monthly average of approximately 1.5 per cent of letters were 'treated' and 0.24 per cent 'stopped' at base.[9] The letters consulted for this work show remarkably little evidence of cutting by censors and much evidence that a surprising degree of latitude was given to soldiers writing from the front.

Australians were able to write fairly openly about their lives in the army mainly because censorship regulations allowed consderable scope for 'complaints, flippant criticisms, grumbling or abuse'.[10] Another reason was probably that unit censors shared many attitudes with their subordinates: a fact which received powerful, and admittedly unique, expression at the conclusion of a letter from Singapore. The soldier-author concluded his description of the situation with a defiant 'We can take it!', beneath which the unit censor (presumably a unit officer) added not merely the usual signature, but also 'And how! – Censor.'[11]

I have divided the book into three main parts. The first, entitled 'The Front Line', deals with how soldiers responded to the stresses of front-line service. The second, 'The Army Way', analyzes the difficulties Australian front-line soldiers experienced less because of the enemy than because of their own army. The final section, 'Mates', is a critical examination of the mateship that was central to Australians' reactions to the strains they felt at and behind the line.

The first three chapters focus on the physical and mental ordeals inherent in front-line service, and an examination follows in Chapter 4 of the circumstances that led some men to collapse under these strains. Chapter 5 offers an explanation of why Australian soldiers seem generally to have been able to cope with battlefield stress.

The second part of the work focuses on aspects of army life that often challenged the soldiers' equanimity: the callousness, inefficiency and inequality they criticized in their own army. This discussion raises the question of whether and why Australians put up with these burdens: that is, how 'disciplined' were Australian soldiers? This is a longstanding issue in writing about Australians at war. Another common theme is that of wartime mateship, and in the last section that cherished icon comes under scrutiny for flaws and inconsistencies.

Readers who want more information about the definition of front-line soldiers, about the organization of front-line units or the chronology of Australia's campaigns, are directed to Appendix A, 'Who Fought Where'.

This book is not intended to deify or demolish the Australian soldier. For the most part I have great admiration and sympathy for the men under discussion here, but my guiding aim has been to present an accurate interpretation of the behaviour of Australian fighting soldiers under the burdens of service in World War II.

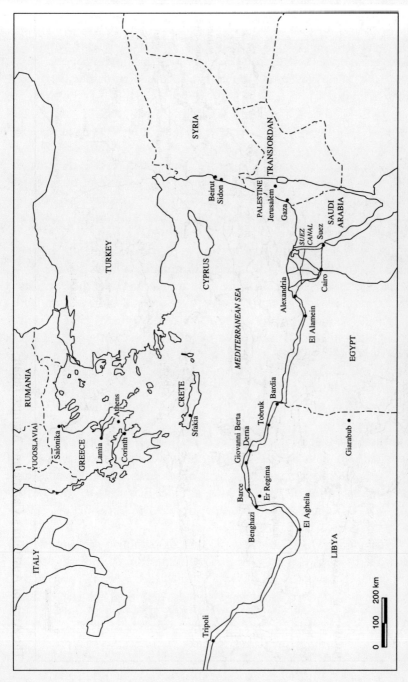

The Area of Australia's Campaigns in the Eastern Mediterranean

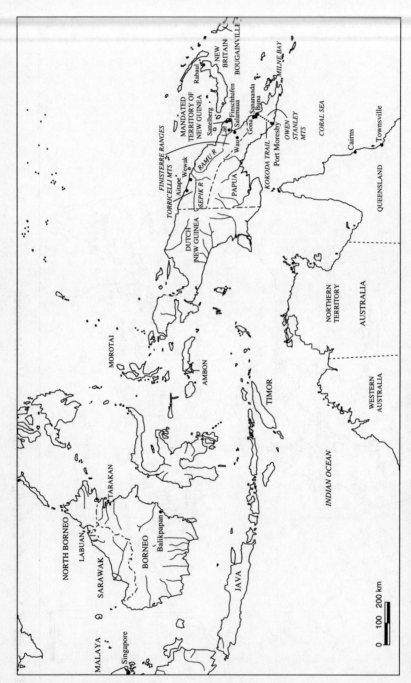

The Area of Australia's Campaigns Against Japan

PART ONE

THE FRONT LINE

CHAPTER ONE

THE UNNATURAL LIFE AT THE FRONT

*S*oon after arriving in a forward area in Papua, a diarist in a regiment waiting for its first action wrote of an encounter with a group of veterans who were being evacuated: 'Those fellows certainly looked "all in". "Yes", they told us, "it's tough up there".'[1]

Front-line soldiering, the life 'up there', has always been the art of the barely possible. In executing orders, the combat soldier frequently pushes himself to the very limits of endurance. His is what one Australian infantryman called an 'unnatural life'.[2] That life's exacting quality emerges again and again in the testimonies written by Australian front-line soldiers in World War II.

FEET AND BACKS

Combat soldiers commented repeatedly on their trying physical experience. Australians marched themselves to exhaustion in almost every campaign. Men in rifle companies, especially, could be sure that in any operation, marching would comprise a substantial and tiring part of their movements to and at the front.

For example, although motorization was important in the Australians' first campaign, in Libya, the infantry covered great distances on foot. During the two main battles, the assaults on Bardia and Tobruk, men of all three participating brigades made wearying marches. At Tobruk on 21 January 1941, for instance, the 2/8th

3

Battalion marched 32 kilometres, the last 8 of them in action. Of the
march preparatory to the assault, one member wrote 'my feet felt as
though they were worn down to the knees'.[3]

Much more footslogging was ahead of this and other units in the
two weeks between the fall of Tobruk and the entry into Benghazi. In
the three days culminating in the fall of Giovanni Berta, for instance,
the 2/8th marched approximately 85 kilometres and the 2/7th Battalion 120 kilometres, mostly over difficult country. Writing home
about this chase to Benghazi, Signalman Neeman, who had travelled by
truck throughout, noted that ' "the infantry god protect them" were
almost marched off their feet in the effort to close up on the retreating
enemy'.[4]

Australians marched further in this than in any other Middle Eastern campaign, although the mountainous terrain of Greece, Crete and
Syria made for treks that were even more gruelling. In Syria, which
probably saw the most physically exhausting campaign of Australia's
Middle Eastern war, Signalman Neeman wrote sadly that his signals
section had had to abandon the luxuries of the truck and, accompanied
by load-carrying mules, proceed laboriously on foot.[5] This was a fore-
taste of things to come, for in the South-West Pacific Area (S.W.P.A.)
nearly all soldiers became foot soldiers.

An official wartime publication reported that any Australian in
New Guinea's jungles would tell you: 'You can't get any place in this
blanky country without going on your flat feet.'[6] In fact, occasionally it
was possible to use air and motor transport, but only as a prelude to
hard marching.

Footslogging in the S.W.P.A. was nearly always exhausting. Most
movement was confined to tracks or trails, which under concentrated
foot traffic and constant dampness were almost universally and per-
petually muddy. Ankle-deep mud was commonplace, and knee-deep
not unusual on these tenuous lifelines. As well as having to drag their
feet laboriously through the quagmire, most soldiers suffered energy-
sapping falls in the mud. Two extracts from diaries kept on the Kokoda
Trail note the difficulty of maintaining one's footing:

> ... we move on over dreadful tracks mud ankle deep added to
> this. it commences to rain. moving down a mountain side
> almost straight up and down. slipping and sliding in all direc-
> tions.

Trail rough steep and slippery . . . Track slippery some place
had to crawl hands and knees . . . Slip, slide slither, Climbing
almost perpen-dicular descent likewise.[7]

Negotiating, and especially climbing, the hills, ridges and mountains of
New Guinea were the greatest physical challenges on these tracks. After
reaching the end of the Kokoda Trail, an infantry officer wrote to his
former headmaster: 'I have seen men standing knee deep in the mud of
a narrow mountain track, looking with complete despair at yet another
seemingly insurmountable ridge. Ridge after ridge, ridge after ridge,
heart breaking, hopeless, futile country'.[8]

'Heart breaking' also figured in another infantryman's compelling
description of the physical demands of the same mountainous trail:

> For a heart-breaking trail I don't think that Hannibal or Napo-
> leon when they crossed the Alps could have wept the tears of
> blood that we did. They consist not of one vast mountain
> range but a series of peaks and valleys which follow each other
> in rapid and monotonous succession. How our legs took us
> over them I am to this day uncertain. The slopes are almost
> perpendicular and the track lay along a native pad . . . The pad
> always passes over the highest point of the mountains – there
> is no way around as the contours do not run true to form and
> on the sides you will be confronted by precipitous slopes.[9]

Watery tears are also said to have been shed over the climbs necessitated by the trail.

Other tracks also imposed arduous climbs. Soldiers in nearly every
campaign had reason to agree with Signalman Neeman's remark to his
wife that there was 'always a damn mountain somewhere ahead which
we have to climb over'. In commenting on a track in the Wau-Salamaua
region, he also pointed out that climbing in the steepest areas was not
merely backbreaking and exhausting, but also dangerous:

> The track over which we travelled wound its way over the
> worst part of New Guinea, what I've seen anyway; just a nar-
> row ledge track around steep sided mountains sheer drops of
> hundreds of feet in places . . . been several lucky escapes . . .
> Capt Scott went over only saved himself from a long drop by
> managing to grab hold of some nettles which took his weight
> for long enough for somebody to give assistance.[10]

Writing from the same area, a 34-year-old officer told his wife: 'You should see me scrambling up almost vertical slopes in the mud, hanging on with everything but my teeth. Tarzan of the Apes would have to go into severe training to stand up to this country.'[11] New Guinea was essentially a young man's country, particularly in the steep areas that sometimes had to be ascended without the benefit of a track. Campaigning in inland regions was largely a matter of capturing the high ground that dominated tracks and valleys. However, despite the drawbacks of mountain life, some found it preferable to the denser vegetation and greater heat of the coast.

Wherever they experienced jungle warfare, Australians sweated so profusely that compensatory salt tablets became regular issue in the S.W.P.A. If the need to travel almost exclusively on foot was a major reason for this, so was the need to carry virtually all one's requirements when marching. Unlike the operational areas in the Middle East, those in the Pacific were generally inaccessible to support vehicles. Moreover, in circumstances that often decreed units would become widely dispersed or would advance rapidly, men could leave fewer of their possessions in organized dumps. One's home tended to be on one's back, especially in mountainous areas.

Thus troops advancing on various tracks in the S.W.P.A. faced the prospect of going into action at any moment loaded with up to 32 kilograms of gear. Table 1 gives a sample of what men carried in the New Guinea campaigns.

These weights alone ensured the rapid exhaustion of their bearers, but other factors increased the loads; for instance, the mud which gathered on boots and the water which soaked clothing, adding 1.5 kilograms weight to webbing alone. Riflemen also frequently had to carry ammunition for Bren guns and mortars, as well as taking turns with equipment such as Brens and tools. For signallers, mortarmen and machine-gunners the loads were often even heavier, although behind the lines in most New Guinea campaigns native carriers helped with the heaviest items.

The physical cost of carrying such weights was high. Some members of the 58/59th Battalion were said to have lost two stone (about 14 kilograms) in an appalling four-day march to the front line in June 1943. The legendary rigours of the Kokoda Trail were arguably due more to the weights carried than to the difficulty of the terrain. Certainly the 7th Division's senior medical officer concluded that the

TABLE 1: Some typical loads carried by Australian soldiers in New Guinea, 1942–5

(Weights are given in the measures presented in the sources. 1 lb = 0.45 kg)

1 September 1942: Riflemen of the 2/27th Battalion at the beginning of the Kokoda Trail.[12]
Haversack: Dixie, rations, toilet gear, quinine, water tablets, mosquito ointment, boot brush, boot polish (3), tea, sugar, half towel, handkerchief, few odds and ends. *Roll on back:* Groundsheet, mosquito net, pullover, long pants, spare shirt, underclothes, socks. *Pouches:* 150 rounds small arms ammunition, 3 grenades, dozen matches, baseplates. Water bottle. Rifle. Bayonet.
Total weight: 65 lb. (An improved walking-stick was also virtually universal.)
Other recorded weights on the Kokoda Trail: 3rd Battalion (a) 15–20 kg and (b) 35 lb and 3 grenades; 2/1st Battalion 55 lb; 2/14th Battalion (a) 45 lb minimum (b) 65 lb; 2/16th Battalion 45 lb minimum; 2/33rd Battalion (a) on 10 September 1942 *c.* 55 lb and (b) from 12 September 1942 40–50 lb; 21st Brigade up to 70 lb.

May 1943: 2/6th Battalion riflemen moving to the front near Mubo[13]
Haversack: 1 tin emergency rations, one field operations ration, one day's ordinary ration, mess gear, towel, anti-mosquito cream, toilet gear, atebrin tablets. *Pack:* Spare pair boots, 2 pairs socks, one singlet, one shirt, one pair underpants, one pair trousers, mosquito net. Groundsheet, blanket. Steel helmet. Webbing equipment, clasp knife, field dressing, 1 tin emergency rations. Weapon, ammunition (50 rounds per rifleman, 100 rounds per Tommy-gunner, 100 rounds for each Bren). Water bottle. One grenade.
Total weight: Over 60 lb.
Other recorded weights in the Wau-Salamaua area: 58/59th Battalion (a) moving to Bobdubi Ridge, 19 June 1943 60 lb and (b) moving to start-line on Bobdubi Ridge, 30 June 1943 60–100 lb; some 2/6th Battalion members carried in excess of 100 lb.

September 1943–January 1944. Forward infantrymen, 9th Division, Lae-Huon Peninsula offensive.[14]
Haversack: mess tin, cigarettes, shaving and washing gear, half towel, emergency ration, mosquito repellent, chlorinating tablets, atebrin, handkerchief, writing material. *Bed-roll:* Groundsheet, mosquito net, gas cape, ration, spare socks. *Pouches:* 2–4 grenades, pair bootlaces, four-by-two to clean weapon, ammunition. Weapon.
Total weight: Unknown.
Recorded weights on Huon Peninsula: 2/32nd Battalion on way to attack Pabu, November 1943 up to 80 lb; 29/46th Battalion 80–90 lb.

February 1945: 2/6th Battalion march over the Torricellis.[15]
(In this campaign, the 2/6th generally carried less than earlier, for they had better access to supplies.)
Packs: mosquito net, shirt, trousers, 2 pairs socks, pullover, towel, laces, mess gear, day's ration. Half-tent shelter. Gas cape. Weapon and ammunition.
Total weight: Over 60 lb.

prevalence of haemorrhoids in the Owen Stanleys campaign was 'undoubtedly related to the excessive straining in climbing hills with heavy loads'.[16] A brief diary entry, written on the first full day of one man's Kokoda experience, said simply:

Most strenuous day of my life
heavily loaded

The three subsequent entries started with the word 'ditto'.[17] A similar trial emerges in a soldier's account of a move up the Sattelberg Track, a year later:

We are all loaded up with our personal equipment plus bed rolls which are wet and weigh a ton plus a bag of rations each. It's bad enough climbing mountains with only a small pack on your back, but with all this gear is going to be tough going. What a hell of a load to lump uphill all the way through mud and slush. Some of us loose our footing and finish up flat out in the mud. One feels like just lying there for ever. I don't think I have been so exhausted in all my life. After hours of agony we at last reach Coy H.Q. .... [18]

Another participant in that campaign was one of many soldiers who have drawn parallels between Australian troops and beasts of burden: 'If ever I see a man overloading a horse in future there'll be trouble. But no horse ever carried as much as an infantryman does.'[19]

Officers in the field often considered higher headquarters to be unrealistic or vague in their expectations concerning loads and, in the light of their experiences, devised scales of equipment for their men or even told them what to reduce. The men needed no prompting, and from the first New Guinea campaign not only took the approved actions of cutting towels, blankets and toothbrushes in half, but also jettisoned equipment they did not want. The general attitude of veterans in this matter was well summed up by an old campaigner who, on being invited to speak to men of a militia unit newly arrived in New Guinea, advised them to drop, 'accidentally', all surplus gear in the first river they crossed.[20]

Gear considered surplus often included helmets, gas masks (still being issued to reinforcements in mid-1943), anti-tank rifles, 2-inch mortars, blankets, and spare clothing. So intolerable was the combination of weight and terrain that even personal effects were discarded. By 1945, the army was in a better position to enable men to retrieve gear quickly and to replenish food and ammunition periodically, rather than take everything on their backs. However in 1945 soldiers still had to carry great loads, for even ruthless reductions could never safely go below a certain heavy minimum or prevent the army from adding more to the lighter loads.

On arriving in the S.W.P.A., desert veterans generally found the loads heavier than they had previously experienced, but there had always been something to carry in the Middle East too. For instance, Australians went into the assault on Bardia with loads of 22 to 32 kilograms each, and at least as much at El Alamein the following year.

DIGGING IN AND OTHER HARD LABOUR

Once the burdened and tired infantryman had reached his destination, he usually had to join in preparing a defensive position. In the jungle, for instance, he would probably be engaged in cutting any scrub that hampered observation and accurate gunfire (at least beyond grenade-throwing distance), placing barbed wire and tripwires with attached tins and booby traps, clearing spaces for headquarters, latrines, reserve ammunition, and, most arduous of all, 'digging in': that is, excavating weapon pits, a platoon headquarters, latrines, an ammunition pit and, if possible, crawl trenches.

Digging in was regarded as an even stronger imperative in the open spaces of the desert than in the more confined world of the jungle. Australian digging efforts in the desert alone would have been enough to justify the persistence of the nickname 'digger'. A shortage of excavating machinery and the fact that solid rock lay only 30 centimetres or less below ground in many areas at Bardia, Tobruk and Alamein usually made digging wearying and disheartening work.

In many places it was also never-ending work. Where positions were relatively static, notably in Tobruk, soldiers were ordered to improve and extend them through excavation. When soldiers were on the move, positions had to be dug afresh. So incessant was the digging at Alamein, for instance, that one tired diarist was struck by similarities with other burrowing animals: 'we are honestly worse than rats, at least they only use one hole but every time we move we immediately start to dig, either another one or deepen one already there'.[21]

During an earlier desert campaign, an artillery officer tried to quantify the digging, and also exemplified attitudes to it:

This war so far has consisted of 2% fighting and 98% digging.
You dig gun pits and holes to sleep in and holes to crawl into if
shelled or bombed and just when everything is finished and
with sighs of relief you relax orders to move come down. After
moving a few miles the same old digging starts all over again,
and so life goes on. There is no doubt that the digging has
saved many lives so far but it gets awful tiresome after a
while.[22]

Towards the end of the war, some four years later, another 6th Division
veteran made a similar point in the jungle: 'One gets very tired of
putting up tents, cutting bamboos making beds digging weapon pits
only to move on again a couple of days after.'[23]

As important, constant and tiring as digging was the chore of
carrying supplies. Few if any members of combat units entirely escaped
this labour in each campaign, for there was a steady demand for rations
and ammunition to be brought into the most forward positions. The
work was often done by men already tired from other exertions. After
several days of fighting in Syria, for instance, Corporal Clive Edwards
wrote of being included in a party carrying rations to other men within
his battalion: 'Dog tired to start with, we set off on a nightmare trip
which led us over the worst hills we've climbed and over some seemingly impossible obstacles.'[24]

In New Guinea, native carriers were invaluable in supplying the
front, but they were not supposed to be sent into the firing zones and
there were rarely enough of them to fill all other requirements. Thus
Australians regularly had to be sent back to make the carry from dumps
one or two hours behind the line. Aircraft dropping or landing supplies
nearby might reduce the carrying time, but still longer trips were
required of Australians when there were few or no native carriers at any
point on the supply line. The latter was the case in the Lae-Finschhafen
campaigns, wherein certain combat units did little else but make
exhausting journeys supplying other combat units that were in contact
with the enemy.

Corporal Jack Craig, who at Finschhafen endured both combat
and carrying, offered a vivid description of the latter:

Today we are carrying rations up to B Coy. and what a bastard
of a job. The track up the mountain in some places is perpen-
dicular and we are down on our hands and knees, pushing
boxes and bags of rations up a foot at a time Christ! the places

they pick for us to fight in. It took us hours just to go a few hundred yards. Yesterday the ration party had to carry wounded back down this track. How they managed, I do not know.[25]

Over extended periods such labour was naturally harmful to health. A 9th Division brigadier even described such work as 'worse than fighting'.[26]

'Fighting' was never less than physically exacting. The marching involved in moving to and at the front did not end when combat began, for a feature of World War II combat on all fronts was, that regardless of the weight of fire from supporting arms, victory had ultimately to be won by the foot soldiers who advanced and took enemy ground. When Australian attacks failed to achieve that goal, physical exhaustion was often a factor.

The wide gaps between front lines in the desert campaigns – at Alamein, for instance, they were about ten times further apart than the average forward trenches in World War I – ensured that a day's fighting demanded wearying movement there. Similarly, reaching the point of contact in Syria's mountains or the jungle was often an ordeal that left men exhausted even before they began to fight. We already have noted that it was tiring to march at a steady pace in the jungle: add to that a need to charge or take cover and the enervating nature of jungle fighting becomes clear.

SLEEP LOSS, DISEASE AND HUNGER

Combat often entailed not only tiring exertion but also loss of sleep. A World War I veteran participating in the fighting on the Kokoda Trail noted in his diary: 'Lay down on ground Slept till daybreak. first sleep for over 30 hrs : Had held up Japs for that period.'[27] During the Battle of El Alamein, some went without sleep for four to five days. Others endured the same period with just three or four hours' sleep in the fighting on Singapore. Their one consolation in its surrender was that they could at last get some rest. The Malayan campaign was for many not just a matter of costly and ultimately unsuccessful fighting, but a wearying mixture of fighting and withdrawing. Retreat was always exhausting.

Men at the front also lost sleep because of nocturnal patrols, sentry duty, the noise of shelling and bombing, lack of adequate bedding, the

hard ground of the Middle East and the damp ground in the tropics
Australians in North Africa often spent their nights fighting, patrolling
or digging so that they had some concealment in the desert's open
expanses. They then had to try to sleep during the day, in great heat,
and plagued by flies and fleas.

A powerful source of insomnia during the fighting in Papua were
the mites that caused 'scrub itch', which consisted of intensely irritating bites scattered over the body and especially around the feet and
ankles. A still more potent enemy of vigour in the tropics was the mosquito; this was not only a 24-hour pest but a source of debilitating
disease. After 1942, malaria was by far the greatest pathological threat,
and arguably the greatest military threat, facing the Australian army. It
accounted for 44 per cent and 83 per cent respectively of the 9th and
7th divisions' casualties from all sources in the New Guinea campaigns
from September 1943 to January 1944. Eighty-six per cent of the average posted strength of the 9th Division, and 96 per cent of the 7th
Division, were evacuated sick at some time during these operations.
Virtually all who served in the Papuan campaigns of 1942 and 1943
contracted the disease.[28] One might argue that because the victims
were evacuated, their sickness is not relevant to the physical strain of
soldiering. Yet thousands were treated in their own lines or treated
themselves, and were evacuated only at the last possible moment. This
was also the case with other debilitating diseases on all fronts. For
example, many soldiered on with bowel diseases, which were very common in Tobruk, Alamein and on the Kokoda Trail.

Front-line soldiers who had no experience of being weakened by
sickness were very fortunate. Less common, but far from unknown,
was the experience of hunger and thirst worsening one's plight. This
was clear in Bombardier Adeney's account of the gruelling withdrawal
across Crete:

> We had marched 65 miles in two days the last day and night in
> which we had no water and one tin of bully beef which we
> wouldn't open because it makes you thirsty . . . Its an experi-
> ence I never want to go through again Ive been on some dry
> tracks but never one to touch that. I don't think anybody who
> took part in that march will ever forget it.[29]

His conclusion was verified in his commanding officer's correspondence: '. . . that 53 miles over the mountains with water scarce and in

the conditions it was made was the worst experience of my life'.[30] The march to Sfakia beach drove most 'close to the limit of endurance'.[31]

In the New Guinea campaigns of 1942 and 1943, difficulties and mistakes in the organization of supply condemned Australians to long periods with little food. Of the Kokoda campaign, the official medical historian writes: 'Most of the troops on the trail from Uberi to Wairopi felt the constant urge of hunger'. The word 'starvation' seemed appropriate to one veteran of the trail when he looked back later in the war. His diary of the Owen Stanleys operations offers some evidence for that impression, with references to a meal consisting of half a raw potato, and to men going without food for 24 hours at one point.[32]

In the Lae campaign, the initial ration scale set by the 9th Division's headquarters was inadequate, and circumstances forbade planned increases in rations after the landings on 4 September 1943. As a consequence, the 9th Division's first two weeks of campaigning in New Guinea's exhausting conditions were undertaken on reduced rations. Private Murphy wrote at Lae on 18 September: 'We are still living on hard rations and I think that only for Jap rice and vegetables we find in their gardens we would starve'. The problems continued after the subsequent landing at Finschhafen. A participant noted wryly in his diary: 'Finschafen fell on the 2nd Oct. Not. a bad record Lae and Finschafen in four weeks. What would happen if they fed the lad well on fruit, beer etc.'[33]

Hunger made itself felt in other campaigns, too: notably, in Greece, Syria, Malaya, Singapore and Wau-Salamaua. However, cases of malnutrition were uncommon, even amidst the privations of the Kokoda Trail. Generally, Australian troops had enough food, but considered it disgusting or monotonous. In fact, its monotony, and especially its lack of nutritional variety, seems to have been at least partly responsible for the 'mindless exhaustion' of men on the Kokoda Trail. In several other campaigns – Tobruk, Wau-Salamaua and the Huon Peninsula, for instance – the limited range of food supplies produced or threatened vitamin deficiency. The yeast extract Marmite was introduced to fill a need for Vitamin B at Wau and also at Tobruk, where ascorbic acid tablets and vitamin-reinforced margarine were used to provide other necessary supplements. Nevertheless, at least one front-line defender in Tobruk considered the consumption of tinned food the prime reason for a general 'lassitude'.[34]

EXHAUSTION

What soldiers meant when they wrote of being 'exhausted', 'dog tired' or 'done' varied, but in several campaigns participants reached a state of physical exhaustion that was extreme by any measure. At the conclusion of the retreat on the Kokoda Trail, for instance, Clive Edwards noted 'we all had a bath in the creek and I've never seen such a mob of wrecks in my life. I look so skinny that I frightened myself. . . I've lost 2 stone over this terrible trek.'[35] A corporal who was in reserve during that withdrawal said of those of his unit who were ordered forward that 'it is no exaggeration to say that I hardly knew some of the men when they returned. Capt Smith looked like a slim boy. Capt Fraser lost 3 stone.'[36]

On the retreat, many became so tired that they were barely aware that they were moving, and some had hallucinations. Even after the tide turned on the trail, most men reached much the same state at the conclusion of their advance as their colleagues had at the end of the retreat. Thus the medical officer of the 2/1st Battalion calculated that on average each member had lost 18 kilograms in the 1942 campaign. The men of the 2/2nd Battalion were so debilitated on being relieved in December 1942 that they were incapable of carrying their automatic weapons.[37]

The official history says that some Australians engaged in the fighting on Singapore actually died of exhaustion. More often, campaigning soldiers collapsed, dropped out or were evacuated because of physical fatigue. Some men succumbed to the need for sleep, even in the most unlikely places. For example, a medical officer with an infantry unit in Malaya noted in his diary: 'I was so fatigued by this time that whenever I went to ground I immediately dropped off to sleep, in spite of bursting shells and mortars'. During the fighting on the Kokoda Trail, some men of the 39th Battalion were so tired that they were 'falling asleep over their weapons even as their enemies pressed them closely'.[38]

Front-line soldiering could be as much a battle against fatigue as against the enemy. This was almost literally true at Sanananda where, in order to combat the powerful desire to sleep, some men on watch in perilously forward positions pulled the pins from grenades and held down the levers, knowing that sleep, and the release of their grip, would bring death.

Another Australian soldier's attempt to inflict mental defeat on his fatigued physical self emerges in this diary comment concerning a march during the Aitape-Wewak campaign: 'Knocker Mackenzie was my inspiration, not wishing to give him the satisfaction of seeing me crack first, I kept going, although I would have sooner sat down at more frequent intervals and rested the weary body.'[39]

Sometimes the mind was barely able to struggle with physical exhaustion, which, especially in the form of sleep deprivation, could sap powers of concentration and logical thought. The soldier might be capable of no more than telling himself that he must go on. One artillery regiment's history describes those driving its trucks during the retreat through Greece as becoming 'so drugged by exhaustion that they were insensitive to all feeling save the vital one of movement.'[40]

Battle seems often to have 'galvanized' tired Australians – one unit war diary uses that very term to describe the effect on its members of an order to make a bayonet charge during the Cretan campaign.[41] Because of this stimulation, men sometimes recognized their own exhausted state only as the fighting ended. Frank Hole recalls reaching a safe area behind the lines after barely avoiding encirclement by advancing Japanese troops in Malaya. Only then realizing how totally exhausted he was, he lay by the road and slept in his full battle equipment, including helmet.[42] Captain Laybourne Smith had a similar reaction at the end of his first, hectic day of action, the decisive day in the capture of Tobruk: 'It was only when I arrived back at the bty. position that evening that I found out what a strain all this had been as when I got out of my carrier I felt absolutely done and could only just walk.'[43]

When soldiers had to force themselves to persevere in physically trying circumstances, a concomitant was mental stress. This was clearly so among those who cried and despaired on the ridges of the Kokoda Trail. It appears too in a letter from a soldier who had been evacuated to hospital in Tobruk with a temperature of 102°: 'the Drs . . . give it various medical names, but I think that really, though the Germans couldnt kill me the desert nearly did, after 4 months trying. Many went before me. Thank God for a rest from eternal dugouts sleepless nights and all the other hardships I've told you about.'[44]

A further illustration of this point is a diarist's note written at the end of Alamein: 'So "done" that I trembled uncontrollably for 1/2 hr.' So too is an officer's diary note from the retreat in Greece: 'Bombed and machine gunned for over an hour in the pass before reaching our destination. Absolutely rooted.' Physical fatigue was a predisposing factor, though not a prerequisite, for mental breakdown.[45]

Mental struggles and stress often bore a direct relationship to physical strain, but there was in many cases little or no connection between the two. The mental battles fought by soldiers were frequently less a matter of the spirit fighting the flesh than the spirit fighting itself; not so much mind against body as mind against itself.

CHAPTER TWO

EXPERIENCES OF FEAR AND DEATH

*W*hen considering enlistment, the Australian civilians who eventually became front-line soldiers must have pondered that many of their counterparts in World War I died violently. Once in the army, and even before they reached the front, the predominantly young members of combat units had further reason to give unusual attention to the possibility of dying prematurely. In making a will they speculated as to whether it would ever be required, and when from a troopship they watched Australia's coastline fade into the distance, men asked themselves whether they would return. One of them later reflected as a prisoner of war: 'The memories of seeing the Sydney Heads fade out will never be forgotten We wondered if we would ever see them again.'[1]

Australians also thought of death whenever they imagined their first battle, for like all soldiers, they wondered whether they would 'prove' themselves in the face of danger. A lieutenant waiting to take his troops into their first action described the untried soldier as a 'man who half expects to lay down his life for his country'.[2]

A NEW PERCEPTION OF DEATH

Although death had already assumed an unusually prominent role in the soldier's mind, arrival at the front and exposure to enemy fire transformed attitudes to it. The possibility of sudden death ceased to be abstract and distant, and became instead tangible, distinct and much

17

more threatening. In this new world staying alive could no longer be taken for granted. Rather it was a demanding task, to be undertaken while obeying orders in perilous locations.

All around him the soldier saw the inadequacy of others' efforts to dodge bombs, bullets and shells while simultaneously fulfilling their tactical role. The novice might be protected by his naivety about war, as Private Hackshaw's account of Bardia shows: 'when we were moving forward we saw our first dead men, a couple of them had been left where they were with blankets over them. It was a fairly cold morning and someone said in all innocence "I bet they're cold sleeping out there".'

However, such innocence could only be temporary in the front line; soon the soldier would stumble on such horrors as the headless body seen at Bardia by another member of Hackshaw's battalion.[3] On the Kokoda Trail, where the regular flow of outgoing wounded was a persistent reminder of the cost of war, Lance-Corporal Spindler first came into contact with death in action as he passed the many Japanese and Australian bodies beside the track: 'dont like passing these bodies awful sight, smell dreadful ... more bodies. just skeletons right on track, awful sight. close my eyes as I pass.' Some three years later, Captain Lewis wrote of his first exposure to war dead, seven Japanese at Balikpapan: 'they had been well fed, well-dressed; now they were somewhat ballooned out; the smell was the same as that of most dead animals; there was no dignity in death.'[4]

The Australian's initiation to front-line soldiering reinforced his desire to live, as exemplified in a lieutenant's words after his first major action: ' ... I discovered that I shared the common desire to see tomorrow in spite of the army and income tax and mothers-in-law'.[5] Commenting on the arrival of untried reinforcements at Sanananda, Trooper Ben Love collected his thoughts after his first three weeks' campaigning: 'This glorious game of war is going to give them a nasty jar – but we all must "live and learn" they tell us – oh yes we learn all right, it's the "living" that is the snag in this game.'[6]

One can readily accept Love's argument, based on his personal experience, that expectations derived from civilian life received 'a nasty jar' when they collided with reality. Battle was a learning process, in which preconceptions were shattered. However, becoming better educated about the nature of war did not remove the obstacles to surviving its dangers.

The practical education of the battlefield could provide tactical and technical lessons, which helped to win the war. However, as far as individual protection was concerned, few if any veterans regarded their new knowledge as more than a flimsy shield against the enemy's weapons. Experience also brought familiarity with the sight of violent death, and hardened many towards it, but this knowledge did nothing to help witnesses avoid the same fate. The vastly increased threat to the front-line soldier's own life, and his repeated exposure to the violent termination of other lives, both ensured that after his first experience of action an informed and intensified fear of death was never far from his thoughts.[7]

Experienced Australian soldiers have testified to the universality of that dread. Michael O'Brien concluded from his campaigns with the 18th Brigade in North Africa and New Guinea: 'I am sure that every man has a certain amount of fear. If any man told me that he was never afraid in action I would call him a liar.' John Lovegrove, who as a member of the 9th Division fought at Tobruk, Alamein and in New Guinea, wrote of 'that sickening, gut-wrenching fear that grips every-one facing an enemy in combat, under fire, or even when crawling stealthily close to enemy defences on reconnaisance No man is spared – everyone feels it in varying degrees.'[8]

At times even those whose courage was officially recognized acknowledged fear. Tom Derrick, V.C., D.C.M., whose feats of bravery were legendary, emerges in his personal diaries as a man concerned with his own mortality. In Tobruk, at the end of his first month at the front, he reflected: 'Has been a month of disappointment, from a mar-velous time at Derna to something rotten and fearful, never knowing when one will come over with your S.X. [your number] on it.'[9] So Derrick's hopeful expectations had also been dashed by a 'rotten and fearful' reality. A few weeks later, he complained that one was 'always waiting, never knowing if your going to wake the next morning'.

The following year on the Alamein front, Derrick wrote of his conviction that an order for a recent attack had meant 'she was cur-tains'. In December 1943, one month after his V.C.-winning action at Sattelberg, he mused: 'My 4th Xmas overseas . . . I don't care where I spend the next one I only hope I'm still on deck.'[10]

Derrick could sometimes be seen chewing on hard biscuits – his battalion's favoured method of countering 'tension'. The battalion concerned was the 2/48th, the most decorated Australian battalion of the war, and the fact that it had 'a favourite ploy' in this matter illustrates the universality of front line fear. So too does the fact that in reporting on medical aspects of a period of heavy fighting in the Aitape-Wewak campaign, the regimental medical officer of one of the proud and illustrious 6th Division battalions could write of the troops' 'continual fear of death'.[11]

Some Australians asserted that during combat they were too busy to be frightened. Yet even if the combatant did become so involved that fear disappeared, prior to battle men could hardly avoid reflecting that some of their number would be dead by the end. During that waiting period, soldiers often suffered an overwhelming need to urinate frequently. The practice was called, tellingly, having a 'nervous'.

Another unwanted physical symptom of fear occurred during action. In wartime studies concerning American troops, up to one-fifth admitted losing control of their bowels because of fear, and Australian front-line soldiers suffered the same reaction. A decorated veteran of the 2/6th Battalion recalls a Japanese mountain gun causing 'numerous cases of enforced diarrhoea' in his company near Mubo. John Barrett quotes an ex-soldier as thanking God that Australian underpants were khaki.[12] Direct wartime statements about the matter are, understandably, uncommon, but there is a hint in a Tobruk defender's quip about a civilian acquaintance: 'I wrote to Harold he seemed disapionted at not coming over tell him he doesn't know how lucky he is, he also asked did I get a thrill well I dont know so much about a thrill but I felt like doing something in my pants'.[13]

Furthermore, the concluding sentences in the two following quotations – one concerning the advance on Sidon, in Syria, the other written in the Western Desert – may have more than a figurative meaning:

... by now they were dropping shells and mortors amongst us I was always wondering when one was going to lob under me the cobber would say when one lobbed rather close, 'By Jesus the bastards are dinkum'. I was too shit scared to say anything.

Stukas over this morning. They dived down on us with 'screamers' on their wings which make a high pitched noise like a 'banshee'. It is a horrifying noise and made to scare shit out of us and it sure did.[14]

Whether or not the Australians' talk of being 'shit scared' or 'shit frightened' was metaphorical, those expressions show that many could not forget fear during action. So too does the even more frequent use of the word 'hell' to describe experiences in combat. Private Clarke applied it most effectively in his little diary at one of the darkest moments of the fighting on the Kokoda Trail: 'hell on earth amongst the clouds in the mountain[s]'. In more prosaic terms, Corporal White added a logical conclusion to the use of that metaphor: 'we have been through hell since [entering Greece] I've seen all the action I want to see for a long while'.[15]

The fear and strain felt during battle also emerged in Australian soldiers' frequent expressions of relief at surviving the enemy's attempts to kill them . Nowhere was this feeling stronger than after El Alamein, as these comments suggest:

> Jerry was completely finished in our sector. What a feeling it was. The boys were laughing and joking and going on like a lot of kids who were just about to start on their Xmas holidays from school . . . How good it was to feel free and alive, to be able to walk about in daylight with [sic] the fear that was consistently in our hearts.

> Settle in on beach, after walk across mine fields German dead with booby traps. Glad that I survived. God! What a mess a dead man is after a day in this world, unburied . . . still enjoying the fact that I am alive.[16]

Many who during the action had been able to shut out the risks of what they had been doing now suffered terrible reactions. O'Brien writes: 'When a fellow is in close fighting or in an attack he really has not much time to think about anything else but what is just ahead of him and to do the jobs set out for him. I have been very jumpy and afraid for a few days after a hand to hand fight.'[17]

These men needed complete rest for recovery. Campaigning soldiers' oft-expressed yearning for the relief that would permit such rest is further evidence of the mental strain imposed by front-line service. Private John Butler, who had longed for action before entering Tobruk, wrote three months into the siege: 'I don't think I'm alone in wishing [a wounded comrade] a speedy recovery and although we would welcome him back amongst us, a speedy return to Australia. No matter how selfish I am I would not wish for anyone to return to the fighting lines.'[18]

On the eve of the battle of El Alamein, Cobber Craig's experienced mates were 'cheerful and happy' after being told of their tasks; several days later they were 'praying we would be relieved'. In New Guinea in December 1942, Trooper Love recorded the elation of the men of the 2/7th Cavalry Regiment on hearing that they were to be committed to battle after two years of waiting; 16 days later, after participating in the 'ghastly nightmare' of Sanananda, he greeted news of forthcoming relief by American troops with the word 'Whoopee!'[19]

The concern with survival lasted for the duration of men's service. Thus the day after the war ended, Captain Gordon Combe, M.C., wrote to his wife: 'perhaps the great relief at the disappearance of that subconscious yet ever-present question, "Am I destined to return to my loved ones?" from our minds is the most significant change which the news of peace brings to us'.[20] Whether it had been subconscious or conscious, the fear of violent death was a burden for every front-line Australian soldier to bear.

The mental stresses associated with danger emerge in the soldiers' writing as even more burdensome than those accompanying physical fatigue. Thus, wherever physical tiredness and a sense of danger were at odds, the latter almost invariably prevailed. This was surely the main reason that combatants often became aware of their physical exhaustion only at the end of a battle, when the source of their sustaining nervous energy had evaporated. The precedence of danger over tiredness certainly struck the Australian sergeant who reflected on his participation in the long retreat through Greece: 'How we kept going so long without food and rest is amazing, but there is something which keeps you going Dick – the love of life is strong and its amazing what you can do when things are desperate.'[21]

FATE AND HOPE

No combat soldier could long avoid contemplating his chances of violent death, for that fate was inseparable from the front-line experience. One of the main stances or beliefs was really disbelief – a refusal to accept the possibility. For while assessing the deaths of others as part of 'the game', many told themselves that they were outside the rules. Some in this group felt that their survival was assured because of the protection of something supernatural, Lieutenant A. H. Robertson, for instance, wrote to his wife from New Guinea: 'You know, with all the narrow escapes I've had and still to be without a scratch, I'm beginning to think that some Power is watching over me and is going to bring me back safely to you in the end . . . It has happened too often now to be luck or chance.'[22]

After being wounded in Syria, Corporal Edwards wrote from the hospital: 'Like you Mother, I'm convinced there is some unseen power looking after me for I was very lucky indeed to come out of the show slightly wounded as I did for there were literally thousands of bullets all round me and yet one chose to hit me in the thigh.'[23]

Men often thanked God for their survival. In Tobruk, where shirts were seldom worn, the rosary beads that some Australians wore around their necks were a highly visible sign of faith in the protective power of Christianity – and probably also a sign of hope that they would be spared. Others, though probably relatively fewer than in the American army, held that non-Christian lucky charms had the power to protect them. For example, Private Zuckur wrote home from Tobruk: 'Have you seen that long photo I sent you from Bonegilla of my old company well the whole mob have gone except four lucky cows, no doubt Mona about your lucky charm it still hangs around my neck.'[24]

A former company commander recalls an attack in New Guinea being delayed so that his 'lucky' scarf could be found, at the insistence of the sergeant-major.[25] Some claimed that they were naturally lucky. A soldier who would die nine days later wrote from Tobruk: 'I am always very optimistic about everything, even when I am chewing gravel lying on the ground with a dirty big bomber from the "faderland" hovering about overhead, it's a lucky bomb that picks me out.'[26]

A belief in one's personal inviolability derived strength from the numerous instances in which soldiers felt that their survival of a campaign or battle or patrol was surprising, or even miraculous. A good example occurs in Eric Lambert's Alamein diary: 'Almost as soon as our own barrage began the Hun replied and he was right among us . . . How I came thru' it God only knows; men on either side of me were falling and I became convinced I bore a charmed life and no longer bothered to go to ground.'[27]

In this instance, belief in 'a charmed life' clearly threatened to end it, yet one wonders how firm was the faith many had in their stated conviction that they were invulnerable. While near Buna, Gunner

Sunley wrote in his diary: 'I am sure no bullet has my name on it, but the Tojo may not be able to write and he might mistake me for some one else so I take no risks – that are not necessary.'[28] Private Allan Jones wrote to his mother in a more serious tone, but also with an element of doubt: 'I've got a feeling that I'll come home without a scratch. If I don't remember that plenty of better men than I am, have gone west . . . '.[29]

Gullett says that 'we in the battalion knew that luck was the only thing to hope for really', and although that is an overgeneralization about attitudes, many certainly did regard, or come to regard, fate as blind rather than benevolent. Writing from Tobruk in the fifth month of the siege, Private Aldridge told a friend:

> We hope we are out of here by Xmas . . . It's a bit far to look ahead but, considering a bloke is only alive hour by hour. A mate of mine was telling me about his plans when he got home, 30 minutes later they dropped a shell on him that's how it is here. We don't seem to look at it on the bad side wev'e seen so much and been so close to death that a lot of us are 100% fatalists.[30]

Fearnside gives further insight into this fatalist philosophy in a fine passage concerning preparations for the battle of Ed Duda:

> The more sensitive, and the more imaginative, thought of life and death, of the coming battle in the stark and simple terms of who would live and who would die. The exhilaration of the first encounter was long since gone; each exposure to danger had shed a husk from an inner resolution and revealed a being who doubted and hoped and feared. The game of war was in perspective now, a numbers game. Some to live and some to die, with every man taking an equal chance.[31]

The prevalence of this fatalistic outlook is apparent in soldiers' discussions of postwar plans, which often included the caveat 'if I get home'. An important aspect of this way of thinking is conveyed in a vivid description of dive-bombing written in Tobruk: 'Most of us grit our teeth and wish it were over, clinging desperately to a resigned fatalistic attitude of mind.'[32]

As the last phrase implies, there was sometimes a forced, affected element in Australians' fatalism. One can easily imagine men saying they were fatalists because it helped them to appear nonchalant and unafraid – in other words, to strike an honourably masculine pose. The 2/28th Battalion historian writes of a 'veneer of fatalism' which vanished among Tobruk's defenders soon after they heard that they were to be relieved. Further evidence of this 'veneer' is Medcalf's comment about soldiers on Bougainville: 'Outwardly we were fatalistic – if you were going to get it, you'd get it. But each of us thought, "It will not happen to me".'[33]

Nevertheless, there is no doubt that many did feel that they were dependent on fate. They felt especially that the longer they campaigned, the greater the odds against their survival. This was one factor in the tendency for enthusiasm to diminish in the course of a campaign. That attitude is typified in a diary entry written by a veteran sergeant near Salamaua: 'We are well aware that we are overdue for being relieved, if they don't soon get us out there will be nobody left to take out.' Even within a single battle a soldier might speculate that: 'A couple of us are killed or wounded each day. I can't help wondering if my turn is coming.'[34]

Veterans were generally able to regain their martial eagerness between campaigns. For example, Aldridge – quoted above on 100 per cent fatalists – reported that his group was 'eager to start' on their return to the line 11 months later.[35] However, by 1945 many veterans were running out of reserves of enthusiasm, largely because they believed their chances of survival were decreasing. Early that year, when the Minister for the Army reported to the Prime Minister of Australia on interviews he had held with veterans of the 7th and 9th divisions, he referred to their 'fatalistic outlook', and noted: 'These original members stated that in consecutive campaigns they had seen their numbers gradually decimated, and expressed to me their doubts that if they should again proceed on active service, there was every possibility that they, the remaining members of the "Old Brigade" would become casualties and never return to Australia.'[36]

Paul Fussell writes that 'every front-line soldier in the Second World War' passed from a belief in his own personal inviolability to one in which he recognized his vulnerability but took care to protect himself, and finally to a conviction that departure from the front was the only means of avoiding premature death.[37] It is simplistic to say that all soldiers passed through these stages, but clearly many did reach a stage where they felt that their chances of survival were dwindling rapidly.

Statistically, these fears were unfounded. From a comparison of the number of men who passed through various infantry battalions with those units' wartime casualties, it appears that a soldier in a typical front-line infantry battalion had one chance in 14 of being killed (see Table 2). Yet, for most of the war, front-line soldiers had no idea that these would be the final odds – for despite their confidence about victory, they did not know when the war would end. Most importantly, they could not know who the unlucky one would be.[38]

Ultimately, the fatalists were right: the front-line soldier's survival was a matter of blind chance. Roland Hoffmann acknowledged this in a letter discussing the battles of January 1941: 'I was very lucky in both shows. Its only luck one way or other. You can help yourself by prudence a bit – e.g. going down flat automatically with the shell burst etc. – but that only helps in special circumstances.'[39] Steward says that among Australian soldiers 'luck' was one of the most frequently used four-letter words, and indeed 'tough luck' or 'bad luck' appear to have been standard phrases in descriptions of the deaths of comrades.[40]

Death in battle was appallingly arbitrary. One platoon might suffer heavy casualties – as did 16 Platoon of the 2/33rd Battalion, which had the battalion's highest casualties in the Owen Stanleys, then lost all but two members in a plane crash, and on being rebuilt was reduced to six men after a few days in the Ramu Valley – while other platoons of the same unit could have spectacular success and few or no casualties in the same campaigns.

A lone shell landing amongst a closely packed group of men might cause appalling casualties, like the one which killed or wounded almost all the men of a platoon of the 2/13th Battalion at Ed Duda, or it might fail to explode, like the one which landed amongst D Company of the 2/48th Battalion as it formed up at Alamein.

Some men were hit by bullets that detonated grenades they were carrying, while others experienced bullets hitting grenades or passing through clothing and equipment and remained unharmed. One man might be killed by a chance shot at night, like the 2/43rd Battalion's only fatal casualty on Labuan, while another man in that battalion could have a Bren gun blown out of his hands by an anti-tank shell at Alamein and be unhurt. Those who appeared to be favoured by chance had no guarantee of survival, as Major Harry Dunkley indicated in a letter from New Guinea: 'One bloke survived a sword wound, a bullet

TABLE 2: Casualty rates within selected battalions 1939–45

Unit	No. passing through ranks	Killed*	Wounded	P.O.W.	Total	Per cent killed	Per cent wounded**	Per cent P.O.W.	Per cent casualties
2/2 Bn	2796	167	409	167	743	6.0	14.6	6.0	26.6
2/3 Bn	3303	174				5.3			
2/6 Bn	2900	137	337	351	825	4.7	11.6	12.0	28.0
2/11 Bn	3000+	183				6.1-			
2/12 Bn	3491	285	608?		893	8.2	17.0?		25.6
2/16 Bn	3275	224	455	0	679	6.8	13.9	0.0	20.7
2/33 Bn	3065	107	323	26	456	3.5	10.5	0.8	14.8
2/30 Bn	1300	83		1049		6.4			
2/13 Bn	2706	245			875	9.0			32.3
2/43 Bn	2711	243	556	35	834	9.0	20.5	1.3	31.0
2/23 Bn	3187	315	711	101	1127	9.9	22.3	3.2	35.4
2/24 Bn	3000+	252				8.4			
39 Bn	1666	132	266	0	393	7.9	16.0	0.0	23.9

* Includes died of wounds and missing in action. Except for 2/11, 2/13 and 2/24 bns, these figures include only those killed as a result of enemy action.
** These figures have not been adjusted for men wounded twice. Their presence would slightly reduce the likelihood of any individual being hit.

and a grenade to be killed by a bomb from one of our own planes. Tough luck.'[41]

The arbitrariness and ghastliness of death in combat made a frightening combination, as these extracts from a letter written after the Greek campaign imply:

> ... I don't want to come back to you a nervous wreck, and my nerves up to date are still standing up to the lot and will try hard for your sake to be always that way, although its hard at times when men are blown to pieces not very far away from one ... may [God] grant that I be one of the lucky ones, to come home to you ... [42]

Naturally, many of those who believed that the odds were mounting against them became more careful over time: showing, for instance, a 'calculating outlook' towards raiding and patrolling at Tobruk.[43] Moreover, there was widespread acceptance of the principle, derived from the previous war, that one should not volunteer for anything.

However, there was not much one could do to take care while advancing across open ground or in a jungle patrol. This was ensured both by the physical realities of the tasks and by one's sense of honour. Somehow most men survived such ordeals with body, mind and self-esteem intact. Others did not.

CHAPTER THREE

MAJOR SOURCES OF FRONT-LINE STRESS

*F*ear had many faces in combat. Occasionally the faces were the human ones of the enemy soldiers, though to Australians their Japanese opponents were especially frightening because they seemed less than human. The jungles in which the enemy was encountered increased the terrors of the life-and-death struggle.

Often the foe's presence was indicated only by his terrible long-range weapons, and the impersonality of these planes and big guns added another dimension to fear. The need to obey orders and to fulfil one's military objectives despite these threats also heightened the stress of front-line service, as did the confusion that was always a part of battle.

AIRCRAFT, ARTILLERY AND ARMOUR

Until mid-1942, aircraft were the first hostile agents seen by most Australian soldiers. The initial contacts were usually not especially dangerous for the men on the ground, but in the course of the early campaigns aircraft became an awesome threat. In Tobruk, Greece, Crete, and South-East Asia, Australians found themselves with little and eventually no air support, so that the enemy was able to bomb and strafe virtually at will.

Enemy aircraft were a source of fear wherever they appeared. 'One gets contemptuous of what comes from the front', Corporal Stoner

29

wrote home from Malaya, 'but we all have a dread of what drops from above.'[1] A source of extreme dread was the screaming sound of aircraft and bombs, which appeared to be directed at the listener.

Many also felt depressed and frustrated by their inability – and their air force's inability – to retaliate effectively against enemy planes. For instance, a corporal noted in his Tobruk diary: 'We were dived bombed. About 50 planes over like a swarm of bees. Three bombs about 15 paces from me, one dud about 7 paces. Nerve racking to say the least . . . They just have an open slather. Terribly demoralising.'[2] In writing to his wife about his experiences in Greece, another corporal asserted that: 'we can fight man to man on the ground and hold our own with the best, but when it comes to hundreds of dive bombers at you and you can't hit back at the swines, by god its nerving dear . . . it makes the strongest man feel as helpless as a baby'.[3]

The inability to retaliate against powerful weapons has been one of the chief sources of stress for twentieth-century soldiers. Prolonged exposure to the aerial version of this ordeal left men talking of 'what a hell on earth aeroplanes can make'. An Australian staff nurse's diary entry concerning the men being treated in Egypt after the Cretan campaign encapsulated her countrymen's experience of air attack in the early campaigns: 'Australians whom we thought of as fearless have been afraid and it is no wonder, fighting the foe in the air from the ground'.[4]

After mid-1942, aerial superiority passed gradually and then overwhelmingly to the Allies. Aircraft were never again as great a single component of the threats bearing down on the soldier's mind, although as one Australian's 1943 letter from New Guinea vividly showed, they were still there: 'I'd rather face a hundred nips on the ground than have those blinkin' planes dropping eggs on you. Nerves, cripes if we hear a insect buzzing now we go like hell for a slit trench.'[5]

A more traditional source of mental strain that troubled Australians in the early campaigns was artillery bombardment. Shelling of Australian forces in World War II never reached the dimensions of the largest barrages of the Great War.[6] Nevertheless, as in 1914–18, it posed a threat to soldiers' minds, as well as bodies. The following descriptions, concerning respectively a large German gun at Alamein and a group of German guns in Greece, could well have been written in World War I:

It is a terrifying weapon. You hear the dull explosion as it is fire from many miles away and then the sound of a locomotive turning over and over coming at speed towards you. The noise makes the hair on the back of your neck stand up. They have been at it for over half hour now and looks like it will never stop. We are all cowered down in our holes waiting for it to stop, for that is when the enemy attack and we have to get our heads up and open fire. They land very close and dislodge the sand and dirt in on top of you. It's in your eyes, ears, nose and mouth and you wish like hell it would cease.

Jerry opened up on us with his artillery from Lamier early in the morning and continued firing on our spot till 1700 hrs that day. Needless to say the hill was in a hell of a mess and I am pretty right in saying there was a shell crater every 15 yds. over the whole of the area . . . We lost about 12 chaps killed and a few wounded and altogether we were all practically shattered by the time the firing ceased.[7]

Considering such ordeals it is not surprising that soldiers continued to use the World War I term 'shell shock' to explain the evacuation of men with no physical wounds, despite the strenuous rejection of the term by army medical authorities.

Like the aircraft, the artillery piece was a weapon against which most front-line soldiers could not retaliate. They could take certain precautions, especially in defensive positions, but under shelling men generally had to 'kiss the ground' and hope. Shelling might be sporadic, with the danger of a random shell hitting one's dugout or the palm tree above, or it could take the form of the 'veritable hell' of an extended barrage, under which survival might seem a miracle. In either case, men under fire asked themselves 'Who is going next?'

Corporal White considered the 'hardest few minutes of his life' those in which he had run the gauntlet of German artillery fire at 'Hell fire corner' during the retreat through Greece. He only had to do this once, but soldiers in static positions, such as the Tobruk fortress, had to endure bombardment as a regular feature of life. Incomplete but illuminating figures exist concerning the volume of shells that fell on Tobruk. In the relatively quiet period 26 June–6 August 1941, an average of 650 shells fell each day on the three forward sectors. Nearly two-thirds of these landed in the western sector (which included the salient), one-quarter in the southern, and only one eighth in the east. The total increased in August, and the weight shifted to the south and the east: the latter received 1000 shells on 29 August. By September, a daily average of 1000 shells were hitting Tobruk. For an 80-kilometre front this was not heavy by Great War standards, but it was not negligible, either.[8]

That fact is clear in a diary entry written in the salient during July, after some of these shells had found their mark:

> Since yesterday morning I've had the worst time I've ever had. Yesterday morning about nine o'clock the Hun shelled us with big stuff . . . Brian had his leg nearly blown off and I had to carry him about half a mile on my back . . . While I was at Company the section post was shelled again and many parts of it were completely smashed in. Bluey and Dead Eye were buried and had to dig themselves out and Ted was thrown against the wall with the force of the explosion. Most of the boys are a bundle of nerves . . . Anyone who reckons he's not scared of shells is a blasted liar.[9]

On the eastern sector two months later, a young reinforcement recorded similar impressions of his introduction to the routine of front-line soldiering and shelling: 'Arty Biltz bloody awful . . . Shell fire heaviest ever on perimiter. Night was hell . . . I am shit scared steady shell fire.'[10]

The volume of shelling suffered on various other fronts was similar to, or even greater than that endured at Tobruk. While in a purely defensive role during the Syrian campaign, the 2/33rd Battalion was hit as many as four times daily by concentrations of 200 and 300 rounds. Up to 500 shells per day landed on one company's positions near Jezzine during the last two weeks of the campaign. Approximately the same daily total fell among a company of the 2/48th Battalion during July 1942. Over the 46 days spent by the 2/17th Battalion on the Alamein front between major actions there, a daily average of 188 shells struck the unit's defensive area. Understandably, the battalion historian talks of this period becoming 'a strain'.[11]

One of the most powerful Australian evocations of the stressful experience of sustained shelling in World War II is a brief and emotional one concerning the fighting at Ed Duda, a low knoll outside Tobruk. Towards the end of the siege, the 2/13th Battalion advanced outside the fortress perimeter to Ed Duda, where they underwent an ordeal described in Private A. Armstrong's diary under the heading 'This Was Pure Hell': 'After we took the position we were shelled continuously for two days. Had we not been relieved after the second night I think half the coy. would have gone shell happy. It was terrible I can't describe it.'[12]

Friendly artillery could also put nerves under strain. The noise worsened the plight of men already jittery from enemy fire, and its close proximity could attract enemy fire. The fear of nearby guns 'drawing the crabs' contained an implicit recognition of a frightening danger faced by the gunners themselves, for counter-battery fire – the attempt to knock out each other's guns – was a regular feature of the artilleryman's war. Guns were also vulnerable from the air, as Captain Laybourne Smith's letter concerning Greece testifies:

> My troop was moving down the road . . . and everything was lovely when thirty feet above the trees the air became black with planes . . . and they gave us the doing of our lives. Before a man could move every vehicle in my troop was on fire. True we saved one gun but nothing else. The vehicles blazed and the ammunition in them exploded and the bastards came back and back until the ground around us seemed alive with explosive bullets. The final count showed one man killed, fifteen wounded, only three badly, and everyone scared stiff.[13]

Laybourne Smith performed the most perilous job in a field artillery regiment: namely, that of forward observation officer (F.O.O.). This job required its incumbent to go ahead of the guns and direct their crews – if he could survive the enemy's attempts to seek him out. Death or terrible injury were also relatively common for men in anti-tank units, which in the Middle East generally used guns much weaker than those on the tanks they encountered.

Enemy tanks, which figured in most of the pre-1943 campaigns, posed a frightening threat. Australian infantrymen regularly lacked effective means of resistance to tanks, which, like aircraft and artillery, tended to induce a sense of helplessness in their targets. Although more vulnerable than planes or guns, enemy tanks were more likely to direct accurate fire at the individual, to seek to crush him – a favourite tactic in the Alamein campaign – or to force his surrender.

Japanese tanks were seldom encountered, but they had a powerful impact at Milne Bay. Here, in a reserve position, Major Matthews recorded his impressions of Australians drifting back after an initial rebuff: 'Stirring tales of sudden attacks, frights, but mostly about tanks that got amongst them with their lights blazing.'[14]

German tanks were decisive in the single biggest disaster suffered by any Australian battalion in North Africa: the 2/28th Battalion's loss of 554 men killed, wounded or captured at Ruin Ridge, on 27 July 1942. The following day, an Australian elsewhere on that front wrote a diary entry that would surely have been endorsed by many Australians who encountered tanks: 'I had a good look at a German Mk. IV tank last night and the only description I could give it is that it is an enormous hideous demoralising monster'.[15]

When defending in the desert, Australians usually remained under cover, but in attack they had to cross ground that was generally flat and open. Even if their advances made optimal use of the little available cover, concentrated on the points of enemy weakness and were undertaken at night, participants felt disconcertingly exposed. Men were encouraged to fire back at the enemy as they advanced, but though this may have kept some defenders' heads down, it was advised for psychological rather than military reasons. Ninth Division training instructions issued in the light of the Middle East campaigns of 1941 recommended the practice not because of any tactical benefits but because: 'In the attack it has been found that, by firing their weapons as they advance, advancing t[roo]ps sustain their morale.'[16] In other words, it mitigated the sense of helplessness inherent in so much of the infantryman's combat experience.

THE DREADFUL JUNGLE

In contrast to the openness that made desert advances daunting, the claustrophobic atmosphere of the jungle tried nerves in the Pacific area. The dense vegetation made it difficult for all but the smallest groups to remain in contact, so jungle fighters stalked and killed each other in frightening isolation.

Enemies could remain hidden in much closer proximity than in earlier campaigns. Where the opposing lines became relatively stable in the jungle, they were often less than 100 metres apart. Lance-Corporal Spindler wrote of the 'dreadful' strain of being so near to Japanese positions at Gona that the Australians had to talk in whispers, and nrrvn were on edge wherever the lines were static and close together.[17]

It could be even more stressful when the enemy's presence was possible rather than certain. This account of a New Guinea patrol gives a perfect example: 'We patrol very cautiously up the steep track, keeping watch on each side for an ambush. Our mouths are dry and the hair on the back of our necks are stiff, expecting any minute to be blasted down . . . All along this track there were ideal places for an ambush and at everyone a man aged another year'.[18]

This sense of danger created 'a constant feeling of strain' in many of those who marched on the Kokoda Trail.[19] Indeed soldiers faced a possibility of ambush in every jungle campaign, because jungle tracks were scarce and militarily important. Thus one of the best evocations of soldiers' emotions on the tracks was written during the New Guinea campaign in 1945, as Private Wallin recalled his earlier experiences there as a rifleman at Wau-Salamaua:

> . . . after the open ridge is travelled and I enter the dim lighted jungle, dripping foliage squelching mud and water, I often feel sort of depressed and suffocated. Maybe memories of other days patrolling along similiar tracks always waiting for that ambush to be sprung on oneself. Knowing that any moment one can be down in the mud of the track, to rot away, the same as many enemy dead are that lie in similar circumstances on these tracks . . .[20]

Little wonder that in the tropics, some desert veterans suddenly found campaigning intolerable, and gave as the reason 'the hunting, hiding, listening part' of jungle warfare.[21]

Listening in the jungle created a sense of unease upon which Australians frequently commented. Some were struck by an eerie silence; others were troubled by the constant sound of moving insects and animals or creaking trees. Loud noises tended to denote death or danger, as this comment on a Wau patrol suggests: 'Rather typical of the country is that the only noise we heard for the whole patrol not made by ourselves was a sudden mad death screech in the jungle as something went west.'[22] The danger of 'going west' at the hands of a hidden foe was the main reason that the jungle was eerie.

The combination of a nearby enemy and the strange noises or uncanny silence of jungle nights made sentry duty a nerve-racking job.

For example, Trooper Love wrote in his dugout at Sanananda: 'It is a
strain on the old nerves doing the hour "watch" through the night . . .
every time a branch shakes or leaf falls everyone becomes tense, rifles
and Owen-guns are grasped tightly as we crouch down in our holes –
you cannot see, only listen – and wait.'[23]

This strain gave rise to 'itchy finger', which was probably responsible for most of the numerous incidents in which soldiers taking their
turn at sentry-go at night shot other unrecognized Australians. A development late in the war rendered the nocturnal atmosphere even more
disturbing for sentries: namely, regular attacks made by individual
Japanese soldiers on the Australian lines after dark. Arthur Wallin
described the aftermath of one such raid, in which 'Charlie the bomb
thrower' hurled a picric bomb and a grenade at a nearby tent: 'A hell of
a row, black smoke everywhere as I reared up out of a dead sleep
grabbed the rifle and made for the weapon pit – for three and a half
hours we sat there, waiting for more to be thrown and to add to the
discomfort it poured rain.'[24]

Private Clement Johnson was lying in his tent in northern New
Guinea when:

> . . . a Nip Lieutenant paid me a visit at about half past nine,
> came into my tent, I was in bed but awake, and saw him come
> in, he came in close to my bed, and was just going to pick up
> my rifle which I had close to me, when I flew out and grabbed
> him by the throat, and struggled on the ground with him, and
> choked him unconscious, during the fight he tried to get me
> with a hand grenade, but I was lucky enough to see it and
> throw it away before it exploded . . . I am o.k. except of course
> that I got rather a big fright, my nerves havn't been the best
> since, but I guess I will come good in time.[25]

Not surprisingly, Private Tommasi wrote, on moving back from the
front at Bougainville, that it was 'great to be able to just lay back and go
to sleep without fear of Nips crawling up on you'.[26]

A FRIGHTFUL ENEMY

The jungle brought Australians closer to their enemies in physical
terms, but in human terms there was always a great distance between

them. With that distance came mental strain. When the war against the Japanese began, Australians considered themselves physically and mentally superior to their new enemy. The ordinary soldier's racist contempt during this pre-contact stage is encapsulated in a comment reportedly made by a private to a friend leaving on a reconnaissance shortly before the first clash in Malaya: 'Hey Merv – bring me back a bloody little Jap I can piss on.'[27]

Such attitudes made the Malayan retreats and the surrender at Singapore especially humiliating for the Australians concerned. Contact with real Japanese must have led these Australians to modify their opinions of their enemy's abilities. Nevertheless, it seems that because Australian units had performed relatively well against the Japanese in this fighting – suffering far fewer battle deaths than they inflicted – many Australians in the 8th Division continued to consider themselves superior on a man-for-man basis. They were often frightened in these campaigns, but because of the odds against them rather than any aura attached to the individual Japanese soldier.

However, news of the defeats of early 1942 transformed the Japanese image in the eyes of many Australians elsewhere. From the first days of fighting in Papua there was talk of Japanese 'invincibility' and 'supermen', and clearly fear was among the emotions behind that talk. There were Australians who, like their compatriots in the earlier campaigns, entered the fray in Papua expecting to meet incompetent 'little toothy buggers with glasses', but this expectation was frequently shaken by contact with reality.[28] For there was more than a grain of truth in the frightening tales of Japanese skill and guile that greeted new arrivals to New Guinea. At that stage, the Japanese were more skilled, experienced and tenacious than the Australians. However, the image of the terrifying 'super soldier', like the one that preceded it, was a stereotype, a distortion.

The inaccuracy of the stereotype should have become apparent in the Milne Bay battles of August 1942, as this revealing extract from a brigade commander's report on the campaign affirms: 'The operation shows the superiority of our troops and weapons. Great determination to close with the enemy and destroy him must still be developed and is expected to follow now that our troops have proved the Jap is not a superman.'[29]

Australians participating in the subsequent Kokoda campaign seem not to have drawn the same conclusion until they saw evidence of it in their own operations. But to their relief they did see it, and by the end of the fighting on the Buna-Gona-Sanananda beaches, the comparison made by an artilleryman at Buna was probably widespread: 'the Tojo's are tough and great jungle fighters, and have given the infanteers a hard job but they have met their masters at that game'.[30]

Even so, when in 1943 the 9th Division entered the fight against the Japanese – the last A.I.F. division to do so – its members had heard many stories of the 'superman' ilk. Thus, although some sailed into action supremely confident, others had believed the stories they heard, and they anticipated the forthcoming campaign 'with considerable trepidation'.[31]

When they did come to grips with the Japanese, men of the 9th were surprised and not a little self-satisfied that this enemy was not as formidable as other veterans had led them to expect, and was in fact markedly inferior to their German opponent of earlier campaigns.

However, even the overwhelming victories of 1943–4 did not kill fear of the Japanese jungle giant amongst the civilian manpower pool: in the last year of the war, the administrators of the Jungle Warfare Training Centre at Canungra in Queensland felt that infantry reinforcements still had to be reassured that the notion of the Japanese super soldier was a myth. From late 1942 onwards, Australian troops had the upper hand over the Japanese in every aspect of jungle warfare. The ratio of battle deaths was roughly ten-to-one against the Japanese, and Australians new to the front must have soon discovered that fears about comparative ability were unfounded.[32] However, there continued to be frightening features peculiar to this enemy.

In the Middle East, Australians captured by the enemy could reasonably expect humane treatment. The thousands of Australians who surrendered to the Japanese early in 1942 subsequently received treatment that was notoriously inhumane, but at least had their surrender accepted in most cases. Any Australian who fell into Japanese hands after March 1942, however, had virtually no hope of surviving the experience.[33]

During the first protracted Australian action in the S.W.P.A., at Milne Bay, Australians saw evidence that if caught by the enemy, they could expect to be treated savagely: there are numerous eyewitness accounts of the discovery of Australian bodies that had been disembowelled, beheaded, emasculated or used for bayonet practice. Gratuitous and frightening atrocities reappeared in later campaigns, together with mutilation motivated by need: for from the Owen Stanleys campaign until the end of the war, starving Japanese ate portions of dead Australians.

Great mental stress must have weighed on men such as the diarist who wrote 'One of my best mates was killed and eat by the Japs' or the eyewitnesses who recounted to a postwar inquiry that they had been able to recognize a fellow battalion member, whose 'body had been terribly mutilated', because his head was still intact.[34]

Similarly, stories of Japanese mercilessness and sadism must have frightened Australians. For instance, one member of a three-man group that became separated from their unit at Milne Bay proposed that they commit suicide rather than be captured. On a broader scale, the 2/33rd Battalion historian tells that when the unit was about to enter the fighting in the Owen Stanleys, and was told that any wounded would have to fend for themselves, the order came as a shattering one, 'coupled as it was with the information the Japs were known to take no prisoners on the battlefield, and invariably bayoneted wounded'.[35] This fear probably affected campaigning soldiers in Malaya, too, for presumably many heard some news of Japanese atrocities committed against the wounded there.

Further evidence of this fear of vicious treatment emerges in the Australians' comments on the Japanese. During the Milne Bay battle, Brigadier Field wrote in his diary: 'The yellow devils show no mercy and have since had none from us.'[36] The Australians' relentless killing of Japanese then and thereafter owed much to a determination both to retaliate in kind and to take revenge for Japanese atrocities and rumoured maltreatment of POWs. However, a desire to destroy what they feared was another factor. The most direct statement of that fact appears in an infantryman's letter written late in the Papuan campaign. He first contrasted the Australian attitude towards the Japanese with his feelings about previously encountered enemies: 'My regard for Tony [the Italian] was always impersonal and for Fritz . . . tinged with admiration, but none of us know anything but vindictive hatred for the Jap.' Then followed an explanation for that hatred: 'Apart from his merciless way of waging war I suppose it is because we fear him and his policy of conquest brought so near to Australia.'[37] The Japanese were often described with animal metaphors, notably that of the rat. This implied a sense of fear and of loathing that was probably behind much of the Australians' eagerness to kill or – to use another popular wartime expression – to 'exterminate' Japanese.

At least one senior Australian officer in New Guinea seems to have tried to encourage such an eagerness based on fear. Lieutenant-General Herring, General Officer Commanding New Guinea Force in July 1943, is said to have told newly arrived troops that if you did not kill the Japanese first 'he would not only kill you, he would eat you'.[38]

The Australians' eagerness to kill their enemies in the S.W.P.A. ranked only slightly behind that of the Japanese, and included the killing of sleeping, wounded and even captured enemy soldiers. Capturing Japanese troops was certainly perilous and nerve-racking, but the tendency to shoot first and ask questions later owed something to fear of a ruthless, incomprehensible and often hidden enemy.

It was also due to the frightening logic of jungle warfare, for where opponents were in close proximity, one often had no choice but to shoot first and ask questions later. After a successful ambush by some comrades at Sanananda, Ben Love described jungle warfare as 'pure murder'.[39]

KILLING AND THE TASKS OF WAR

The necessity of 'murder', of killing in war, was a source of strain for some Australians – even in the war against the Japanese. On this question, one diarist in New Guinea asserted that 'this is not murder killing such repulsive looking animals'.[40] Yet some had mixed feelings or regrets about killing Japanese, and powerful anxieties emerge in the following recollection of one soldier's first battle, wherein he encountered a hideously wounded Japanese lying beside the Kokoda Trail: 'then came the beginning of some of the terrible things that happen in combat. Our officer didn't have the stomach to finish off the dying "Nip" – instead he detailed me to do it, and I have lived to this day with those terrified eyes staring at me.'[41]

In the Middle East, men had stronger reasons for anxieties about killing fellow men, especially as nearly all Australian troops shared a Christian faith with their enemies there. Australians in that theatre of war are said to have depended much on the heat of battle to bring their killer instinct to the boil, for they generally felt little hatred towards Italians, Vichy Frenchmen or even Germans. The latter were still called 'Huns', were still hated by some and distrusted by more, but surprisingly there was not the widespread, sanguinary hostility that one might expect given the reported Australian attitudes of the previous war. There is also some evidence of anxiety about killing these and other enemies Australians encountered in the Middle East, notably one diarist's description of a man 'tormented by the recollection' of bayoneting three Germans, and the fact that Australians were somewhat 'squeamish' at Bardia.[42] Nevertheless, it seems from the soldiers' own writings that on the matter of killing, most were not stricken by guilt about this essential feature of war. They might be detached, eager, proud, or even exultant, but rarely anxious; or rather, seldom openly anxious. Physical distance from the victim, such as the target of an artillery piece, mortar or machine-gun, worked against empathy and remorse, and where soldiers were close enough to see the men they killed, the desire to survive the experience, and relief at doing so, was stronger than qualms about 'murder'.

Whereas killing protected the killer, other tasks common to campaigning on all fronts threatened him, and were accordingly more stressful. In every campaign, Australians had, for example, to patrol into 'No Man's Land' and beyond. Naturally, there were variations in methods between Middle East and jungle – notably in the addition in the Pacific of the extremely dangerous and stressful job of forward scout. Nevertheless, in all areas the principle was the same: small groups of men trying to remain concealed while they advanced to reconnoitre or cause havoc amongst enemy forces, which were almost invariably larger. The ever present dangers of discovery, ambush and exploding mines created tensions in the Australians, as these varied descriptions reveal:

> Bob and I went on a patrol to Nip positions. I was stepping like a cat by the time we reached home and believe me my hair was bristling.

> . . . at 1 am we are sneaking along the wire when machine guns opened up on us the fire was very heavy the Germans threw grenades and we crawled on our stomachs to get away. He sent up flares and the suspense was dreadful . . .

> These patrols are carried out every night to keep Jerry jittery and on his toes but it is very nerve wracking for us and we hate the guts of the 'heads' that bung them on I suppose it is necessary but we have to do them, not the 'brass' and have to take the

risk of running into an ambush at any time. I have been out on
a few and always dread the next one.[43]

Considering the final quotation, it is not surprising that the strain
found expression in a lack of enthusiasm for patrolling amongst veterans, complaints when it was felt that units had 'copped the crow' too
often, and expressions of doubt as to whether the benefits outweighed
the costs. An example of those costs appears in a diarist's description of
the aftermath of a patrol that had been ambushed three weeks earlier,
in Tobruk:

> ... the corporal of our squad ... has not yet straightened up
> but gets about with a perpetual stoop and anxious glances
> enemywards; it jolted his nerve badly. Another member of the
> squad has been in hospital and I admit I felt a bit jittery for a
> couple of days ... [44]

Capturing enemy territory necessitated stressful combat on a scale
larger than that of patrols. Merely reaching enemy ground was often
dangerous; taking that ground was nearly always a dreadful prop-
osition. Substantial man-made defences faced Australians in their
assaults at Bardia, Tobruk and El Alamein. In Syria, apart from forti-
fied positions, Australians faced mountainous terrain that was sometimes said to be worse than Gallipoli.[45] In the S.W.P.A., Australians
had to tackle daunting natural obstacles defended by a tenacious
enemy skilled in camouflage and fortification.

Australians also did their share of defending. This was a source of
stress throughout the war, for even after the strategic initiative passed
irrevocably to the Australians and their allies, their opponents were
still eager to attack at every opportunity. Although the Germans were
generally on the defensive in North Africa after July 1942, it was taken
as a matter of course that they would quickly counter-attack in an
endeavour to recapture any ground lost to the Australians. During the
Battle of El Alamein, for example, one position held by Australians
withstood approximately 50 German attacks. Australians also had to
expect counter-attacks whenever the Japanese were on the defensive:
there were eight such attacks on Mount Tambu on the night of 16–17
July 1943, and the following month saw 15 counter-attacks within four
days at Old Vickers.

Fighting off these assaults was physically and mentally draining, as
was defending against the materially and often numerically superior

enemy earlier in the war. Moreover, when Australians were defending, even temporarily, the initiative necessarily rested with the attacker, and this left the defenders waiting, anticipating and worrying. Private Butler expressed the feeling well during the siege of Tobruk: 'This is a nerve racking game we're on and the worst part is the days of inactivity and waiting – waiting for one knows not what.'[46]

The waiting and anticipating must have been even worse for the Australian island garrisons that lay in the path of the Japanese advance early in 1942, for they had no prospect of success. The discomfort of the Rabaul garrison emerges in a member's recollection written soon afterwards: '. . . one day we heard there was a Jap convoy heading this way . . . Most of the boys played cards to try and take their minds off it.' Of the day following the Japanese landing he wrote: 'Daylight came and we wondered how long we had to live.'[47]

CONFUSION, DEFEAT AND RETREAT

Even in actions where an eventual Australian victory was likely or assured, the burden of uncertainty about enemy intentions was stressful. For instance, among men advancing towards the coast against intense opposition at Buna in December 1942, the possibility of a heavy counter-attack suddenly emerging from the jungle 'caused a high mental strain that has to be experienced to be realized'.[48] Perhaps the most poignant illustration of this phenomenon comes from Bougainville. In February 1945, an infantryman there recorded that he and a company of his battalion had become separated from the rest of the unit, and had dug in for the night. He expected the Japanese to counter-attack, for 'They always do.' The next morning's entry revealed the expectation to have been incorrect, but also a source of anxiety: 'Well the night passed O.K. the only thing that disturbed us was the screaming when one of our boys nerve gave, He is all right now. It was horrible.'[49]

The 'hellish' nature of the combat that did come to pass was enhanced by its inherent confusion. The noise of battle drew descriptive language very apt for something likened to hell: 'terrific', 'pandemonium', and 'inferno'. A diarist chose to summarize 72 hours of the battle of El Alamein with the expression: 'Shocking three days of noise, death and fear.'[50] Respite from such clamour was often mentioned as one of the chief benefits of battle's end. 'It seems terribly strange not

having any Huns over and its great to find things so quiet as all our
nerves are just about done', wrote Lieutenant Chrystal after barely
surviving the Greek and Cretan campaigns and the bombing of the ship
that evacuated him to Egypt.[51]

Apart from noise, other sources of confusion were the desert dust,
the jungle vegetation, the dark of night, the lack of reliable communications, the soldier's inability to know what all but his nearest comrades were doing, the difficulty of identifying friend and foe, and the
'screaming bloody nightmare' of hand-to-hand fighting.[52]

In a note on the timely reinforcement of Australians surrounded at
Slater's Knoll, on Bougainville, a diarist intimated the strain that could
arise from the uncertainty of a defensive battle: 'I believe the boys cried
when the tanks arrived and no wonder they had been fighting for their
lives for three days not knowing what had happened to the rest of their
Bn.'[53]

The confusion and the stress tended to multiply when actions
ended in defeat and retreat, as can be seen in each of five major Australian withdrawals. The retreat of the untried 9th Division before the
Afrika Korps in April 1941 took a heavy toll on nerves, for the Australians were keyed up for a first battle which was repeatedly post-
poned, were caught up in a chaotic, exhausting series of movements
and were aware that their military careers were close to ending before
they had really begun. A lieutenant recalled soon afterwards that 'when
we were withdrawing from Benghazi, we were outflanked and never
expected to see home again'.[54]

Australians who escaped the almost incessant air raids and the
other torments of the retreat in Greece could scarcely believe their luck,
as this note from a captain taken aboard a British destroyer suggests:
'Such a feeling of relief I don't think you could imagine and we were all
giggling like a lot of kids over the beer and cocoa the ships officers gave
us.'[55]

Those retreating across Crete suffered air raids and anxieties
already noted, while in Malaya the Japanese encircling and infiltrating
tactics created a sense of great insecurity amongst retreating Australians. A survivor of one such encircling action intimated to his wife
the harrowing nature of the ordeal:

> How it happened was the Japs got all around us in biger num-
> bers than what we were. So we had to break out and get around

in front of them again. After breaking out away from them we had to walk through jungle. rubber and swamp, at times we were in mud and water to the knees. I reckon we must have walked about 70 miles in all . . . I dont think any body who never seen us could realize how lucky I was to get out. It was so terrible.[56]

Another participant noted that the Malayan routine of 'fighting by day and withdrawing by night stretched our nerves and bodies near to breaking point'.[57]

Relentless pressure also characterized the retreat on the Kokoda Trail. Clive Edwards superbly evoked the uncertainty and tension prominent in this and the other withdrawals:

Confusion was the keynote and no one knew exactly what was happening but when the sounds of battle came from in front we were told that the others were trying to fight their way through. We stood by to help but they failed and a general withdrawal was ordered . . . It was pitiful – the rain was coming down, and there was a long string of dog tired men straining the last nerve to get wounded men out and yet save their own lives too. Bewilderment at the turn of events showed on every face and as the long line faltered and halted those at the back became affected and sent messages along the line to 'keep moving, the Jap is on us' . . . [58]

There were other sources of fear not so far discussed here. For instance, there were the acute dangers faced by men in certain specialist jobs: engineers, who often took the positions of maximum risk in clearing and blocking paths between friend and foe; signallers, who frequently had to repair damaged lines under shelling or amidst the threat of ambush, and who in action were a high priority target; mortarmen, who faced retaliatory fire from enemy mortars and artillery, as well as the hazards of premature explosion; and Bren carrier crews, whose aggressive use of their thinly armoured vehicles led men in one battalion to dub their carrier platoon the 'suicide squad'. And there were also fears attached to enemy weapons not already treated: for example, machine-guns, mines and snipers' rifles. Fear is so amorphous, its causes so numerous, that it is possible to deal in detail only with those most prominent in the minds of Australian front-line soldiers. Somehow most of them coped.

CHAPTER FOUR

WHEN FEAR BECAME UNBEARABLE

*I*n a wartime account of his experiences during the Greek campaign, Signalman Neeman reported sadly:

> after a day of continual enemy aircraft patrols, some of the chaps really started to crack up; it was terrible to see how some of them went; I myself was scared, but a few of the chaps went really haywire, digging ridiculous holes in the bottom of creeks into which water seeped, and going bush until dark didn't care about meals ...[1]

FEAR STATE

All men were 'scared', but fear was a burden too heavy for some to bear. Not surprisingly, the term 'bomb happy' was in common usage – even among medical officers – to describe sufferers, although the officially preferred medical terms for neurosis associated with combat stress were 'fear state' and 'exhaustion'.[2] The symptoms could be less dramatic than those described by Neeman, but some were at least as tragic. For example, the 'amazing' amount of terror-inspired stuttering among patients in an Australian hospital after the battle of El Alamein; or the behaviour of the officer in New Guinea who 'could not resist the impulse to pick up tin hats from the ground, attempting to place one over the hat which he was already wearing'; or the actions of a front-line soldier hospitalized after suffering acute stress at the jungle front:

[He] became almost speechless, and would communicate with others by use of the incomplete, ungrammatical speech of young children. Instead of saying 'please take this', he would simply hold out his hand and say 'take'; he would repeat 'I-frightened' or 'me-hungry'. He refused to leave a friend who brought him down the trail to the hospital, and the latter stated that at night the patient would whimper and would not sleep till he was allowed to curl up in the arms of his friend.[3]

Although these cases were unusual, even the typical victim's behaviour, described below in the sober language of a senior army medical authority, is heart-rending to contemplate:

After a certain period of stress, the affected individual begins to sleep badly, his concentration wanes. He shows at first a normal fear during the actual stress . . . Gradually as the stress continues his alertness becomes over-alertness and increases to an incapacitating degree. Appetite wanes, sleep becomes impossible. He loses weight, becomes rather wild-looking, unkempt and haggard, jumping at the least sound and rushing to cover. Gradually, the state of over-alertness deepens so that any sound, however remotely it resembles the sounds significant of danger, evokes flight or the so-called 'startle reaction'. A sudden loud noise, the back-firing of a motor or a careless whistle, sends the affected individual rushing headlong to a shelter. During bombing he may lie quiet and immobile, the picture of 'frozen fear' in animals. He may exhibit slow, coarse tremor of the head and extremities with an immobility of expression strongly resembling that observed in Parkinsonism. On the other hand, the soldier may become confused, and shout and run about, endangering his own life. After the stress has passed he does not recover his poise, but continues in the misery of apprehension and alertness. If he is able to sleep, it is a sleep tortured by terrifying dreams of battle and flight. Even in his half-waking moments he may have brilliant reminiscences of his recent experiences, which assume an almost hallucinatory character. His judgement is impaired and interest in his environment is lost in the total preoccupation with his fear.

The author of this passage stated that with adequate hospital treatment, the sufferer commonly recovered within two or three weeks.[4]

Indeed a surprisingly high proportion of 'fear state' casualties were not only released from their private hells, but restored to the public one of the front line. In some cases, the fighting ability of those who broke down was revived very rapidly. This emerges in Sergeant Lovegrove's account of an incident involving a Bren gunner in a group of six Australians surrounded on a basin-shaped hilltop in New Guinea:

> [He] had a narrow restricted field of fire through jungle for some 150 feet down a slope to where 2 tracks crossed . . . and along which every so often a Jap would pass. At intervals he 'collected' three of them, then suddenly his nerve 'snapped' and he rushed back down into the basin. As he uncontrollably sobbed, I comforted him, cradling his head on my chest, he was trembling violently, then after about 20 minutes he stood up, tensed himself, thanked me and said 'I'm O.K. now' and strode back to his position on the Bren.[5]

Lovegrove had become an experienced patrol leader in the Middle East, and when detailed to give a talk on the subject to incoming officers there, he made some illuminating points about swift remedies for breakdown:

> To control a man who 'cracks' when on patrol close to enemy defences the Leader's reaction must be instantaneous. Either of a couple of alternatives usually has the desired effect. (a) a sharp hit between the shoulder blades or on the jaw with a rifle butt – he will most certainly cease crying noisily, stifle his sobbing and regain control of himself. (b) a firm open-handed left and right slap to the face can achieve similar result . . . On return the offender often will seek out the patrol leader and sincerely apologise . . . The apology thus accepted he is unlikely to offend again . . .[6]

Although men showing signs of breakdown were usually sent to medical help, the principle continued to apply that one should treat such men as far forward and as quickly as possible. Sedation, rest and good food were the three chief treatments. These methods were highly successful, but some men had to be sent back further than their regimental aid posts for treatment. These most serious cases included soldiers described by an Australian nurse after the evacuation of Crete: 'Some of the boys who have been there were absolutely nervous wrecks and they will never get over it.'[7]

Yet even men evacuated from the forward area were treated with some success. More than half of those sent to medical treatment behind the regimental aid posts at Tobruk eventually returned to front-line service or units.[8] Two samples from Australian general hospitals in New Guinea in 1942–3 and 1943–4 showed figures of 48 per cent and 37 per cent, respectively, as fit to rejoin their combat units.[9] A senior army psychologist felt sufficiently confident about Australian methods to assert of 'fear state' cases that: 'If ready recovery does not occur, one usually finds evidence, either of an overwhelming stress continued for a long time, or of the presence of weaknesses in the personality structure of the individual which makes him less able to assimilate or adjust himself to the experiences of battle.'[10]

Most campaigning soldiers underwent what could be described as 'overwhelming stress continued for a long time', but the point about weakness in the personality structure is valid and significant.

Like men in other armies, some Australian soldiers found themselves incapacitated by fear in, or even immediately before, their very first action. It appears to have been a regular occurrence for a few men in each battalion to find it impossible to cope with the strain of battle from the time of their first experience of it. Naturally men with a previous history of neurosis were most likely to 'crack' at this time, and there is reason to believe that the Australian army contained more such men than it would have with more careful screening of recruits. Rigorous psychological assessment of new recruits was only introduced in 1942, and numerous men who were mentally unsuited to service were accepted before that date. A psychologist who researched the matter in 1942 concluded that 10 per cent of accepted recruits should have undergone further psychological investigation, while 3 to 5 per cent were 'mentally unfit for overseas service'. The problems of many recruits may have emerged soon after enlistment, for in a large sample of reviews by nearly 300 A.I.F. medical boards for 1940–1, the single disability for which most men – 26.7 per cent – were boarded out was 'mental and nervous disorders'.[11]

Not only did many of those who broke down in action have a previous history of nervous disorder, but numerous such soldiers suffered psychiatric breakdown that had no apparent relationship to combat: 51 per cent of one group of psychiatric casualties during the Borneo campaign broke down without ever experiencing battle stress. These breakdowns, which also affected some men with no history of neurosis, had numerous causes, including an inability to adapt to structural features

of everyday army life, such as its communal nature and discipline.
Another survey, from New Guinea, concluded that in only 14 per cent
of cases were the psychoses and neuroses concerned attributable solely
to war service. The exception to this rule appears in a medical article
about Tobruk: it notes that fear was the dominating emotional reaction
amongst all neurosis patients in the fortress, and that the 'anxiety and
terror inevitably associated with modern warfare are the exciting
causes of psychoneurosis in almost every man who breaks down under
stress'.[12]

Unfortunately, few reliable figures for combat-related breakdown
have been recorded. We do know that in the Middle East in 1940 there
were just 308 hospitalizations for 'psychoneurotic conditions', and that
in 1941, with the commencement of combat – a potential first or aggra-
vating cause – there were 2678 cases. There are also some statistics
available for the Tobruk siege: despite the extended lack of rest and
exposure to danger, the average breakdown rate recorded over three
months in infantry battalions was just 1.13 per cent. Another survey
put the figure for the entire garrison as one psychiatric casualty to 800
men in the field. This figure is remarkably low, even taking into
account its exclusion of men with physical disorders created by psychological illness, and those men who 'carried on' during the campaign and
broke down thereafter.[13]

The official medical historian says that exhaustion and fear states
were fewer in number in the S.W.P.A. than in the Middle East, but it
seems probable that such states, and certainly psychiatric casualties in
general, were in several instances higher than at Tobruk. For example,
a wartime analysis of casualties admitted to a dressing station at
Kokoda and Soputa throughout November 1942 shows 6.3 per cent of
casualties (13 of 207) to have been 'N.Y.D.(N)' – Not Yet Diagnosed
(Nervous).This was a general term for psychiatric casualties. Of probable relevance here is a battalion historian's comment that of the unit's
138 casualties evacuated from the Kokoda Trail by the end of September 1942, possibly 4 to 7 per cent 'were those whose presence would not
be missed'.[14]

The figure quoted by a medical officer concerning Borneo is more
authoritative. Psychiatric casualties there, most of whom were not
battle-related, comprised 4.86 per cent of all Australian casualties. The
compiler regarded this as a 'high figure', and indeed it is one of the
highest known Australian totals. Nevertheless, it is considerably lower

Exhausted and strained Australian troops rest after the charge that captured Gona, in December 1942. Dozens of Japanese corpses lay around this position. (A.W.M. 013845)

An Australian writes home from front-line Tobruk in August 1941. (A.W.M. 020484)

Reminders of death. In January 1945, men of the 9th Battalion move past temporary graves of Australians killed in recent fighting on Bougainville. The battalion commander, Lt-Col Matthews, faced serious morale problems in the week after this photograph was taken. (A.W.M. 078599)

At Sattelberg, November 1943. Infantrymen are tensed to go 'over the top'.
These were always stressful moments. (A.W.M. 060600)

Pre-battle reflections. In December 1943, two privates wait pensively for the order to advance on Shaggy Ridge, once the preliminary aerial bombardment is over. December 1943. (A.W.M. 062325)

Relief at relief. Happy Australian infantrymen, some of them wounded, have disembarked at Alexandria after leaving Tobruk in September 1941. (A.W.M. 020460)

Taking it. Australian infantrymen on Bougainville in January
1945 await a possible Japanese
raid in their water-filled
dugout. (A.W.M. 078551)

The errie jungle: forward
observation post in the
Sanananda area, January 1943.
(A.W.M. 014184)

Observers often noted the cheerful courage of Australian wounded. This private has just been wounded by a Japanese grenade on Shaggy Ridge in December 1943. (A.W.M. 062296)

The new diggers. Tired but proud victors of Bardia, where the Second A.I.F. tradition was founded in January 1941. (A.W.M. P0643/12/07)

An Australian looks reverently at the Tobruk grave of Corporal John Edmondson, V.C. In winning the first Australian Victoria Cross of the war, Edmondson saved his officer's life and killed at least three Germans during an attack that cost him his own life. Such actions helped to create new military traditions, and inspired similar leadership and self-sacrifice in others. (A.W.M. P0426/05/05)

than British and American ones; for instance, in the British Second
Army between D-Day and the end of the war, psychiatric casualties
fluctuated between 8 per cent and 20 per cent of all battle casualties.[15]

Lack of comprehensive and precise figures on the number of
Australian combat-related psychiatric casualties is frustrating, and in
part a reflection of a traditional reluctance among military and medical
authorities to confront the issue. The official medical historian considers it 'curious how reluctant we have been to acknowledge fear in
medical terminology. We . . . recognise it as a primal instinct, yet we
hesitate to be frank when it obtrudes its universal influence into diag-
nosis and prognosis.'[16]

Yet the medical history itself is disappointingly indirect in its discussion of the role of fear. One point reiterated is that the soldiers
deserve credit for not sustaining more psychiatric casualties than they
did – a view that depends on the dubious notion that men had choice in
the matter.[17]

Medical writing about Australian psychiatric casualties reflects an
anxiety to find explanations in the individual rather than the war. It
concentrates on the fact that many psychiatric disorders among
soldiers had nothing to do with combat, while the combat-related cases
seem to receive less than their due. On the other hand, any highly
stressed soldier who claimed to be sick was probably likely to receive
more sympathetic treatment from his regimental medical officer than
from combatant officers. Thus one commanding officer exclaimed,
after noting that his R.M.O. had defended a 'sick' soldier who had
refused to go on patrol: 'Once cowardice was punished by death but
now we give them medicine!!'[18]

ATTITUDES TO COMBAT EXHAUSTION

Those in command had every reason to regard 'fear state' as a threat to
the army's morale and cohesion. Their concern was reflected in the
policy that sufferers under 40 years of age were retained in the army to
discourage imitation. The same attitude emerged when members of the
army's general staff expressed reservations about the effect that a proposed medical article on a war neurosis clinic in Tobruk would have on
morale. The article contained descriptions of a type widely published
and freely available overseas.[19]

The idea that breakdown was a sign of moral weakness had been strong amongst the officer class – or, at least the European officer class – during the previous war. The following comment, written by a lieutenant after the siege of Tobruk, illustrates its existence amongst Australians in World War II: 'I find that "bomb happys" are more or less of a type – no guts. Four of my men were blown clean out of a dug out – and emerged laughing. A fifth (not one of mine) wasn't nearly as close but suffered from "shell shock". Nerves and fear mostly.'[20]

Some men in the lower ranks also regarded breakdown as a sign of moral weakness. John Lovegrove described an incident that occurred immediately prior to a company attack in New Guinea: 'As we were moving off a recent re-inforcement, fit, robust looking and about 6 feet tall, collapsed on the side of the track sobbing. He was from another of our platoons, and his own group as they strode passed were unsympathetically abusive. A couple even spat on him'.[21] Lovegrove's friend and fellow platoon member, Allan Jones, recalls feeling not disgust but annoyed embarrassment on seeing another acquaintance paralyzed with fear at Alamein. And in a wartime note about a different mate, Jones showed yet another attitude to those incapacitated by fear:

> I had a letter from M – a couple of days ago and he doesn't seem to be exactly in the pink at all. According to his letter he has Neurosis Anxiety noises in head, squint and incorrect focus of left eye So you can see what is a young lad's reward for being one of the 'heroes' of Tobruk. It didn't affect me that way but there are lot of kids like M – ...[22]

These contrasts in the other ranks' attitudes are most obviously explained by the fact that while the despised man was a reinforcement, M – was an established friend. Yet there was more to the matter than degrees of acquaintance. The central reason emerges in Peter Medcalf's moving account of a group's reaction to the breakdown of a young but established comrade before a patrol on Bougainville:

> A strange thing happened. A feeling of terrible sadness and compassion touched all of us. We gently helped him up, and led him to Perce the Boss, holding his hands and guiding him like a small and helpless child. Among us were men of many backgrounds, hardened men who had seen the worst in their fellows; but the same feeling affected all of us – there but for the doubtful grace of God or providence go I.[23]

In other words, those in the ranks knew that the strain of front-line service was capable of breaking them all, and they were accordingly sympathetic to the man who, after sharing the burden with them for some time, finally succumbed.

Medical authorities, despite their preoccupation with factors that predisposed men to break down, sometimes conceded that background and personality were not certain guides to reactions to stress, and that 'even men of reasonably sound personality may break if the strain is sufficiently severe.'[24] Breakdown often happened to initiates, and could happen out of the blue – the result of a near miss from a shell or bomb in particular – but it was also the inevitable culmination of prolonged exposure to strain.

For the men at the front, the fact that not even the bravest individual could cope indefinitely with the strain became more painfully obvious as their period of service lengthened. A private's Tobruk diary contains the reflection: 'I wonder how long men, even Australians, can stand the unrelieved tension'.[25] The question 'how long' must have been a virtually universal one among Australians, for it is clear that in combat positions all soldiers, 'even Australians', stand somewhere on a continuum that ends in mental breakdown. The vast majority of Australian troops left the front before reaching that end-point but many endured stress for protracted periods. During operations, units were generally rotated between forward and reserve positions, so that it was most unusual for a man to be in the front line throughout a campaign. Nevertheless, numerous units spent much longer in the line than the optimum period of about one week at a time.

For example, the 2/9th Battalion spent a month – roughly twice the usual period – in the notoriously dangerous Tobruk Salient, and during one four-month period in the fortress, the 2/23rd Battalion was in the front line for all but two days. The 2/43rd Battalion spent nearly two-thirds of their siege as forward troops. Some battalions of the 9th Division were in the line near Alamein for at least seven consecutive weeks from July to September 1942. Relief came to the 58/59th Battalion only after 11 weeks of daily contact with the enemy during the Salamaua campaign. On his unit's relief during the Papuan fighting, a militiaman noted proudly: '3rd Batt have been in action . 13 weeks. twice as long as any other Batt.'[26] The 2/3rd Battalion's 15 weeks in action was one of several very long spells for Australians in the Aitape-Wewak operations, while the 36th Battalion spent some 30 weeks in forward positions on New Britain – a unique record made possible by the relatively quiet nature of that front. Periods of more than a few weeks without rest seem to have been unusual in most campaigns, but a few weeks was enough to leave most front-line soldiers feeling mentally and physically drained.

Indeed by the completion of their rotations many were nearing the end of their tether. Jack Craig saw a graphic illustration of that fact when he rejoined his unit immediately after Alamein, during which he had been in the pool of replacements: 'God! they all looked tired and worn out. They were nearly white with dust and sand and all old and ashen faced. There were no boys left now. They had aged years.'[27]

Australian commanders generally ensured that relief from the front came in time, and it is interesting to note the medical historian's comment that when exhaustion and fear states occurred in the S.W.P.A. it tended to be in actions from which 'relief was not to be expected'.[28]

The British army estimated that the average rifleman would suffer breakdown after an aggregate of about 400 combat days. The American army, which tended to rest troops less frequently during a campaign, and which in most respects was less akin to the Australian army than was the British, calculated an average figure of 200 to 240 aggregate days.[29] Bearing in mind that thresholds varied between individuals, and that many broke down well before these periods expired, it is interesting to compare these figures with the Australian record.

The infantry battalions of the 6th and 7th divisions were all in action for periods ranging from 200 to 240 days, counting campaigning as opposed to contact days, while only the 9th Division and the 18th Brigade saw 400 such days. Very few individual members of those two formations would have done so, however, and it is doubtful that a majority of members of the 6th Division and remaining 7th Division units saw 200 to 240 campaign days. The infantry battalions of the 6th, 7th and 9th divisions each sailed for the Middle East with some 1000 'originals', but by 1945 few seem to have retained more than 100 of these men. By April 1945 only 1359 of the 52 243 men in these divisions – that is, 2.6 per cent – had been in the Australian Imperial Force since April 1940 or earlier. It appears to have been common for more than 3000 men to serve as members of a battalion over the course of the war.[30]

AVOIDING BREAKDOWN AND DEATH

Not only does this high turnover of personnel suggest that most soldiers escaped suicidally lengthy service, but it raises the question of whether men actually sought to transfer out of combat units in order to avoid it. It is also pertinent that huge numbers of men were discharged from the army throughout the war. By late October 1941, 13 per cent of men who had so far enlisted in the A.I.F. had been discharged. The late war rates were even higher.[31]

The vast majority of these transfers and discharges had nothing to do with combat stress. Men rarely had any choice about leaving their unit. Illness, wounds and age limits resulted in many thousands of unavoidable medical downgradings, transfers to non-combatant duties and discharges. Deaths and losses through capture also ate into battalion membership – often to the tune of 10 per cent – but anecdotal evidence suggests that as the war progressed, veterans increasingly sought and found positions that would increase the odds of mental and physical survival.[32]

The evidence concerning desertion also hints that veterans became increasingly keen to leave the firing-line. After coming home from the Middle East, more than 200 men of the 2/33rd Battalion did not return from leave on time, and indeed most never reappeared. Other battalions seem to have had similar experiences. In 1944, the desertion rate in the Australian army appears to have been nearly four times that in the British. Presumably, some or most of these men were keen to avoid further combat.[33]

Desertion was one of several illegitimate ways of avoiding mental breakdown. The fact that the 'illegal absentee' or desertion rate among Australian soldiers appears to have been higher than in the British or American armies seems important, but the Australian army was unlike the other two in that it suffered very little desertion from the front line. The official history suggests that there were never more than a few hundred 'absent from the fighting formations'.[34] On the other hand, desertion was more practical in the combat zones of Europe than in those of North Africa or New Guinea.

Another illegal means of evading breakdown was to disobey an order to go into a forward area. Individuals and small groups occasionally refused to man a post, to patrol or to attack: as many as a company of men were included in several such incidents on Bougainville. A less obvious method of evasion was to court illness. Steward reports seeing dermatitis sufferers in hospital at Port Moresby scratching their skin in the hope of getting home. And while the vast majority of the soldiers who contracted malaria did so unwillingly, some undoubtedly monitored their intake of suppressive tablets, timing a malaria relapse to coincide with the end of their leave, which would consequently be extended. Another instance of men encouraging the disease seems to be indicated by the fact that when regulations stopped the practice of sending men to Australia on contracting the disease, the sickness rate fell. According to Steward, the army classified such cases of malaria as a 'self-inflicted wound'.[35]

The self-inflicted gunshot wound was the last resort of men prepared to use illegitimate means to halt their slide towards madness or death. These wounds mostly affected fingers – especially little fingers and those of the left hand – and toes, but also included suicides. The true incidence of these wounds will never be known.

Only 62 cases of self-inflicted wounds (S.I.W.s) are recorded in the official casualty registers – 40 of them fatal. There were clearly many more than 22 cases in which men survived. The official history notes that 30 cases – chiefly affecting hands and feet – were reported within five days at Tobruk. Among the soldiers represented in this study, six cases of other soldiers' self-inflicted wounds are discussed, some of which do not appear in the official registers. Those registers show that one A.I.F. infantry battalion alone had five, possibly six, cases in Papua, and it is hard to believe that no other battalion suffered similarly there.[36]

Part of the difficulty with records of self-inflicted wounds in the Papuan campaign was that medical officers were ordered not to label wounds as self-inflicted unless they had seen the shot fired. Conversely, the medical history asserts that some men were unjustly accused. Certain medical officers claimed that true S.I.W.s were 'rare or practically non-existent' in Papua.[37] This and other such claims about the phenomenon were too rosy, but clearly it was an expedient that directly involved a very small minority.

The negative attitude of one powerful member of the majority towards the practice appears in a pre-battle speech of the C.O. of the 2/23rd Battalion, who noted the absence of 'the usual broken reeds who committed self-inflicted wounds'.[38] In a diary entry written in a convalescent depot in Palestine, a private from the same battalion implied similar feelings, although he also showed the presence of an opposing opinion in the lower ranks: 'A bloke in the next tent has just cut his throat. I see him being carried away on a stretch: the conversation turns to S.I.W's and suicides, some say they must be game, am afraid there is too much loose talk on the subject.'[39]

Allan Jones believes that in the Australian army sympathy was nearly always given to anyone under such strain as to commit a self-inflicted wound. That 'strain' emerges in a touching scene described by Captain J. J. May, who served in the Australian hospital during the fighting at Wau:

> The wounded lay there bandaged, no sound coming from them. In a bed near one of the propped up shutters a soldier kept sitting up an looking down into the conflict . . . He had a self inflicted wound . . . he had shot himself in the foot. I felt a great sympathy and understanding towards him and I went over to speak to him but he was oblivious to us locked in his own private world of terror. He would lie still for a few minutes, then prop himself up to arms length and stare into the valley . . . [He] had shot himself because of his panic and was still held up not able to get away from it all.[40]

This passage suggests that at least some who wounded themselves were not calculating cowards, but men driven to desperate straits.

The army relieved soldiers to prevent them from going mad. The individual front-line soldier desired relief for that purpose, too, but also wanted it to prevent his own, objectively insignificant death. The same dual purpose informed the methods – legal and illegal – by which the individual sought to secure his own release from the front. Circumstances or, more often, a sense of honour prevented most from taking the illegitimate paths, but the fact that others were willing was a reflection of a widespread preoccupation with death.

TWO CASE STUDIES OF FRONT-LINE STRESS

Two diaries of the Bougainville campaign provide extraordinary insight into the process by which front-line service propelled men towards, and eventually beyond, the limits of their endurance. The diarists were men of the same brigade, but of very different station: one the commanding officer of the 9th Battalion, the other a private in the Intelligence Section of the 61st Battalion. The disparity of rank between the lieutenant-colonel, G. R. Matthews, and the private, J. H. Owen, permits the reader to observe from two different perspectives the unfolding of related and similar developments in central Bougainville in 1945.

The earliest relevant entry is Lieutenant-Colonel Matthews' description of his men as they took over an American outpost late in November 1944: 'They were all excited and glad to get into it.' The following week, after his battalion had captured a Japanese outpost he exulted: 'Our boys were wonderful, no hesitation and right into it. I am proud of them.' Then and on an occasion early in December he noted a 'marvellous' response from headquarters troops asked to help carry ammunition to the foremost combatants.[41]

On 18 December, the mutilated body of a battalion member was discovered in the jungle, but during a visit from several high-ranking officers the following day, Matthews' troops were said to be 'well shaven and dressed correctly and all cheerful'. On Christmas Eve, Matthews mentioned a well-attended memorial church service, remarking: 'The tps sadly feel the loss of their pals.' Four days later he noted the inefficiency of several battalion officers.[42]

In the course of the following month, the battalion came under Japanese shelling, suffered casualties on booby traps and, perhaps most stressful, advanced over terrain where there was 'a constant sense of danger', and from which sprang several Japanese ambushes and attacks.[43] At the end of January, serious morale problems emerged. On 29 January, a man in a section that had previously been ambushed ' "accidentally" shot himself in the foot', and another refused to go on patrol. At this time Matthews was being urged from above to 'push on as quickly as possible'. The following day, the medical officer reported that men of one company were exhausted and suffering from diarrhoea and very low morale. Matthews sent the company back for a rest.[44]

The next morning Japanese shelling landed close to battalion headquarters. Matthews ordered a second company to go forward and capture the enemy artillery pieces at first light. The company commander reportedly told Matthews that his men were too fatigued. The testimony that follows in the diary is dramatic and telling:

I ordered him to do it and rang off. 1/2 hr later he rang to say
he had told his Coy and no man would leave his posn, all

refusing duty. I asked why and they said they were all too tired, they were cut off from the world and could not get casualties back and weren't prepared to get any anyway. I told Coy Comd to order his officers fwd and he said he knew they wouldn't but would give it a go.

His 2 i/c [second in command] rang shortly after and said Coy Comd cracked up, mental strain, crying.

Amazed by these events, Matthews relieved the company commander, whom he blamed for the general disobedience. He then sent the company their packs and cooking gear, stating that this made them much happier.[45]

The following day, Matthews was disappointed when men of a third company 'came home' soon after contacting Japanese troops. When he told the platoon commander concerned to go back and complete his task, the latter said 'his men were frightened', but he completed the job to Matthews' satisfaction. This was only the beginning of the day's troubles: another company commander reported that his officers and men were openly expressing dissatisfaction with Matthews, the men of another company were said to be complaining about lack of support from other arms, and a lieutenant took up a belligerent attitude to the C.O.[46]

On 2 February, battalion spirits lifted with the capture of a Japanese gun. Matthews' intentions of resting his companies were thwarted on 3 February by orders from higher command to get moving. Matthews recorded no further morale problems in the subsequent three weeks, although on 16 February he wrote that his unit deserved a rest, and when on 21 February he criticized the performance of a company of a nearby battalion, he added: '. . . must be no better than some of my Coys'.[47]

The nearby battalion was the 61st, and just the day before Matthews' comment, Private Ewen had written about the unit's morale in his first Bougainville diary entry. He remarked that the men, having been in action for about six weeks, were hoping for relief within a week. His description of the effects of protracted front-line service is memorable: 'we are all just about had. Living on your nerves in mud and rain, sleeping in holes in the ground soon wears a fellow down. I have watched the boys faces get drawn and haggard, and their movements slow and listless.'[48]

On 25 February he recorded that morale was high, but the men very tired. He also noted enviously that the 9th Battalion was being relieved.[49] That same day, Matthews was recording that his 9th Battalion was indeed to be relieved: 'Loud cheers from everyone when news was spread.' This was a reversal of the battle-hungriness of 23 November. The joy continued in the rest area, where Matthews also received a message from the brigadier expressing appreciation of the battalion's 'wonderful effort'.[50]

While 9th Battalion rested, 61st Battalion soldiered on, to the point where in March Ewen could write of one company: 'this Coy . . . has had it. Most of the boys nerves have gone, and they just can't take any more. About a month ago if they bumped trouble they would hop in and have a go, but now it takes the offrs all their time to get them to hold their ground.'[51]

He blamed the company commander. Brigade command recognized this dangerously low morale, and on 19 March Matthews was told to relieve the 'completely fatigued' 61st Battalion as quickly as possible. He was warned 'of possible infection of 61 Bn low spirits on [his] troops'. 'My troops should be O.K. for a while', he reflected, 'but if the going gets tough they may crack too.'[52] On 21 March, Matthews recorded that a senior brigade officer had told him: 'troops when fired on rush back in disorder leaving their officers. They are frightened to move out of their perimeters. Patrols go out and do not complete their tasks; sit in jungle and wait for time to elapse and then come in.'[53]

The 61st Battalion was relieved, but three weeks after Matthews reported the brigade officer's comments, the unit was back at the front and, according to Ewen, in much the same condition:

> The Bn is in a bad way as the men are all cracked up. To-day 9 from D Coy and 3 from 'B' refused to go on patrol, and I believe that 'A' Coy patrols only go 200 yds out and sit down. If they send us in again the Coys are going to refuse to go. So things are in a very bad state. Already two officers have been sent back for standing-up for the men. Nearly all the boys have a vacant look in their eyes and look dazed.[54]

During the changeover of late March, Matthews reported that his men had been told horror stories by 61st Battalion, but that they seemed unaffected. Yet within three days, one officer had 'dropped his bundle a bit'. Many of one company had reported sick, and one-third of them were put on light duties.[55]

Three weeks later, the men of another of Matthews' companies were said to have 'the jitters', and 'would not go on' Led to believe that they were about to stage a 'sit down strike' after hearing much enemy fire ahead, Matthews went among this company and persuaded them to go on. He recorded an instance of similar nervousness among a platoon on 20 April, but on 22 April said that the arrival of Australian tanks had raised morale 100 per cent. At the end of that month his diary shows that he had been recommending men for decorations, and he reflected on 'some mighty work done'. The following day, with some men being relieved, he noted that their morale was now high.[56]

A final indicator of the point to which front-line service had driven these battalions is comments on leave granted to some of their men on their relief in May. Matthews noted on 2 May that 76 men had been given 24 days of the 60 or more days of home leave they had accrued. He commented: 'A lot won't come back until their full credit of over 60 days is exhausted and I don't blame them.' Ewen made a similar prediction, adding to it: 'This Bde will never do another show after the way the Bde has been treated. Even the officers have given the game away.' Indeed he himself made a resolution: 'I've made up my mind that I will not go into action again without I get my leave.'[57] His last wartime entries were made in May, during a rest period. The next entry followed eight months later, in January 1946:

> Since coming out of action I've did 3 months Field Punishment, and even if I had to complete my full sentence it would be worth it.
> Seventy-five of us refused to go back into action until we were again given our leave. Its a long story of Bad Army Adm. All the officers had leave and half the Bn were on leave when we were ordered back up. We refused to go – 3 days later Peace was declared – luck? – X and I got 18 months.[58]

Although the incidents drawn from both men's diaries involved more than 1000 men, a case could be made that these soldiers were not representative. For a start they were of the original Citizen Military Forces (though the 61st Battalion was entitled to the Australian Imperial Force title by 1945), whereas most units that saw front-line service were originally A.I.F. (See Appendix A 'Who Fought Where' for definition of front-line solders.) There seems to be no evidence of entire campaigning A.I.F. units even considering disobeying orders. In fact, it is difficult to imagine them doing so, even though they endured longer and far bloodier campaigns than the 9th and 61st Battalions undertook on Bougainville, and despite the fact that resting A.I.F. units sometimes dreaded being recalled to the line.

Yet it would be unfair to dismiss the experience of these two battalions as entirely unrepresentative. On the only occasion that they fought alongside A.I.F. units, at Milne Bay in 1942, the efforts of the two fledgling militia units did not suffer by comparison with the veterans, as Ewen noted.[59] It is important also to recognize that in 1945 neither unit seems to have been held by senior command to be in disgrace. Indeed, Matthews recorded that in an address in May, a very high-ranking officer gave 9th Battalion 'the highest praise any unit could have' and that something similar occurred when the Commander-in-Chief visited in June.[60] This strongly suggests that these units did not perform below general Australian standards.

Perhaps the behaviour of the original A.I.F. units would have been like that of these two battalions had they also been engaged in the protracted, pointless campaign on Bougainville. In fact, the official historian says that in the Aitape-Wewak region, where the 6th Division did undertake a similar type of campaign, the A.I.F. veterans were even less enthusiastic than the Australians on Bougainville. Long made that assessment despite being acquainted with many of the facts outlined above: he had access to, and made use of, Matthews' diary.[61]

Moreover, the inescapable fact is that the Bougainville experience is relevant not just to the Australian C.M.F. but to all men who have ever entered the front line. For the evidence of other armies shows that all combatants are on a slippery slide to breakdown. Whether in original C.M.F. units the slide tended to be unusually fast, and propelled by some internal dynamic, is a matter for conjecture, but they should be presumed innocent until proved otherwise. The chief blame for the undisciplined behaviour in the two battalions should be laid at the feet of the authorities who were obviously too slow in recognizing and reacting when these soldiers had been driven beyond the limits of military efficiency, and beyond their capacity to endure.

CHAPTER FIVE

TAKING THE STRAINS OF
THE FRONT LINE

*D*espite the mental and physical burdens of campaigning, Australians were generally effective front-line soldiers. They were regarded as formidable fighters both by their enemies – even in defeats such as Crete and Malaya – and by their allies. Cases of individual fear developing into group panic were most unusual among Australian combat troops. Although the typical Australian soldier never regained the naive enthusiasm of his first campaign, he was usually willing to enter the fray as each subsequent operation approached. Clearly, then, most Australian troops coped with the physical and psychological stresses of 'this unnatural life'. The question is 'How?'

TOBACCO, ALCOHOL AND OTHER DISTRACTIONS

There were ways of minimizing thoughts of death. A diarist reported that as the garrison of a Tobruk outpost waited for a German attack in October 1941, 'everyone smoked like trains to calm their nerves', and indeed the vast majority of Australian soldiers were smokers. In calculating distribution of tobacco and cigarettes, the army worked on the assumption that 90 per cent of the members of any one unit smoked. In many instances, men took up the habit or smoked more heavily mainly to be sociable or to fill in time, but the fact that 'tobacco became a compelling and almost universal addiction during the war years' was due also to its capacity to reduce stress.[1]

63

So strong was the dependence upon tobacco that on the frequent occasions that supply to the front was unreliable, it imposed an added strain. Reference is often made in the literature to the discontent of men left without tobacco or cigarettes, and to Australians resorting to expedients such as those described by a survivor of the Cretan campaign: 'All the cigs. we had we "ratted" off dead Fritzies but most of us smoked grass or grapevine leaves rolled up in any paper we could get, or a pipe made from bamboo.'[2]

An eyewitness's retelling of an incident that occurred in perilous circumstances at Buna suggests that this craving could even override considerations of self-preservation: 'Our sargent-major was laying about five yards from "Scotty" Wright and he said to "Scotty" I must get a light off your cigarette even if I do get killed and he crawled over to "Scotty" and lit his cigarette off "Scotty's". About half an hour or so later he was killed . . . '[3]

Alcohol could also take the mind off death. John Butler saw it serving that purpose in Tobruk:

> To-night at 9.0 p.m., I see the remnant of 'B' Coy, after a day and a half of action. All the officers have gone – prisoners or killed, and only 25 men left, they are sitting round a jar of rum – getting drunk . . . drunkenness on such an occasion is excusable – it brings their nerves back – nerves that have been shattered by frightening scenes and experiences – scenes and experiences that are best forgotten quickly. Rum to a war-shocked soldier is like a slap on the face of a hysterical woman.[4]

In the first Libyan campaign, it had been policy to distribute rum before rather than after action, and, during the battle of Bardia at least, its effect on some soldiers' mental activity had been more powerful than desired by the authorities. However, there were not large numbers of Australians intoxicated by rum at Bardia, and still fewer in subsequent actions. On the whole, rum was rarely distributed, and on those occasions was usually issued in very small quantities.[5]

Officers and sergeants had access to liquor in the final jungle campaigns, and in the Middle East, where it was especially valuable as 'air raid tonic' during the Greek and Cretan campaigns. Captain Chrystal described the end of a day of fearful shelling in Greece: 'When Hal arrived from B.H.Q. about 2000 hours he brought a bottle of whisky the

M.O. had sent up and a dozen of us had an unforgettable nip which pulled us together.' Although there is no evidence that drunkenness was a major problem amongst officers and sergeants in the line, an incident noted after a night of enemy shelling at Alamein was surely not unique: '1000 hrs X evacuated – drunk – Y took over.'[6]

Italians at Alamein had an image of Australians as men 'rendered bestial and brutal by drunkenness.'[7] No doubt this was essentially an excuse for the Italians' poor performance, but it may have contained a grain of truth. For officially-sanctioned alcohol was available in unprecedented quantities at Alamein from July to November 1942. The rank and file received a regular issue of beer, and in at least one battalion were permitted, if they had the funds, to buy spirits (usually whisky). However, two bottles per man per week was usually the maximum quantity of beer available, and even if one could somehow obtain extra supplies, this was hardly the stuff of bestial drunkenness. The whisky conceivably could have been another matter.

Men who possessed it at or near the front had the means and of course a motive to get drunk. One diarist referred to a group doing so with 'scrounged' bottles of whisky and gin within firing distance of the enemy in July 1942. To obtain spirits men normally needed money and an opportunity to go back to the source of supply, usually the rear echelon of their unit. According to Bob Anson, these opportunities were rare. He recalls no drunks on the Alamein front, but remembers that the 'Battle of Alamein did see some fellows with a bottle of whisky'. Indeed, one diarist from Anson's battalion noted on the opening night of the battle: 'Gave the boys in my section a shot of whisky – it was good.' This 'shot' was unlikely to have engendered drunken brutality, but the behaviour of another diarist, who recorded on the same night that he and a comrade had decided to share a bottle of Scotch, was presumably affected in some way.[8]

However, unless there has been a vast conspiracy of silence, the great majority of Australian participants at Alamein 'took' its stresses without the comfort of alcohol, or with insufficient quantities to affect their behaviour and perceptions. In the earlier assaults on Bardia and Tobruk, some men drank from the huge Italian supplies captured there, but in general the other ranks in the Australian army never had access to sufficient alcohol to inebriate them at the front.[9]

In the S.W.P.A. alcohol was officially prohibited for most of the war, and scarce for the remaining time, so the concept of the inebriated

Australian warrior was irrelevant there. Various alcoholic home brews
were concocted in rear areas, but this was usually impractical in forward zones: a tragic exception occurred in 1945 when six Australians
died after drinking methyl alcohol from ruptured drums at Balikpapan.
Tea, with its oft-noted capacity to revive men's morale, was a more
widely used 'nerve solace' at the battlefront.[10]

Apart from these drugs of varying strength, prayer and thoughts of
home served to block out contemplation of death. The hard-bitten Bert
Sawford said after barely escaping capture or death in Malaya: 'The
thought of such a good little Wife and Son waiting for me back home
kept me going. I am not ashamed to addmit I said prayers and I am sure
they helped me.'[11] Also, as already mentioned, some even chewed hard
biscuits in the desperate attempt to do something other than contemplate the end. However, while biscuits, cigarettes, alcohol and prayer
helped in the moments of direst need, for most Australians these were
not the main considerations that made them persevere and succeed in
the face of extreme exhaustion and their primal fear of sudden death.
The chief explanation as to why Australians could 'take it' lies elsewhere.

ADAPTING TO DANGER

One plausible answer is that after a time the 'unnatural life' became
natural to the men living it: that the soldier became so accustomed to
physical exertion and danger that his body and mind accommodated
them and permitted him to continue. In the case of physical strain,
there is evidence for this hypothesis. In particular, many Australians
clearly developed an ability to sleep through virtually any noise and
under almost any conditions. For example a sapper wrote to a female
correspondent after the first Libyan campaign:

> Personally, I've slept in neat holes, I've slept under bushes,
> I've woken with aching bones from dossing on hard rocks, I've
> curled up in a furrow of a plowed field – damme, I think I'd be
> as comfortable hung on a barbed wire fence as I would be in
> mother's soft bed – I've even slept perched precariously on a
> steep cliff face – when one has to one can get used to every-
> thing ... [12]

There is a sense of adjustment to other elements of the soldier's
physical burden in this note from New Guinea: 'our chaps have

certainly got the hang of this country now carry full pack and equipment over tracks and distances which a few months back appeared
impossible',[13] John Lovegrove's diary comment on leaving Tobruk
suggests that he and others had become so much 'at home' in the fortress that the life outside seemed to be unnatural: 'we had become so
accustomed to unhygienic conditions, unshaven, unwashed, flies, fleas,
rats and the repetitive daily rations . . . filthy khaki shorts and shirts,
threadbare socks and bleached unpolished boots that the extreme contrast with the superb cleanliness of this ship and its officers and crew
seemed to us unrealistic'.

He went on to contrast the 'dream' of the ship with the 'harsh
reality' of the previous months.[14] That juxtaposition illustrates the
chief limitation of the argument that men became so immersed in the
front-line world that it seemed natural. Men's imagination and memories frequently took them out of the 'harsh reality' and into thoughts of
past and future times with family, good food, baths, comfortable beds,
female companionship, and alcohol. Occasionally they also had frag-
ments of these things at the front: beer rations, books and magazines,
and, of paramount importance, mail from home. For most, the civilian
life they remembered, wanted and maintained tenuous but precious
contact with was the 'natural' existence; the standard by which the
unnatural and unpleasant qualities of front-line life were defined and
measured.

The nature of their civilian backgrounds enabled some Australians
to adapt to the heat, drought and dust of North Africa more quickly
than their European allies and enemies, but most still found the desert
an alien and loathsome place. Libya, in particular, was considered a
'God-forsaken desolate hole', 'the country God didnt have time to finish', 'a bastard of a country'.[15] Conditions in the jungle were even less
familiar and, if possible, less popular.

Nevertheless, the suggestion that soldiers became increasingly
attuned to the unfamiliar physical demands of soldiering has some
validity; always bearing in mind that deprivation of sleep could never
be overcome as a problem, and that no-one could become used to
marching over long distances with insufficient food or while suffering
dysentery.

Even before they reached the front, many Australian soldiers were
well prepared physically for what was to come. The training of recruits
helped them to a considerable extent to endure the trials ahead of them.

A favourite wartime adjective for describing Australian training was 'hard'. 'Severe' is the adjective used by the official historian to describe the four-week course at the Jungle Warfare Training Centre at Canungra, Queensland, through which nearly all reinforcements to fighting units passed from December 1942.[16]

While veterans sometimes praised Canungra's training because of its effect on the quality of reinforcements, they tended to be less enthusiastic about the day-to-day training in which they themselves, and the majority of Australian troops, spent most of their war. In part their dissatisfaction arose from the repetitive nature of the work. However, it also derived from a feeling amongst experienced soldiers that exercises were very limited models of 'the real thing'. To the other ranks, participating in an exercise was 'playing' at war, largely for the benefit of the officers. Yet to the front-line officer, too, it was 'Rather boring trying to paint pictures of battles when you've been through a few shows.'[17] This criticism reflected an insight that however 'hard' reinforcement or daily training became, there would always be an unbridgeable gap between it and the combat for which it was supposedly a preparation. This missing element was surely the emotions battle inspired: particularly fear.

Inoculating men against fear was a task that the trainers might have labelled not 'hard' but 'too hard'. And whereas the experience that followed training could eventually make much of the physical strain seem normal, if not natural, this was far less the case with the mental strain associated with danger.

Lengthy acquaintance with danger did allow men to cope to a limited extent. The official history states that 'familiarity caused air attack to lose some of its awe for the great majority' of the Tobruk garrison.[18] The exact nature of this loss of awe is exemplified in a note from an infantryman in Tobruk: 'we used to run like hell for a hole as soon as we saw a plane but now we are used to them and stand and watch the devils dive bombing and machine gunning, if they don't come too close alls well but when they head for us we break all records for a hole'.[19]

As this passage implies, familiarity helped men to cope with fear not by making them blasé about it but by making them better able to assess the presence or absence of danger; rather than get rid of fear, it told men when there was something to fear. Experience could also exorcise the initiate's fear of the unknown, but it could not eliminate the fear of being killed.

War was a learning process, and one might expect that such an education would enable men to cope with danger and the other strains of front-line existence. Yet the lessons learnt at the front were more in the nature of a series of apocalyptic revelations than a survival course. The essence of the front-line education was the message that it was more difficult to accommodate battlefield actualities to one's world-view than had been anticipated, for those realities simply did not match one's hopeful expectations. As mentioned, 'living' and 'learning' – or more precisely, surviving and learning – were quite different things, and the latter did little to remove fears surrounding the former.

The popularity of the expression 'We can take it' was an indication that stress was an issue that had to be consciously tackled, and not an obstacle that would disappear naturally over time, or that could be avoided altogether by suitable preparation of the recruit. 'We can take it' was similar to the Great War's 'Are we downhearted?', and was not unique to Australians. It was often used simply as a convenient saying: added, for example, to a comment that it was raining or that the war might take years to finish. In part, too, it could be seen as a slogan used in a contrived way by people behind the front line for encouraging those who were in it. Consciousness of this artificial element is evident in a rifleman's note from the Tobruk Salient: 'We often wonder just how long "we can take it." Not too much longer we hope.'[20]

Yet the expression was also taken up with a will by Australian soldiers, who saw in it a means of stating that they were in a predicament and that they were prepared to take the risks necessary to endure it. The catchcry is heartfelt, poignant and courageous in this diary entry from Singapore:

> If we are here another 3 days we will be wiped out to a man, as there is no way of evacuating us. The Jap Navy is behind us, their soldiers in front of us and their Air Force overhead so what chance have we got. But all our boys are keeping their chins up. We can take it.[21]

Another moving expression of determination appears in a diary written by a private as the Malayan campaign drew to a close: 'Struggling back to Singapore. Feet all. raw and. festered. But have to. carry. on. living in hell. but. still smiling'.[22] Such statements show that men fought consciously against circumstances they considered not natural but ghastly. Unfortunately, they do not answer the questions 'How could they "take it"?', and 'Why did they "have to carry on"?'

DISCIPLINE AND LEADERSHIP

Perhaps the most immediately apparent reason that soldiers put up with the strains pressed on them in action was discipline. Obedience and group discipline were indispensable in the Australians' steady marches towards the enemy guns in North Africa, in the successful withdrawal under enemy attack in Greece, and even in the small unit actions in New Guinea, where coordinated fire and movement were essential. Like all soldiers, Australians faced stiff penalties if they refused to obey orders or tried to flee. Perhaps they 'took it' because they had no real choice in the matter.

On occasions some did desert or refuse to obey, as we have noted in Chapter 4; this incident recorded by a provost on Bougainville is a further example: 'a number of men from 58/59 have deserted and are given themselves up. – two walked in tonight and said they would stand .anything but the shelling and would rather do 3 or 4 years than go back again'.[23]

Why did huge numbers of men not show the same preference for a period of safe detention over the risks of permanent extinction? One could answer, rightly, that circumstances were against fleeing in the desert and jungle. However, it is clear from other evidence that coercive discipline was not the only key to endurance.

In fact, leaders in Australian combat units could not readily coerce their men into risking their lives. Discipline there was less strict and formal than in the British army. Usually any new officer's authority was quickly acknowledged, but some platoons exerted sufficient informal pressure to ensure that lazy, selfish and incompetent officers either left or changed their ways. Moreover, while officers had wide legal powers over their men, until these leaders proved their mettle in combat, they were themselves on trial with their subordinates.

Some failed, but a large majority of combat officers passed the test. They proved themselves skilful and adaptable tacticians, they led by courageous example, and took such care to preserve the lives of their men that front-line officers died in battle at a much higher rate than the 'cannon fodder' under their command.[24] At the front, Australian soldiers usually found in their officers leaders as dependable as those praised by Corporal Stoner in a letter from Malaya: 'Our officers (platoon commanders) have been "trumps" and have kept up the morale of the troops despite the fact that they have had the gravest responsibilities and a greater physical strain than most.'[25]

The officers' ability to lead, rather than their formal authority, caused men to follow them into frightening situations. It was obedience based on respect and consent, rather than – or as well as – coercion.

The informality of Australian officer/men relations, as well as the volunteer status of most Australian fighting soldiers, undoubtedly made coercion less important in their army than it was in others. However, leadership is likely to be important to soldiers in any army once battle commences. Even though the fear of punishment and the instinctive obedience so important to discipline can easily falter in the terror and confusion of combat, men's need for direction becomes stronger and so they become more likely to follow instructions. Thus, in recording his impressions of the battle of Bardia, an Australian infantry officer observed: 'The men went extraordinarily well and will do anything you ask them. Under fire they are continually looking to their superiors.'[26]

In the Australian army, direction was provided not only by commissioned officers. Non-commissioned officers generally had closer contact with the rank and file, and an inspiring example of the work they could do to help men persevere appears in Jack Craig's vivid account of his initiation to shelling, at Tel el Eisa:

> Shells were landing in our position one a second and I knew everyone was aimed at me. Lying on the bottom of the weapon pit, with my hands over my ears trying to block out the terrible crash of the shells and sand falling in my eyes nose and mouth I felt I would never survive another minute As every shell burst it seemed just outside my pit. When my nerves were at breaking point and my prayers weaker, I faintly heard another noise, strange to all the bursting of shells and screaming shrapnel. With my mouth open and ears alert the sound grew stronger and I recognised it as someone whistling . . . I found the courage to lift my head above the parapet and through the bursting of shell, cordite smoke, shrapnel and whirling dust, a figure casually approached and when a few feet away stopped whistling long enough to say, 'How are you going down there' . . . When I looked up and saw the calm features of my platoon sergeant I wasn't scared any more.[27]

A feature of the Australian military experience in World War II was that on the numerous occasions when no officially qualified leader was available, someone of lower rank would almost invariably step in and provide the necessary direction. Such men were 'obeyed', even more than were officers, because of leadership qualities other than those associated with formal powers.

But 'leadership' and 'discipline', however broadly they are defined, were not of primary importance in battle. In an American wartime survey of what motivated soldiers to persevere and succeed in combat, only one per cent of the other ranks nominated 'leadership and discipline' as the key factor, and although the structures and experiences of the American and Australian armies varied greatly, this figure reinforces a strong impression that other factors were also more important to Australians.[28]

PATRIOTISM AND THE ANZAC TRADITION

Another possible source of the Australian's determination and ability to 'take it' is his commitment to ideals. Most obvious of those is patriotism. Unless an army is composed of men who share a general belief in the justice of their country's stance in war, it has little prospect of maintaining cohesion and achieving military success. Australian front-line soldiers were no exception to the rule that most troops adhere to a national cause. A sense of patriotic duty was the single most important factor influencing Australians to volunteer or to accept call-up without demur.[29] Many of these men must have expected to be sustained in battle by their willingness to risk all for a cause: in the early years of the war, that of protecting Britain, Australia, the Empire and even the world from the Germans; from late 1941, when enlistments shot up as they had after the fall of France, that of protecting Australia from the Japanese.

The eulogies written by officers and men for dead colleagues suggest that these ideals did provide sustenance. Thus, a lieutenant-colonel said of the Australians killed in Greece: 'Those lads freely offered themselves knowing what price they might pay to keep the Nazi hooro away from Australia.' While returning to Port Moresby after the Kokoda campaign, Lance-Corporal Spindler recalled dead mates 'who gave their lives to keep Australia free', and a captain on Bougainville wrote to the relative of a dead soldier: 'I know in my heart that the cause

Jim died for and the rest of his mates are fighting for is a good one'.[30]

In one sense it is clear that men killed in Australian uniform died for the cause of nation or empire. Yet whether they consciously fought for and were sustained by that cause in battle is debatable. Australians serving overseas did develop an oft-expressed longing for Australia's way of life and especially for their own intimate domestic circle. Yet in contrast to this enthusiasm for 'home', little was stated openly about fighting for Australia. Early in 1942, Australians in the Middle East became openly anxious to move to where they could defend Australia, but this does not necessarily mean that, when in action, their patriotic urge helped them to fight on.

Australians in the Middle East rarely described themselves – aside from their mentions of other, usually dead, men – as fighting to preserve the well-being of their family, nation or Empire. Their compatriots fighting in the Far East early in 1942 were more likely to find meaning and encouragement in such notions, for many must have shared the worried awareness of the private who wrote shortly before the Japanese assault on Singapore: 'if only we can smash him here the threat to Aussie will never materialize'.[31]

There is little contemporary evidence, however, that this threat inspired the soldiers who fought the strategically important battles for Milne Bay and Kokoda. In fact, during the Kokoda campaign, war correspondent George Johnston wrote in Port Moresby: 'Great excitement up the track when the A.I.F. got the news of the 8th Army's smashing victory against the Axis in Egypt on the El Alamain front. Everybody wishes he were over there!!'[32]

Participants in the Papuan campaigns said subsequently that patriotism had been a motivating factor there, and some historians have taken up that idea. For example, Humphrey McQueen nominates the Kokoda Trail as the location of the birth of Australian national consciousness, or at least as 'a focal point in a decade of rebirth'.[33] The A.I.F. units that did most of the fighting had come almost directly from the Middle East, where the desire to return and protect Australia had been strong, and their new field of operations was clearly strategically menacing. It is almost inconceivable that thoughts of national survival were entirely absent from their minds in New Guinea. Perhaps the best wartime evidence that such considerations were significant is the previously quoted statement that Australians in Papua hated the Japanese partly because of 'his policy of conquest brought so near to Australia'.[34]

Yet thoughts about defending Australia were not necessarily prominent when the firing began, and Australians were fighting for their lives. Indeed, one veteran implies that even before men reached the front such considerations were not as important as they might have been, for he argues that officers hid the critical nature of the Kokoda situation from the troops.[35]

The following wartime assessment of the role of patriotism in the Papuan fighting was made by a medical officer who apparently served with a C.M.F. rather than an A.I.F. unit there, but it rings true as a widely representative statement: 'I don't know that we ever thought at the time that we were saving Australia and keeping our wives, sisters and mothers from slavery. These thoughts had come before.'[36]

If this was the case in the campaign that came closest to Australian soil, what could one expect of the campaigns that followed, after the threat to Australia had effectively passed, or of the earlier, distant Middle Eastern campaigns? A battalion newspaper printed in Tobruk offered an explanation of the place of patriotism similar to the medical officer's:

> We have a justifiable pride in our country, and in our mode of life; otherwise we would not have thought it necessary to give up our liberty and endanger our lives for the preservation of our country and its institutions, and what it stands for. In this environment, *we do not think so much of these things*, but the fact remains that all the thoughts and aspirations of our pre-army life are still within us.[37]

As the two previous quotations suggest, Australian front-line soldiers were not without patriotic motivation, but it was by no means their final reserve when their resources were stretched to the limit in battle. One could argue that the 1945 campaigns are proof of this, for Australians fought well then despite their realization that the operations were contributing little to Australia's safety or the war's end. Yet in his memoir of one of these campaigns, Peter Medcalf names 'an unspoken patriotism' as one of the two main motivations of men in infantry battalions.[38] It is impossible to disprove this notion, and it is obvious that most soldiers were in some sense patriotic despite the scarcity of positive evidence of patriotism's motivational power at the front. Furthermore, as a famous study says of a similar phenomenon in American troops, the fact that the emotion was seldom mentioned probably restricted the degree to which it could motivate men in combat.[39] Some commentators may have exaggerated the antipathy or apathy that Allied soldiers held towards nationalism and other ideals. Nevertheless, the most credible conclusion about Australian soldiers is that their chief source of courage and determination was not nationalism, and still less broader ideals such as internationalism and the fight against fascism.

If fighting for Australia's safety was not a primary motivation at the front, perhaps fighting for Australia's military tradition was. The Anzac tradition seems to have been a factor in the enlistment of most Australian volunteers. The military prowess shown by Australians in World War I inspired confidence that Australian arms would be successful again. Yet while the individual might believe that Australians would perform well, this was no guarantee that he himself would. His initial fears might be eased by knowledge that men like him had 'proved' themselves in the First A.I.F., as it did for the gunner who wrote to his veteran father immediately after the battle of Bardia: 'My first bombardment I couldn't describe. But as I ran and flattened, ran and flattened, one of my main thoughts was – "My dad has done this hundreds of times." When things get "hot" and bombers come diving, too, it's thoughts of you that make things so much easier.'[40]

Yet this feeling was unusual. More often, knowledge of earlier successes put added pressure on individuals to succeed. This is clear from a war correspondent's note on the night of victory at Bardia: 'More than one man came up to me that night in Bardia and said: "Correspondent, eh? Well, when you write to the papers tell them we're as good as the First A.I.F."'[41]

The 6th Division's success at Bardia probably facilitated the other divisions' attempts to emulate the old tradition, for members of those formations regarded Bardia as a sign that the Second A.I.F. was in the same mould as the First. Nevertheless, each division had to endure its own rites of passage, as is clear in a poem about the 9th Division's first action, at Er Regima:

> The boys took up their possies:
> Their faces keen and brown;
> Their Dad's had licked the cows before;
> we must not let them down[42]

This extra burden possibly made men willing to endure more than they might otherwise have. However, it may have made some feel even less worthy as Australian soldiers when they came face to face with the frightening realities of war. It is likely that at that point, history ceased to matter.

Regardless of the extent to which the Anzac tradition was an inspiration to men going into their first battle, it quickly faded thereafter. The Australian combatant in World War II soon discovered that his pre-enlistment conceptions of war had been unrealistic. He had derived these conceptions from his knowledge of World War I, and in discarding and modifying them, he was sure either to re-evaluate or, more probably, to forget his Great War illusions. This loss of interest in the Great War tradition was a significant development. The firing line's revelatory education was just one of its elements.

The initial successes of all four of the Second A.I.F. divisions caused members to regard the new A.I.F. and its constituent parts as worthy successors to the old. From the time of its first action, each unit began to create a tradition of its own, and for members this provided a folklore and precedent far more compelling and immediate as a spur to good performance, or at least to pre-battle determination, than anything from a war they had not experienced. New traditions are, for example, central to a poem entered in T. C. Derrick's Tobruk diary. Entitled 'Standing By', and devoted to the dead of the author's and Derrick's battalion, it concludes:

Youve founded a tradition for the 2nd 40 eigh[th Battalion].[43]

In his first campaign, an incident or location might remind the average Australian soldier of something he had read about World War I; in subsequent campaigns, it would prompt comparisons with his own earlier – and usually victorious – experiences. For instance, a soldier wrote in 1941 that 'almost impregnable' Italian posts at Bardia reminded him of 'the things I've heard about the posts of Gallipoli'; in New Guinea, on the other hand, when Australian veterans captured strong defensive positions with relative ease, they did not look to 1914–18 for comparisons, but said how the Germans of their experience, or they themselves, could have held such ground for much longer than had the Japanese.[44]

Ironically, the World War I veterans who re-enlisted in World War II probably contributed to this development by putting Australian achievements of the earlier war into a less awesome perspective among their younger comrades. Though generally respected, these men were seen to be only human, and some declared the World War II campaigns in the Middle East even harder than their experiences in the 1914–18 ordeal.[45]

Nevertheless, these veterans provided a tangible link with the past, and their virtually universal departure after the Middle East campaigns probably contributed to the fact that the operations in the S.W.P.A. saw a marked decline in soldiers' references to the Great War tradition. Other factors were that in the South-West Pacific, Australians faced geographical conditions a world away from those of 1914–18, encountered an extraordinary and previously unknown foe, and fought for an essentially new cause – country rather than empire.

Units still untried by 1942, including all the C.M.F. units and the 8th Division, probably took the already-blooded Second A.I.F. units, rather than the First A.I.F., as the foremost example to emulate or surpass. Perhaps the most poignant illustration of this trend is that of an 8th Division platoon which, almost certainly trying to equal the 6th Division's famous advance at Bardia, sang as it marched towards enemy machine-guns and annihilation near Bakri, in Malaya. Another reason that the new diggers avoided comparisons with the earlier generation may have been that the major defeats suffered in Malaya and elsewhere were awkward to explain.

Writing of Australian soldiers, Kerr refers to a great 'forgetfulness between generation and generation'.[46] However, even in the S.W.P.A., the Great War was not entirely forgotten or ignored by all. In particular, many officers still thought in terms of 'the tradition of the service', and numerous reinforcements must have entered units in the S.W.P.A. inspired by stories of Gallipoli and France.

Yet the ultimate fate of those stories is hinted at in an incident described by Lieutenant Clive Edwards in a letter he wrote home a few days after the war's end. A veteran of four campaigns, Edwards was at the time stationed in Australia, sharing accommodation with several officers who had not been overseas. In his letter he noted: 'Yesterday one of the goats reckoned the Owen Stanley campaign was easy compared to the battles of the Last War and I jumped right down his neck.'[47] Reinforcements to front-line units in the South-West Pacific were likely to meet veterans with a fierce pride in their recent achievements. The war stories the new recruit tended to hear from his new colleagues, and even the lectures he heard from his officers, concentrated on the traditions of his new battalion or regiment, not on 1914–18.

UNIT LOYALTY

With these units and their sub-units we come much closer to finding the best single explanation for the typical soldier's endurance. They filled part of the void left by physical and spiritual separation from the social institutions that had provided support and fulfilment in Australia. Men often used the words 'home' and 'family' in connection with their units, and the official historian says of the Australians in the Middle East at the end of 1941 that 'many had developed a far stronger loyalty and affection towards their units than had been inspired by any institutions at home – outside their families.' This attachment was not as alien to Australians as it might seem, for Bean wrote of the First A.I.F.: 'throughout their services the men . . . lived for their battalions'.[48]

Although in World War II many identified with their division or brigade, the largest organization to which the average Australian felt a strong personal attachment was his battalion or regiment. These units, which generally consisted of some 600 to 850 men, were small enough to enable the ordinary soldier to know many members, and sufficiently large to have an operational role in which he could take personal interest and pride. Generally the battalion or regiment set the outer limits of the member's personal knowledge of the war: he knew little of the workings, actions and personnel of other battalions, especially those outside the 'sister' battalions from his own brigade or state. Members of the unit tended to share one region or state of origin, particularly in the early years of the war, and this was probably a comforting feature.

Battalion and regimental loyalty was not entirely spontaneous: its initial impetus generally came from the higher ranks. C.O.s and their officers, who were usually the most vocal partisans, took every opportunity to create loyalty to their units. They used battalion parades, drill and 'hard' physical training – especially route marches – and appeals to unit tradition.

In the ranks, there was some cynicism about the notion of *esprit de corps*, but most men willingly entered into the spirit of unit loyalty, especially in the A.I.F. Thus although soldiers occasionally directed derogatory comments at their units, more often problems were blamed on those further back; in his unusually frank battalion history, Crooks says that throughout the war he heard not a single seriously meant criticism of the unit. Australians needed little or no encouragement to take pride in the colour patches that denoted their units and that were essential to unit identity. One battalion historian writes: 'It is imposs-ible for anyone who has not belonged to an infantry battalion or other front line unit to realise the significance of a unit colour patch'.[49] As well as embracing the official symbols of *esprit de corps*, the lower ranks created their own traditions, in the form of stories about events and personalities.

The result of these various processes, together with the existence of supporting associations in Australia and unit newspapers in the field, was a strong sense of unit identification. This became apparent in the heartbreak caused whenever battalions were dissolved, amalgamated or had men transferred to make up losses in other units. Even with constant changes in personnel, unit pride and character tended to per-petuate itself, once established, with help from a nucleus of veterans. A battalion historian says of the 2/23rd in April 1944: 'Despite new faces, it was still the original battalion, and God help anyone who dis-agreed.'[50]

Attachment tended to be even stronger to the sub-units of bat-talions and regiments: notably, companies, platoons and sections in infantry; batteries, troops and sections in artillery. Officers and N.C.O.s in charge of these sub-units fostered a spirit of loyalty, especially through competition. However, the most important reason for the development of unit identity at this level was that an individual tended to come to know personally each member of these organiza-tions, especially platoons (or troops) and sections. The few members of these units were the people with whom, barring accidents or pro-motion, one was destined to spend most of one's time in the army.

A man's best mates were almost invariably members of his section or platoon. And although his circle of friends within these groups might at first be small, it widened as cooperation within the unit became increasingly necessary. This mutual support, initially part of the job of soldiering, eventually became a habit of life carried into the soldier's rest and leave. It became, for instance, a widespread custom that indi-viduals shared amongst their section or platoon any parcels received, even when the addressee was absent sick or wounded. Transfers from groups of this size were often painful, regardless of rank. Corporal Clive Edwards described as his greatest disappointment since joining the army the decision to put him in charge of a section outside the platoon in which he had served for 17 months.[51]

The time when the front-line soldier most needed support of the kind lost in separation from home was in combat, and for our purposes the key question is whether unit identity helped men to endure. Like the Australian military tradition, it could have done so either by giving men more confidence or by making them more determined.

An experienced Australian army psychologist stated in November 1944 that in the mental struggle against fear in battle, the individual combatant gained 'tremendous help' from unit membership, for: 'He is enabled to identify himself with the strength of a mass personality, which, if it is well trained, is not subject to the fear reactions of the individual and which has a well-defined goal.' The psychologist argued that only in units where the goal was less distinct – that is, where morale was low – would the individual not receive this support.[52] As almost all Australian fighting units quickly established a reputation for martial success and valour, their morale was generally high during campaigns. Even in the depressing pre-invasion atmosphere in Singapore, a soldier offered evidence of the phenomenon described by the psychologist: 'There was a feeling of safety there knowing that the Unit [the 2/30th Battalion] would fight as a machine when it was necessary with every soldier protecting the other.'[53]

The main purpose of the army's encouragement of *esprit de corps* was not so much to make men confident and secure as to make them fight. That was clear in the commanding officer's speech reported in Captain Cumpston's diary:

> Lt-Col Evans gave boys pep talk this morning – we expect to move fwd shortly and must remember that whole of Aust will be watching us when it knows we are again in battle . . . Newcomers must remember that it is unit and not indiv which is impt in battle – they must not let unit down – the best unit in the AIF.[54]

We cannot know how successful such exhortations were. There is little doubt that regimental norms in other armies' units – British guards regiments or the U.S. Marine Corps, for instance – made some difference to their battle performance, and it is conceivable that the same applied to the Australian army. There is some evidence that divisional pride spurred soldiers on both at Tobruk, where men of the 9th Division wanted to prove themselves worthy replacements of the 6th, and in the advance of the 7th and 9th divisions on Lae, which became something of a race. At lower levels, two battalion historians suggest that brigade and battalion pride caused men at Alamein to react to news of other units' successes by feeling determined to prove that they too could achieve their appointed tasks.[55]

A more detailed example, in McCarthy's volume of the official history, suggests that loyalty to the battalion was an important motivating factor in combat. The 39th Battalion played a vital role in the capture of Gona in December 1942. Amongst those of its men who fought well were some 100 reinforcements from the 53rd Battalion, which had so far performed poorly, and McCarthy argues that the main explanation for their improved contribution lay in a contagious battalion pride developed by the 39th in its earlier struggles on the Kokoda Trail.[56]

Yet there were strict limits to the reach of *esprit de corps* at or above the level of the battalion. This was particularly so in the S.W.P.A., as McCarthy himself hints when he describes the subject-matter of his volume as 'the story of small groups of men . . . who killed one another in stealthy and isolated encounters'. In similar vein, a platoon commander in New Guinea told his wife: 'When you get into action you don't see much of any troops except those of your own company, and very little of those not in your own platoon'.[57] Most telling on this point is the comment, made by the psychologist quoted above on the value of unit membership, that: 'Of course, if the nature of the fighting becomes individual and not concerted, as it most often was in the New Guinea theatre, he is more prone to individual fear reactions.'[58]

It was very unusual in the South-West Pacific for an entire battalion to participate in a set-piece action, or for an artillery regiment to function as a centralized unit. Cooperation at that level was much more common in the Middle East, but it was not universal there, and the fog of war descended just as inexorably on its battlefields. In these circumstances, it is easy to imagine that the confidence and comfort engendered prior to action by membership of a battalion, and the notion of fighting for the battalion's honour, may have quickly faded during combat. Once the fighting began, battalion commanders were rarely in a position to remind men of their unit traditions.

Even when battalion loyalty did appear to be crucial, it may well have hidden deeper motives. A stirring incident that occurred on the Kokoda Trail in 1942 is relevant here. At a perilous moment in the fighting, a group of men evacuated sick from the 39th Battalion returned, without receiving orders to leave the safety of the rear areas, to reinforce the front. The lieutenant in charge of the party told the commanding officer, Lieutenant-Colonel Honner: 'We heard the battalion was in trouble so we came back.' Later, Honner said of this occasion: 'I can think of no incident that reflected more radiantly the great *esprit de corps*, the strong bond of mateship in the battalion.'[59] However, one wonders whether it was in fact this 'bond of mateship', rather than attachment to the unit as such, that called the group back. Was *esprit de corps* loyalty to the battalion or to one's friends in it?

There is even more doubt about the real object of allegiance in smaller units. In battle, companies and especially platoons and sections remained far more cohesive than larger units, but the individual soldier's loyalty was not so much to these virtually anonymous sub-units ('B Company', '12 Platoon', and so on) as to their friends who composed them. American wartime studies found that in combat, soldiers saw themselves not as components of formal military organizations, but as members of small groups of as few as six or seven men. This was probably the case in the Australian army too.

MATESHIP

Whether unit identity was as important in battle as it was before and afterwards is doubtful, and its exact role is problematic. On the other hand, mateship within units was certainly crucial. Together with unit membership, comradeship filled the gap left by the soldier's separation from family and civilian friends and institutions. By the time most men reached the front line, they had made friends within their sections and platoons.[60] As implied in earlier chapters, the circumstances of every-day life at the front virtually forced comradeship on the soldier: heavy loads carried on the march almost cried out to be shared; the intense cold experienced at night often made huddling together and sharing blankets a necessity; posts and trenches often had to be manned by two soldiers; and many weapons were operated by crews of two or more men, who naturally became dependent on each other.

By the time they went into action, men were prepared to take great risks to protect and support their comrades. A section leader recalls an incident in which his patrol ran into a Japanese force at Lababia:

> All hell started to break loose from the Japs, and as a matter of fact a little bit of panic set in, and the men started to bolt back towards our perimeter when one of them noted (I think it was Wattie) that the Bren had been left in the pit. He dived back to get it but the bipod legs were stuck in a root or something and wouldn't come free. He saw the Japs coming so he turned round and opened fire on them. A couple of the boys looked back and saw that Wattie was still there. They yelled out that they couldn't leave him behind, so they all dived back into their pits again, and fought the Japs from there.[61]

Medcalf writes that every combat soldier knew that if he was hit during the fighting on Bougainville, his mates would risk all to get him out, and indeed there are numerous recorded instances of men doing so in various campaigns.[62] For example, during the Kokoda campaign, a corporal at the 21st Brigade Headquarters reported an incident, one of 'dozens', which was preceded by the wounding of an Australian by a bullet that fractured his left thigh and became embedded in his right leg:

> [Tom] had to be dragged up the slope of the mountain several hundreds of feet meanwhile his fractured leg was dragging all over the place and catching in the bushes. He fainted many times with pain but did not whimper once ... The position was dangerous and he begged them to let him remain where he was and make a safe get-away themselves; this they refused to do and after a stupendous job they got him to safety. It took 3 days to get him down through the mountains.[63]

Like 'Tom' in this passage, the wounded were often anxious about being an encumbrance, and their anxiety was expressed in selfless behaviour.

Comradeship not only caused men to defy fear, exhaustion, and pain, but also gave them feelings of comfort and security. These feelings are reflected in the fact that the quality nominated by a large postwar sample of veterans as the one most characteristic of Australian soldiers was 'dependability'. Gullett declares that 'the support and comfort' of friends were essential to coping in battle, and his belief is supported by a section leader's comment on ferocious fighting near Deniki: 'Things were grim at that stage and your comrade alongside you became your mother, father and God all rolled into one.'[64]

Australians' attachment to their comrades was usually strengthened by the experience of battle, for those who survived now shared a unique tie, born of a common ordeal and mutual debts. In January 1942, Sergeant Mitchell described this relationship in words reminiscent of Shakespeare's *Henry V*: 'the memories of the Malayan campaign must live for ever. I saw a veteran of some 40 summers wounded thrice and helping to carry a stretcher. Such deeds are unrecognised by decorations but make us a band of brothers for evermore.'[65]

There was a strong belief that the mateship which developed in combat, like war itself, was comprehensible only to the initiated:

It is hard for people to understand how attached fellows can get to each other after being in action together, fighting for our lives alongside of each other, living in dirt and filth, sharing light rations, but that is how it goes.

The comradeship of men in arms is something very great, which must be experienced before you know the fullness of it, for it is bought with a price, and the price is not gold.

... that profound comradeship and perfect understanding between all ranks which can only be found amongst men who have experienced the severe hardships, terrific strains, and ever present dangers of active service.[66]

Thus although there existed a strong prewar Australian tradition of staying loyal to mates through thick and thin, and although the mateship developed by soldiers before their initiation to combat owed much to that civilian tradition, it was not the source of the comradeship present in and after battle. Instead, life and death on the Kokoda Trail, in the Tobruk Salient, or in any of the other life-sapping and -threatening battle zones gave rise to a form of mateship found only amongst fighting men.

Several prominent Australian writers have defined the mateship of Australian soldiers as part of a national tradition, a feature of a national character.[67] Yet the precondition of the mateship exhibited by

Australian combat veterans in World War II was not to be an Australian male, but to be a front-line soldier, and its presence among the men of other armies is well established. The following scene, a description of a reunion of Tobruk veterans immediately after the siege was raised, is scarcely imaginable amongst civilian Australian mates: 'I saw other chaps meet their particular mates and it was a great sight. Out would go their arms and embrace each other. You could see the emotion on their faces and tears in their eyes.'[68]

Immediately after the cessation of hostilities, Captain Combe wrote home concerning a gathering of his battalion's officers. He wrote of the front-line soldier's distinctive mateship:

> Everybody appeared to be jolly, but there was an unexpressed under-current of emotion born of the knowledge that with the end of the war, something very deep was going out of our lives, something with no parallel in civilian life. That spirit of true comradeship which springs from fighting together for a common cause. It was saddening to think that this great trust in one another, arising from the certain knowledge that your friend here during the last five years has been willing (and has risked his life accordingly) to lay down his life, was soon to be dissipated.[69]

Combe's point about comradeship deriving from shared fighting for a common cause is noteworthy. The cause meant here is the political and ideological one of the Allies, to which, as we have seen, there was an overarching commitment. However, a far more potent one for most Australian soldiers appears to have been comradeship itself. The altruism depicted here as an effect was for many a cause. Combe's language in the concluding sentence recalls the biblical passage that expresses one of the key inspirational principles of front-line soldiering: 'Greater love has no man than this, that a man lay down his life for his friends.'

PASSIVE MATES?

One piece of evidence seems to present a serious challenge to the notion that mateship was a prime factor in Australian soldiers' battlefield endurance. General Iven Mackay commanded the 6th Australian Division in Greece, and shortly after the campaign ended in defeat he asserted:

The number of men who behave bravely in battle is far fewer
than is commonly thought, whilst the number who act in
merely a passive way or who follow a policy of evasion is much
greater than is generally believed . . . In a platoon four or five
men are brave and plucky as individuals, another four or five
might be pretty good and another four or five not so good, and
then you will tail off to the other end . . .[70]

Mackay's figures imply that at least half of a typical platoon (of 30 or so
men) was less effective than 'not so good'. This hardly suggests a great
deal of mutual support, or indeed an effective army. His calculations
should be considered in the light of his recent disappointing campaign.
He was also unlikely to have a detailed knowledge of the battlefield
behaviour of many of the platoons of his division: the rifle platoons
alone numbered in excess of one hundred.

Nevertheless, the point about passivity should not be cursorily
dismissed, for it echoes observations made by S.L.A. Marshall in his
renowned work on the American World War II experience. Marshall
asserted that in any given action no more than 25 per cent of the men
under fire would use their weapons unless 'compelled by almost overwhelming circumstances' or by personal supervision from their
superiors.[71] This and Mackay's comments might together be seen as
evidence that the passive troops – supposedly the majority of all
soldiers – were anything but comradely in their battlefield behaviour,
and that in fact they left their brave comrades in the lurch.

Yet Marshall's argument does not run this way. One of his central
and most famous contentions was that those soldiers who did the firing
were sustained by, and were actually dependent on, the near or presumed presence of comrades; not necessarily by comrades who used
weapons or offered other military support, but by comrades who were
simply present. The firers, he argued, were not fearless, just as the non-
firers were not *ipso facto* cowards. He illustrated the process by point-
ing to the numerous completely defenceless Japanese troops on Pacific
islands who stayed with, and thereby supported, their active comrades
until killed.[72]

Mackay himself told an anecdote that seems to be consistent with
Marshall's thesis. An Australian sergeant was said to have killed every
German who entered a Greek village for almost two and a half hours: he
did the shooting while those around him loaded and handed him
rifles.[73] Those men presumably fell into Mackay's 'passive', 'evasive'
or 'not so good' categories, but by their presence – which one assumes

involved some danger – they quite probably made a substantial contribution to their comrade's persistence.

Thus, even if one accepts the essence of Mackay's criticism – and
one cannot unequivocally do so – it is not inconsistent with an army in
which self-sacrificing mateship was of great importance on the battlefield. The soldiers' own testimonies bear witness to that importance.

COMRADES AND HONOUR

His mates were the most significant reason for the Australian soldier's
perseverance. But the role of nearby comrades in enabling men to
endure was not confined to the self-sacrifice and security they inspired.
The Australian front-line soldier fought bravely in the presence of his
colleagues not just because of commitment to them, as individuals or as
members of a unit, but also because of anxiety about disgracing himself
in front of them.

This was most obviously the case for reinforcements to experienced units, as often they were accepted into the rather cliquish mateship of section, platoon and so on only if they showed enough fortitude
in action. The original members of combat units had themselves faced
the same problem in their introductions to battle. Corporal Hoffmann
wrote of his experience at Bardia, in the first Australian battle of the
war: 'Its a very terrifying experience attacking a position under, not
only the enemy's barrage but your own as well; and I can't believe that
anyone can ever become used to it. You try to pretend to the blokes
near you that its okay, but you don't bother trying to pretend to yourself.'[74]

Michael O'Brien recalled a conversation that followed his first
combat: 'After our first action our chaps started to speak a bit confi-
dentially among themselves and we all found out that we had the same
feelings of being afraid but each of us had kept it from the others.'[75]
O'Brien's memoirs suggest that, despite this instance of post-battle
frankness, men continued to try to suppress signs of fear during the
fight. He wrote that in action: 'I prayed not so much to be protected
from injuries, it was not fear for personal wounds or death but that God
would help me to take whatever came to me without being afraid and
that I would never let a mate down during any critical times in battle.'[76]
The fear of 'letting your mates down', of 'squibbing it', was another

great strain on the Australian soldier. It was also the mainspring of his success in the war.

A willingness to take death before dishonour in the eyes of one's comrades emerges too in Bean's discussion of the perseverance of Australians in the First A.I.F. at Gallipoli. He concludes that analysis thus: 'Life was very dear, but life was not worth living unless they could be true to their idea of Australian manhood.'[77] In fact, this motive, like the special comradeship of the front, knows no national boundaries. In all armies, the individual soldier's willingness to endure terrible danger stems largely from his sense of personal, masculine honour, the essence of which is loyalty to comrades and maintenance of their respect. The fear of showing fear, and thereby dishonouring oneself, is a universal motivator.

In the Australians' case, this factor helps to account for several noteworthy characteristics. One is the readiness, already mentioned, of Australians to follow any individual who set a courageous example and standard, even if he were doing so in an unofficial capacity. If one man acted bravely, others felt compelled by their sense of honour to follow him. Perhaps the best single illustration of that connection comes in the citation for Private Kingsbury's Victoria Cross: 'His coolness, determination and devotion to duty in face of great odds was an inspiration to my men to which they could not but respond.'[78] The fear of showing fear also helps to account for the forced humour often seen in Australians as they entered battle, and for the extraordinary cheerfulness and stoicism of the wounded.

The single most important factor that helped soldiers to 'take it' was a sense of honour, a desperate desire to hide their fear in battle. Yet their determination to endure also derived from motives that were not introspective and self-interested. The sacrifices made by soldiers for each other are an embodiment of altruism.

There was commitment to other external ideals or groups: the unit, the Australian military heritage, patriotism. The significance of these allegiances once the firing commenced is debatable. Clearly they had a role, but it seems to have been a minor one. Leadership and obedience also play a part in every battle, but their importance to the frightened soldier was apparently secondary.

Experience, too, helped men cope better with certain aspects of the front-line ordeal, but nothing could eradicate the mental strain of danger. As exposure lengthened, so did the fissures in the walls that protected men against fear.

PART TWO

THE ARMY WAY

CHAPTER SIX

CALLOUS BIGWIGS AND BOREDOM

*E*ven before members of Australian combat units had reached the front line, soldiering had challenged their equanimity. Like all civilians-turned-soldiers, they found certain aspects of the military life unfamiliar, annoying and even abhorrent. Their Australian identity also affected their responses. They criticized some features common to life in every army, and others that were distinctively Australian.

The mental and physical strains peculiar to front-line service generally came to overshadow these burdens, but the typical Australian soldier continued to be irritated, exasperated and angered by experiences associated not so much with being at the front as with membership of a combat unit of the Australian army. The soldiers' complaints about these elements of military life reveal much about the individual combatant, as does the way he coped with those challenges to his composure. The main sources of discontent were callousness or indifference, boredom, inefficiency, and inequality.

CALLOUSNESS AND INDIFFERENCE

Australian soldiers tended to feel that their army had a callous attitude towards them. In many cases this assessment was grounded in a man's very first experience as a soldier. When he entered camp it soon struck him that every aspect of his life was regulated by others. During his training, orders were constantly shouted at him as he and his fellows

91

were herded round the circuit of exercises known as the 'bull ring'. At
Canungra in Queensland, for example, trainees found a regime that the
most favourable commentaries call severe; the negative ones call it a
prison, characterized by 'testing physical punishment, rude abuse from
some officers [and] deliberate denigration of morale'.[1]

During the non-training hours in most Australian camps, life was
austere, and although new men were invariably greeted with the traditional and jocular warning, 'You'll be sorry!', the new existence came
as a profound shock to many. One soldier probably expressed the feelings of most new recruits when he wrote: 'if there was no war on I
wouldn't put up with a lot we do here'.[2]

Another Australian recorded that the group of recruits with whom
he marched into camp in 1940 was addressed by a sergeant who told
them that 'we were leaving behind our civilian life and name to become
just a number in the army'. Private Young wrote a few days after his
enlistment in 1943: 'I am no longer a civillian but just a thing with a
number.' He added in this letter to his mother that in a depot where he
was living – apparently the Sydney Showgrounds – 'We slept on
wooden boards in the Pig Pens (that is right) with 3 blankets. Our mess
is in the Dog Pavillion not a bad combination.'[3]

Connections with the animal kingdom were often made in Australians' writings. In expressing the feeling that they had lost the respect
due to them as adults, they usually chose figures of speech relating to
the treatment of animals rather than, as one might expect, to children.
Animal metaphors were natural in circumstances such as the following,
and especially if the Australians concerned had rural backgrounds:

> . . . arrived Kantara late afternoon, had tea, and then indignity
> of indignities, we were all packed aboard a dinky die cattle
> train; the moo's grunts from the boys would have done credit
> to a big zoo . . .

> At the station we were piled into cattle trucks., 40 per truck
> and what a squeeze The truck haven't been washed out or
> cleaned and soon we are all filthy. Someone started to bleat
> like a sheep and soon everyone was bleating and we felt we
> were home at Flemington sales yards again.[4]

There was humour in these impersonations, but essentially they were
a waggish recognition of and protest at a loss of individuality and
dignity.

The tone was not humorous but vitriolic when the animal metaphor was applied to the loads of gear that the Australian front-line
soldier was ordered to carry. These have been described in Chapter 1.
Many Australians in the field, including officers, thought the loads set
by higher headquarters reflected a heartless and unrealistic outlook. A
lucid expression of that point of view appeared in a corporal's New
Guinea diary: 'When will the heads realise that men are human beings,
and not mules? It's impossible to carry the loads laid down by those
who don't have to carry them themselves.'[5]

Australians regarded their treatment as callous in that they were
loaded down and herded about, but also in that like Private Young at
the Sydney Showgrounds, they sometimes lived in conditions not normally considered fit for men. One soldier reflected: 'The army idea
seems to be to make the soldier live like an animal, and he'll fight like
one.'[6]

It is in fighting that common soldiers pay the dearest price for any
inhumanity in the higher echelons of their army. Australians at the
front had some reason to feel that others regarded them as expendable
commodities. The Australians sent to Greece and to the islands of
Timor, Java, Ambon and New Britain had missions that no senior
commander could seriously have imagined would have been anything but disastrous for an unusually large proportion of the men
involved.

Politics played a part in decisions about these operations, which
could not be blamed entirely on the army. Yet even the tactics used on
the battlefields of North Africa and New Guinea can be criticized as
reflecting a callous philosophy. German documents captured in North
Africa stated that the British almost invariably sought to capture the
most important ground with the fewest possible troops. This perception was proved time and again in the use of the 9th Division in
offensive operations. One could regard this as a sign of benevolent
incompetence rather than false economy, until one considers the
prospects of those attacking, rather than those temporarily left out.

The existence of this doctrine was exemplified in each of the major
Australian counter-attacks at Tobruk. All set unrealistic tasks for the
infantry, who suffered accordingly. For instance, on 3 August 1941, the
2/28th and 2/43rd battalions attacked a section of the German line 4.8
kilometres wide and defended, on average, by one machine-gun every
46 metres. Two-thirds of the Australians involved in this attack

became casualties. In the Alamein battles, too, Australian infantrymen suffered for their superiors' parsimonious tactics.

Australians were also sent into some forlorn attacks in New Guinea. For example, in the 55/53rd Battalion's first action as a unit, it suffered 120 casualties advancing 90 metres at Sanananda. In the same fruitless battle, the 49th Battalion lost 229 men – nearly 48 per cent of the unit – in its initiation to combat. One battalion historian argues that, in New Guinea, Australian attacks were often completely unrealistic – lacking support and preparation, and using too few men. He states that often an attack in sufficient strength was made only after unnecessarily costly smaller attacks had failed.[7]

The campaigns of 1944–5 gave Australian front-line troops powerful cause to feel that their leaders regarded them as cannon fodder. General Blamey ordered the First Australian Army to abandon the policy of containment that had served the American garrisons well in New Guinea and Bougainville. He wanted a more traditionally Australian policy of aggression, and fulfilling his wish cost lives. The entirely questionable strategic and political value of these campaigns made every life lost further ammunition for those who doubted the humanity of their leaders.

There were Australian soldiers who condemned some of these features of their campaign experience. In particular, they were likely to be angered if they saw their sacrifice as one made for dubious political or strategic purposes. A simple but pungent testimony to a sense of being a sacrificial victim is the reflection of an Australian captured on Ambon: 'Everyone reckoned it was hopeless from the start, with no naval or air support, just a handfull of men dumped and left, and only 600 miles from Aussie.'[8]

The Australians left in the Middle East throughout 1942 were annoyed also at what they regarded as an inhumane, unfair and unwise decision – made by politicians and military leaders – not to send them home. This annoyance was directed at least partly at the British. That is apparent in these two extracts, one written in September at the front, the other during the battle of El Alamein:

> Why can't we be relieved and sent home. Its definitely unfair the way the colonial troops are being used up, the Kiwis more than us. They have a mere handful left now out of all their men, surely there is no reason why they and us should continue to be decimated without reinforcing us.

Why can't our chaps be relieved? Human endurance can stand
so much. This cannot go on much longer. I wonder what the
top brass really want from a human being. It is about time the
Poms had a go.[9]

The political and grand strategic elements of the 1945 campaigns
also drew the ire of Australian participants, who soon became aware of
the dubious value of the operations, and that lives lost were wasted.
Consequently, they tried to minimize risks. In this they were strongly
encouraged by most commanders, who were generally able and willing
to provide much more effective artillery and air support than ever
before.

Perhaps because of a belief that their leaders in the field usually
tried to avoid unnecessary casualties, most Australian front-line
soldiers seem not to have been inclined to criticize battlefield tactics
and the tactical doctrine of their army. Such criticism, however, was
not entirely absent. For instance, some men doubted the value of sending soldiers out on a seemingly endless series of nerve-racking patrols,
and whether the rewards of attacking fixed defences with these small
groups of men justified the tragic losses that occasionally and inevitably occurred. After a patrol from his company lost three of its five
members killed in an attempt to examine Japanese positions in the
Ramu Valley, Sergeant Edwards noted: 'It's rocked us and made us
rotten on the silly cows who, knowing that the position was there and
knowing it to be wired, yet wasted good lives finding out nothing. The
ways of the bigwigs are beyond me I'm afraid.'[10]

Following the failure of a larger endeavour, an attack on Sanananda, Ben Love commented, 'So again we gained nothing, and good
men were just mowed down'.[11] The lack of more such testimonies is
probably due to the fact that the men 'mowed down' were not in a
position to write them.

Another revealing example of resentment comes from a captain's
account of events preceding the capture of Lae, which the commanders
wanted the fighting men to achieve quickly, and which the troops
wanted to achieve safely:

Sick Japs along the track kept holding things up and we
expected to run into something at any moment. Then along
the track and into the middle of us came a jeep crowded with
Brigade HQ . . . The old Brig jumped out and started to urge

the troops to hurry along. The troops weren't very impressed
as they thought the Jap was in front.[12]

Clearly, it is likely that the troops concerned became acutely conscious
here that 'the old Brig' was prepared to risk their lives for his higher
purposes. Ironically, junior officers in fighting units – such as the captain just quoted – were probably at least as critical of the higher
headquarters' priorities and understanding of the front line as were
their troops. These officers knew something of the relationships
between the various headquarters, and were aware that the higher the
rank the more considerations of strategy and prestige came to overshadow the issue of avoiding casualties.

Ordinary fighting soldiers, on the other hand, usually had no ink-
ling of the workings of command – graphic illustrations such as the one
afforded to the troops approaching Lae were seldom provided. Thus,
although many cursed the army or its leaders for their heartlessness or
incompetence, others simply supposed that their senior commanders
'knew what they were doing', and trusted that these doings coincided
with the common soldiers' interests. That trust is poignantly exemplified in a Tobruk diary entry. After the 2/23rd Battalion's costly raid of
22 April 1941, the unit received congratulations from the C.O., the
brigadier, and from even higher up. Private John Butler mused: 'So
there you are, I suppose it was all right but one is apt to become preju-
dicial when ones comrades fall out of the earthly ranks and others
maimed for life: it must have been a greater success than was seen on
the surface – a private's not to reason why.'[13] The raid was in fact a
tactical success, but clearly that outcome, and the degree to which the
venture was justified, were not issues on which this private felt qualified to comment.

Some soldiers did comment adversely on the way the authorities
kept them ignorant or even deceived them about forthcoming movements, operations and even training exercises. Clive Edwards remembers lack of information as 'one of our worst enemies'.[14] The anxiety
created by enforced ignorance is hinted at too in a diary note written by
an artilleryman as his regiment waited to sail from Australia: 'If the
brass hats would only give us some information on the destination
we are bound for it would stop the rumours and also the boys from
worrying.'[15]

The issue of leave, precious to every soldier, also gave rise to accusations of heartlessness. An Australian N.C.O. in the Middle East recorded these standard remarks made by authority whenever there was no leave:

1 Leave is not a right but a privilege.
2 Why did you join up – to go on leave?
3 Its a pity some of you weren't under German discipline. See how much leave you'd get then.
4 I had a thousand days service in the last war and only five days leave.

He called these explanations 'statements which have been repeated to soldiers ad nauseam as long as there have been mugs in the army', and one can easily imagine that they made troops cynical about their army's concern for them.[16] A typical complaint about leave is a remark from a soldier in New Guinea concerning another in the same predicament: 'I hope Vic gets home soon as he needs a rest I suppose the miserable cows will only give him about 9 days leave after they come back from this rotten hole they want at least a month leave to recuperate'.[17]

A related matter in which Australians sometimes sharply criticized the judgement and humanity of higher authority was that of timely relief for exhausted units. Perhaps the most convincing complaint to that effect came from Private Ewen on Bougainville, who wrote in 1945: 'This Bn is loosing men now as all the boys are battle-weary and their reflexes to danger have slowed down, they move to slow now. I dont know why they dont pull us out.'[18] As we have seen in Chapter 4, it appears that many members of the battalion had been made to serve beyond the limits of their endurance, but this was most unusual in the Australian army.

If, as seems likely, most Australian soldiers did not regard their army as especially heartless in its tactical employment of them on campaign, this was a reasonable assessment. Australian commanders often talked of fighting to 'the last man', or of achieving goals 'at all costs', but generally they were keen to avoid loss of life.[19] In this they were relatively successful, if one compares Australian casualty totals with those of their opponents. Where Australian casualties were heavy, it was usually a function of the inescapable fact that wherever Australians were on the offensive, someone eventually had to advance and capture the enemy's positions.

More generally, the size of armies, even one as relatively small as the Australian, necessitates a degree of impersonality in dealings between their members. Of course this is small consolation to the members. On the other hand, impersonality and even lack of consideration are preferable to the malicious and gratuitous harshness – 'bastard ization' – that features in other armies' training, and which seems to have been a rare occurrence in the Australian army.

Yet there were probably numerous instances where Australians were justified in believing that the army had insulted them and deprived them of dignity. Claude O'Dea recorded one such instance in his Western Desert diary. When the men of his unit were asked to submit keys to their kitbags, which were being held at base, he remarked: 'I think most of the men were of the same mind as I . . . I wouldn't trust anybody going through my kit . . . Theres no doubt about this army for muddle headedness. As far as it is concerned you have no private feelings whatsoever.'[20]

On Labuan in 1945 as Private Armstrong waited to go home shortly after his fourth amphibious landing, he had much time to assess the role of callousness in his military life: 'Left Lutong 22nd for Labuan then home to be discharged on long service. Waited Labuan four weeks for boat. Bloody disgrace on Army and Govt part. Not being able to supply boats for us. The bastards find them easy enough when there's a blue for us to go into.'[21]

A fitting conclusion here is the comment of a soldier who, on returning from campaigning in the Middle East, was billeted with a family outside Adelaide and was thereby enabled to see in sharp relief the dehumanizing quality of army life: 'They were great people, had us to table, gave us beds with sheets, even though the army officers told them to move all the furniture out and leave the room bare for us. We felt like human beings again.'[22]

BOREDOM

Tedium was a theme that ran through most phases of the typical fighting soldier's experience, and was often blamed on the 'bigwigs'. It threatened the soldier's composure to a degree equalled only by fear.

In a letter written in Libya in February 1941, Captain Laybourne Smith made a statement that no Australian who saw front-line service in World War II would have disputed: 'The man who said that war comprised months of boredom interspersed with moments of intense excitement was a prophet.'[23] Laybourne Smith explained that his artillery regiment had been overseas for nearly 300 days and had fought for just one of them. He was like thousands of other members of the 6th Division who, after enlistment, had endured up to 14 months of boredom before being granted the 'excitement' for which they had longed.

Australians in some other formations had to wait even longer: for 18 months or more in the 8th Division and in certain 7th Division units. Some militia battalions first saw campaigning after four or more years, in 1943, or even in 1945. A number of 9th Division originals spent only about eight months anticipating their initiation into the mysteries of combat, and certain reinforcements had to wait only a few months, but most Australian soldiers experienced a long interval between enlistment and their first front-line service.

Boredom and its attendant frustration usually set in well before action became a real prospect for untried recruits. For instance, even before his 6th Division battalion had left Australia, one member wrote home:

> The men here are getting disgusted with the slowness of the Empire to do something definate, and talking of going home to their jobs soon. That is bad, and can be taken as a general feeling in the camps in Australia and probably throughout the Empire, lack of interest in their training and losing the spirit of the fight. They will take some holding if they are left in this camp much longer ... You see we are going over now again and again training we did weeks ago ...[24]

This battalion had another year of training to do before it saw action.

The repetitiveness of training made all men sick of it eventually, but many Australian soldiers were probably unusually quick to develop an aversion to it. Some joined the army holding to a traditional belief that the Australian was a natural fighter, who could be made ready for action simply by teaching him how to handle weapons. The realization that this was not the case must have soured many towards training almost from the outset.

After eventually seeing action and having the longed-for experience of campaigning, participants needed a lengthy term to rest. In almost every case they enjoyed such a respite. Indeed, these breaks were usually much longer than the operations they followed. For example, the 6th Division's infantry battalions each campaigned for between three and five months in 1941, then rested, trained and refitted for at least 16 months before their next operations. These new campaigns were of similar duration to the previous ones, and were followed by at least another 17 months of waiting for the following campaign. One brigade, the 19th, waited between campaigns from May 1941 to December 1944.

The 7th and 9th division battalions had slightly shorter breaks between operations than the average 6th Division units, although both groups waited some 15 to 18 months between their penultimate and final campaigns. One can see from these summaries of the operations of Australia's most active combat units that front-line organizations spent most of their time out of the front line. To give two more detailed examples, the 2/43rd Battalion spent 77 weeks of its 266-week existence – 29 per cent – on campaign, and the 2/33rd Battalion spent just 40 of its 296 weeks – 13.5 per cent – campaigning.

Considering the nature of front-line conditions and combat, one might imagine that experienced soldiers would have been grateful for these long periods of inactivity. However, while the opportunity to take leave and to recuperate were initially welcomed, the novelty of breaks from campaigning rapidly waned.

Most of what filled the gaps between campaigns was called 'training', and although the term encompassed a multitude of activities, usually it meant practical or theoretical preparation for action. In general, this preparation was identical or similar to that endured before one's first campaign; in fact it was sometimes known as 're-training'. A.I.F. veterans were perhaps fortunate that the shifting of their war from the Middle East to the Far East necessitated great changes in training methods, and added some variety to exercises. Nevertheless, all training palled before long and, as mentioned, soldiers with campaign experience tended to regard training with distaste. Even General Blamey recognized that 'it is very boring to go on with too much training'.[25]

Other aspects of camp life soon became equally tedious. A picture of utter boredom emerges, for instance, in a 9th Division infantryman's Syrian diary entries of March 1942, six months after his unit's relief from Tobruk: 'This bludging is worse than fighting everyone gets

drunk now every oppertunity . . . another glorious day. and bugger all
to do. we all seem to be going cranky. with the monotony.' The diarist
concerned had hated much of his sojourn in Tobruk, so there was real
frustration behind his comment that the 'bludging' was worse than
fighting. Two months later he could write: 'this bloody dull camp life is
getting boring we want action'.[26]

Many who had longed for relief during campaigns were itching for
new operations within a month or two of that release. Thus in March
1941, Captain Laybourne Smith exclaimed: 'The deep dirty underlie-
ing reason for putting troops in rest camps has at last penetrated my
thick scull. After being here for a fortnight we are all so bored we would
fight anything. The troops are really being very good but tempers are
getting short.'[27] In November 1941, a censorship report on the Australians in the Middle East stated that troops not long out of Tobruk
were already ' "itching for action" '.[28] Fraying tempers were also mentioned in a censorship report of 1945, and particularly in a quotation
from a deeply frustrated sergeant in a machine-gun battalion:

> This idling around, filling in time, as we seem to be doing at
> the present makes the chaps very quick and fly off the handle.
> Even in the Sgts tent that I am in we fly at one another over the
> least little thing. I think we really all feel of a like mind – that is
> send us away and give us a job or send us on leave. This train-
> ing on the same old thing day after day nearly drives us
> crazy.[29]

During the long interval between Australia's penultimate and final
campaigns, inactivity and the associated tedium brought about the
greatest wartime drop in soldiers' morale. In February 1945, F. W.
Forde, the Minister for the Army, reported to the Prime Minister of
Australia that a visit to Queensland had disclosed:

> . . . deterioration in the morale of the Australian Fighting
> Forces that had obviously taken place over the past six
> months. It would appear that this is largely due to their
> enforced stay on the mainland of Australia with no clearly
> defined indication as to when and where they may be likely to
> be called upon to take part in active operations . . . I feel sure
> that if it were not for a feeling of utter boredom and dissat-
> isfaction on this basis, their grievances would not have been
> so pronounced.[30]

Forde's worries were corroborated by censorship reports and individual testimonies. A field censorship report from the First Australian
Army in February 1945 used the following extract from an infantryman's letter to illustrate the point that members of inactive units were
dissatisfied:

> Here I am stuck up here – doing a useless job – why? I'd prefer
> to be right in the front line or right out. If any mug ever tells me
> I am aiding the war effort I'll have much pleasure in calling
> him a liar. If a person was fighting he'd be doing something
> concrete and stand a chance of feeling a man. To be fooled
> about doing useless work – well it's making absolute bludgers
> of many men here who have manly ambitions.[31]

In showing its author's deep concern for masculine self-esteem,
this quotation suggests that men sent into action in Bougainville,
northern New Guinea and Borneo would have been less interested in
the political and strategic arguments about these controversial campaigns than in their own release from 'useless work' in a camp.

Indeed, the field censorship report for March 1945 noted that a
belief amongst units in North Queensland that movement to theatres
of war was imminent had led to a decided improvement in the outlook
of troops who had previously shown 'a general feeling of boredom
resultant from inactivity'.[32]

Throughout the war, individuals wrote of being 'fed up' or
'browned off', and in 1945 that attitude was probably at its most widespread. Yet while the boredom inseparable from life in the Australian
army may have disillusioned some forever, and temporarily lowered
the morale of many more, it was essential to the army's campaign successes. The role of the frustration that Australians felt before their first
campaign is problematic, for one could argue about whether it sharpened or blunted enthusiasm. However, without the long dull periods
between campaigns, Australian soldiers would have lacked the
eagerness that contributed to their battlefield successes. And of course,
the skills acquired in the tiring months of training were also
invaluable.

Yet the benefits of the boredom accrued to the army and its nation
in general, rather than to the individual in Australian uniform. The
alternatives that faced him were both intrinsically unpleasant: few
experiences could be more soul-destroying than living for months in a

military camp, and few could be more miserable than campaigning in desert, mountain or jungle. And as the veteran knew, campaigning was also dangerous; his willingness to escape the boredom of camp was not the naive and ignorant eagerness he had felt as an initiate. According to some veterans, their longing for action when resting, and for relief when in the line exhibited a human characteristic of being forever dissatisfied with one's lot. But it was also a matter of feeling that even the awful alternative was preferable to whichever side of the military lifestyle one was currently enduring.

The fact that men who had experienced the horrors of combat should prefer to return to them rather than endure the boredom of the only alternative seems to indicate that theirs was a bleak existence. With a hint of the buoyancy that enabled Australians to endure that existence for as long as they did, a veteran's note from New Guinea captures the essence of the Australian soldier's predicament: 'either nothing happens or too bloody much. No sweet moderation about this game at all.'[33]

CHAPTER SEVEN

ARMY MUCK-UPS

As we saw in the previous chapter, the new recruit was likely to encounter bewildering and frustrating disorganization and inefficiency from the day of enlistment, which was itself often poorly arranged. Confusion was especially prevalent in 1939 and 1940: years during which roughly half of all wartime direct enlistments into the Australian Imperial Force occurred. A lieutenant organizing a 7th Division unit in mid-1940 wrote of his search among recruits billeted at the Sydney Showgrounds: 'Things are terrible here ... absolute confusion. The flow of recruits is more than can be handled, makes one sick to see men walking aimlessly about nobody caring where they go or what they do, but things must improve, if not Gawd help us.'[1]

Such disorganization was largely responsible for the 'Spartan' conditions, to use a charitable adjective, under which many recruits lived in that formative period. A senior officer in one of the infantry battalions said of the first months that 'the powers that be made a frightful mess of feeding, clothing and equipping us', and remarked that improvement had occurred only after complaints to the Minister of Defence.[2]

Indeed, early on, food was not merely bland, but sometimes literally bad, and was so inadequate as to call forth widespread protest in 1939 and 1940. There were also early shortages of uniforms. Camps tended to be very cold in winter, and to have unhygienic cooking and sewerage facilities. For instance, at Woodside camp in South Australia,

104

one artillery regiment was sleeping 54 to 58 men in huts designed for 34; to their great annoyance, men in various camps were forced to sleep alternately head to foot. For much of 1940, health authorities feared that the camps would be swept by a deadly epidemic similar to one that occurred in 1915. As it was, every A.I.F. camp in Australia seems to have suffered an outbreak of the temporarily debilitating upper respiratory tract infection (U.R.T.I.), variously known among soldiers as 'dog's disease', 'Ingleburn throat', 'Pucka throat', 'Woodside throat' and 'Northam throat'.

A few of the camps were well regarded by some inmates in the early period, as were certain camps encountered overseas from 1940 onwards. Moreover, the organization of accommodation in Australian camps improved as the war progressed. Nevertheless, discontent about living conditions behind the lines persisted throughout the war, and as late as 1944 units in some areas of Australia were effectively having to build their own camps.

Early in the war there grew within the Australian army an abiding and infectious cynicism about army organization. Every new soldier soon became familiar with epithets such as 'being mucked about by experts'. Terms like 'typical army organization' and the euphemistic 'usual army muck-up' also became well established. For instance, Private Richardson described his unit's arrival in Egypt thus: 'The army true to the style we have come to know so well kept us awake half the night issuing rations and orders. Aroused us at 3 A.M. Had us ready at 4 A.M. Walked us 100 yds to await a train scheduled at 9 A.M.'[3]

Australians made wry jokes about their prospects of winning a war with such poor organization, or ruminated that running a business along the same lines would be disastrous. Even an officer in the lofty position of battalion commander could exclaim: 'I hope I'm on hand when "due course" arrives in the Army, because a hell of a lot of things are going to happen on that day.'[4]

Expectations of incompetent organization became so strong that signs of efficiency tended to elicit genuine surprise. Lieutenant Gill described the A.I.F. officers' club in Beirut as 'a remarkably fine effort – for the army'. Clive Edwards wrote with satisfaction of his unit's embarkation on the *Mauretania*: 'the speed has been unlike the army way'.[5]

Most of the inefficiencies that plagued Australians were transient annoyances. The miscalculations, delays and other confusions in the day-to-day life of an unengaged combat unit rarely threatened more than the individual's patience. On the other hand, inefficiency or incompetence in certain matters endangered Australian lives. There are four structural features of the Australian army that demand discussion in this connection: training, equipment, medical treatment and leadership.

TRAINING

The creation in December 1942 of the Jungle Warfare Training School at Canungra in Queensland imposed virtually uniform standards on infantry training. Before this time there was significant variation in the level of training exhibited by men in front-line units.

When the 6th and 7th divisions first went on campaign in 1941, their members displayed a high standard of preparation. The 9th Division, however, was only partly trained when it entered its first actions, in the retreat from Benghazi and the subsequent siege of Tobruk. The remaining A.I.F. division, the 8th, had been in existence for some 18 months when it first saw combat, in Malaya, but its original training was directed to open, North African or European warfare. The efficacy of the efforts to retrain it for the unfamiliar jungle environment is debatable.

It would be harsh to blame any training deficiencies in the 8th and 9th divisions on inefficiency. The information available at the time probably would not have permitted more appropriate jungle training than that given to the 8th Division, which did make use of the little experience at its disposal in that area. The arrival of the Afrika Korps on the North African scene interfered with plans to provide more extensive instruction to the 9th Division. Furthermore, although some of the Australians thrust into the defence of Tobruk were unfamiliar with their weapons, the chief problem was the lack of training of officers and staff in battle management. Indeed the front-line soldiers' level of technical proficiency was sufficient to prompt Rommel, commanding the German forces, to say of Tobruk's defenders early in the siege: 'The Australian troops are fighting magnificently and their training is far superior to ours.'[6]

Various units of Australia's other army, the Citizen Military Forces, also went into action less than fully trained. From the beginning of the war, their training was beset with difficulties: notably, a steady loss of their most able and promising members to the A.I.F., and their replacement by green conscripts, severe shortages of equipment; and fragmented programmes, with different categories of militiamen being liable for varying periods of training, most of them brief.

One might wonder about the wisdom and humanity of the authorities who sent inadequately trained C.M.F. units into action in 1942 and 1943 but, on the question of training efficiency, those directly affected were victims less of incompetence than of the relative indifference of the Australian government and people.

However, inefficiency was unequivocally present in reinforcement training, as illustrated in John Lovegrove's Tobruk diary entry for 24 July 1941: 'We received reinforcemnts fresh from Australia last night and one allotted to my Section . . . was wounded virtually on arrival. I have four others of the newcomers in my Section. All . . . poorly trained, psychologically not prepared and with limited knowledge of weapons!'[7]

From 1940 until 1942, ill-trained reinforcements were consistently sent from Australia to overseas units. The worst case occurred in Singapore, where some of those Australians who arrived in January 1942, just in time to be caught up in the catastrophe there, were 'practically untrained'.[8] A number had arrived within two weeks of enlistment and had reportedly never handled a service rifle.

This state of affairs arose in the Australian army partly because of shortages of trained reinforcements with which to fill requirements. A second reason was that reinforcement training in the Middle East itself was efficient – the A.I.F. Reinforcement Depot in Palestine reportedly served as a model for all Middle East forces – and this encouraged a practice of sending men out of Australia virtually untrained. However, as Lovegrove's example shows, some men slipped through the net of overseas preparation for the front. Inefficiency was responsible for that fact, and was also largely to blame for the Singapore reinforcement tragedy. Wigmore, the official historian of the early Far Eastern campaigns, mentions 'inefficient training depots in Australia', and explains that trainers apparently failed to give sufficient attention to elementary training.[9] Another official historian, Maughan, writes of the period in which Lovegrove saw untrained reinforcements in Tobruk: 'Lack of a sense of pressing urgency to train men and formations to battle-pitch afflicted the Middle East Command and also the staffs of some administrative formations of the A.I.F. beyond the reach of guns, both at home and overseas.'[10]

The majority of Australian reinforcements lived long enough to receive the benefits of training within their units, and the standard of such instruction and exercise tended to be high, especially in A.I.F. units. The notable exception was the preparation given to members of the units that fought in New Guinea in 1942, for although they were trained in the light of some evidence from the Malayan campaign, they were not well prepared for jungle fighting. The C.M.F. units' problems have been mentioned, but the initial reverses suffered by participating A.I.F. units were less a matter of inefficient training than of generally well-trained troops suffering from ignorance of the skills and tactics necessary in an environment that was new to them and that was in many respects quite different from Malaya.

On the basis of their initial New Guinea experiences, units conceived suitable training methods and passed them on. Excellent programmes were developed, featuring 'live out and train' exercises in Queensland's jungles, and ingenious assault courses wherein soldiers had for instance to use rifle, bayonet and live grenade against fleeting dummy Japanese on recreated jungle tracks.

Most importantly, from 1942 the Jungle Warfare Training Centre seems to have almost eliminated unevenness in reinforcement training, although Allan Jones, who worked there as an instructor in 1944 and 1945, writes that many of those on the staff had little or no experience of actual jungle warfare, and criticizes the 'almost complete lack of proper tactical training'.[11] Moreover, it appears that some poorly trained reinforcements were still reaching the front in 1945.

Nevertheless, the Australian army's level of training was generally at its peak in the last year of the war. Most of the lows of previous years had been unavoidable, but many Australians had good reason to feel that in this matter the army had 'mucked them about' in a most dangerous fashion. Interestingly, there seem to be no wartime accounts in which Australian soldiers described themselves, compared with fellow members of the Australian army, as under-trained.

EQUIPMENT: QUANTITY AND QUALITY

One of the most serious training deficiencies suffered by Australians early in the war was that on first going into battle, they were often unfamiliar with weapons and equipment of any complexity above that of their rifles and uniforms. This had little or nothing to do with the quality of instruction. Rather, their ignorance of many weapons and other items of equipment stemmed from the shortages that made these items virtually unavailable for training purposes. A corporal instructing new signalmen at Centennial Park in 1940 recorded one such shortage and the anger it produced: '2.7.40 Issued with four (4) rifles with which to train 55 men in rifle drill, passed remarks that would not stand repeating in diary – result reduced to ranks on 3.7.40.'[12]

There were chronic shortages of rifles in Australia until 1942. Bren guns, chosen for the vital role of section light machine-gun in Australian combat units, were also scarce for training purposes in Australia and the Middle East even in 1941. Machine-guns of World War I vintage had to be used, if available, as if they were Brens. Improvisation was a central theme of weapons training during the first two to three years of the war. Infantry units in the Middle East used wooden representations of missing weapons, which meant most heavy weapons.

Even when equipment was available, live ammunition was so precious that men on specialist weapons – artillery pieces, for instance – had very little opportunity to practise with it. Prior to Bardia, the few available Vickers medium machine-guns had fired only one or two shots. The 2/28th Battalion historian tells of a revealing incident that occurred after the siege of Tobruk had begun: 'One afternoon the men gathered around while the C.O. threw a couple of grenades over the perimeter wire. It was the first time that these raw soldiers had seen a "live" grenade. They had to be shown its lethal radius, because when they themselves threw one it would be against a real enemy.'[13]

The paucity of equipment, and especially of weapons, was one of the main reasons that training was monotonous and disappointing for those who so eagerly enlisted in the early years of the war.

Equipment shortages were often filled just before units went into action. For example, most of the 6th Division's serious deficiencies were made good in the month before Bardia, with some units receiving vital wire-cutters on the eve of the battle. A former 8th Division infantryman recalls that only in December 1941, when his unit went into battle stations in Malaya, was an artificially enforced shortage ended and his battalion's machine-guns, mortars and grenades taken from storage. He was put in charge of a Bren gun, his experience with which consisted of firing five rounds in Australia, some months earlier.[14]

Sometimes deficiencies were made good only after the campaigning had started. The 7th Division, ill-equipped for much of its early history, received most of its required equipment during the first weeks of the Syrian campaign. The 9th Division received its first submachine guns – unsurpassed weapons for patrolling – more than a month after the Tobruk siege had started. On the Kokoda Trail, Bren guns were delivered to the 39th Battalion only after its first delaying actions against the Japanese: a fact which its historian calls 'criminal'.[15]

The reason that units in the Middle East often received equipment just before going into action was that the few available resources tended to be given to formations as they were committed, while disengaging units were commonly required to hand over their equipment. By mid-1941, some A.I.F. specialist units had remained in Australia for many months simply because there was no equipment for them overseas.

Even with the policy of handing available equipment to units as they became engaged, the Australian going into the field was all too often without equipment that he had been told he would have. Occasionally he was even without gear he had trained with, for ironically units sometimes received sufficient equipment for training purposes – enough Bren guns for everyone to have a turn on them eventually, or enough vehicles to move one battalion if three pooled their trucks and then took turns, for instance – but insufficient to provide them on the scale necessary when all the men of a unit went into action.

In the 1941 and early 1942 campaigns, Australian units regularly found themselves short of mortars, anti-tank guns, armoured vehicles, tools, artillery not of World War I pattern, and ammunition. The most worrying deficiencies, particularly amidst North Africa's vastness, were in transport. If not for captured Italian vehicles, the 6th Division could not have achieved its remarkable dash to Benghazi, while much of the 9th Division would surely have been lost in the subsequent attempt to withdraw from Benghazi to Tobruk. In the defence of Tobruk, captured Italian equipment – especially signals equipment and machine-guns – was again invaluable to Australians. Even the following year, at El Alamein, the 9th Division was using approximately 150 captured machine-guns, mortars and other weapons.

At El Alamein the 9th Division's conventional equipment was undoubtedly more abundant than ever before. Late 1942 might be seen as a turning point in the Australian equipment position in the Middle East. The official historian, Gavin Long, seems to argue that it came earlier, claiming that the Australians sent to Greece in March–April 1941 were fully equipped, and that 'lack of equipment was not . . . a serious problem' in the A.I.F. by late 1941.[16] Both of his contentions are disputable. For example, after the evacuation from Greece, a signalman who had participated noted a report on Australian political events: 're W. M. Hughes statement that A.I.F. were not properly equipped in Greece. Mr. Hughes Statement severely criticised by Cabinet . . . Mr. Hughes remarks are substantially correct in this regard.'[17] Following the Cretan campaign, another Australian participant complained: 'We can beat Jerry if we have anything like equal equipment, but we cannot stand up to his hordes when we have nothing to hit back with. It is just bloody murder putting us into Greece and Crete with no equipment except our feet.'[18] This overstated the case. In Greece, circumstances required Australians to discard much of their initial equipment, and they arrived in Crete accordingly ill-equipped. However, there is no doubt that many Australians felt that they had not been 'fully equipped' in Greece, either.

Long's claim for late 1941 is also dubious. In February 1942, the commander of the 9th Division referred to 'this eternal question of equipment', and by June the division was 'gravely short of equipment'.[19] The division increased its equipment stocks in July, but largely through salvage and 'scrounging'.

An upturn in the equipment position was even more necessary in Australia at that stage. For as late as March 1942, with the Japanese threat at its height, there were worrying deficiencies in the weapons needed merely to arm all units then in Australia: there were for example only 1590 of the more than 12 000 Bren guns required; only 4154 of the necessary 11 000 submachine guns; and just 195 of the more than 700 25-pounder guns required. By mid-1942, the equipment position had improved significantly within Australia, to the point where a successful Japanese invasion was extremely unlikely. In the field, an R.A.A.F. corporal reported good news on the Kokoda Trail in October 1942: 'Contacted part of the 2/27th going back into the fray. They say they have never been so well equipped – not even in the Middle East.'[20]

Yet the C.M.F. units on the trail were ill-equipped at the time, as they had been since the start of the war. There were also some equipment deficiencies common to all units in the campaign, notably in tools: one of the most piteous sights in Australia's war was that of soldiers trying desperately to dig vitally important slit trenches with helmets, tins, bayonets and bare hands on the Kokoda Trail. Moreover, a member of the 2/27th who served on the trail put the turning point in the equipment position much later than that operation. In January 1944, after the campaign in the Ramu Valley, Sergeant Clive Edwards reflected:

> And so I've finished a 3½ month campaign which will always be remembered by me . . . for a campaign where organisation and supply were well nigh perfect and miles ahead of anything we have experienced previously. It seems to me that the Army chiefs have at last realised that men will fight better and be far happier when they get good equipment and lots of it . . .[21]

When the turning point occurred is difficult to establish. Allan Jones, who fought in all of the 9th Division's campaigns until early 1944, believes that his unit was never 'really fully equipped' during that entire time.[22] On the other hand, by mid-1943, the army possessed more weapons than it officially needed, thanks largely to the prodigious efforts of Australian industry.

What is clear is that in the 1945 campaigns, Australians were equipped on an unprecedented scale – certainly much better than their opponents – and units were probably closer than ever to what was decreed on their war equipment tables. The following were typical comments from participants in the Borneo operations:

> . . . a continuous stream of material rumbled by us – huge tanks – bulldozers, tractors, amphibious tanks, truckloads of equipment and stores for as far as the eye could see – we had everything we wanted here and more.

> . . . as I look around me and see all the equipment we have I sometimes think it can't be many more months. The Jap was beaten by us when practically all we had was rifles, but now we have so much . . .[23]

Yet even in 1945, such statements were not representative of the entire Australian army. The Australians engaged in Borneo were generally better supplied than those fighting elsewhere in the S.W.P.A. The latter were far less enamoured with the supply system, especially in early 1945, when there were galling shortages of clothing and heavy mechanical equipment.

There were also more significant shortages in aircraft and shipping. The paucity of shipping was the most troublesome, for it forced commanders to send units across defended country when amphibious landings would have been appropriate. This and the aircraft shortage also affected ammunition supplies in a few instances, most severely in the Aitape-Wewak campaign. During one of these shortages, a diarist wrote angrily: 'Nips dug in less than five hundred yards in front and on our left flank waiting here for mortar bombs and air strikes to shift them off five good men killed because sufficient metal couldn't be found to saturate the objective they had to take'.[24]

Transport difficulties also affected the everyday lives of Australians in the Torricellis, who soldiered on with 'beds made from old bags, no blankets, and a half shelter enough to cover half a man, only not waterproof ... clothing and boots a disgrace and no replacements'.[25]

Shortages of shipping were due essentially to American decisions, and one could argue that the equipment shortages suffered by Australians throughout the war were generally less a matter of inefficiency or parsimony than of hard political and economic facts. Under such harsh realities one could include Australia's initial material shortages; its industrial inability, at least for several years, to produce all the necessary weapons and equipment; and circumstances that made it impossible early in the war for Britain, Australia's military model and traditional supplier, to equip any but its own under-provisioned army.

Yet these considerations meant little to men sent into battle with insufficient or unfamiliar equipment. Nearly every quotation in this section suggests that the soldiers at the receiving end felt that in this area they had been 'mucked about'. Indeed someone had apparently erred in calculating that all the units formed could be equipped.[26] Incidents such as the late delivery of machine-guns to the few men on the Kokoda Trail owed more to inefficiency than to industrial limitations. We cannot know the exact cost of such mistakes, but it would certainly have been higher if not for the ability of ordinary Australians to make do with captured equipment.

One soldier's remark about an important item of equipment, the submachine gun, indicates that Australians saw military inefficiency in the quality as well as the quantity of items they received: 'In Crete our chaps were fighting each other to obtain possession of Tommy guns taken from Jerry casualties. At close range the man with a rifle has not a chance against a man with the Tommy gun.'[27]

The bolt-action Lee-Enfield rifle that was the standard weapon of the Australian army was possibly the best bolt-action rifle in the world at the time. The Australians' accurate rifle fire and especially their use of the bayonets that they often attached to their rifles were respected and feared by their opponents in the Middle East. However, as the previous extract indicates, the prevalence of submachine guns among German troops made some Australians very conscious of the limitations of the 'bolt pulley'. In the South-West Pacific, where Americans could be seen using or carrying semi-automatic Garand rifles and M1 carbines, the unsuitability of slow-firing, long-range bolt-action rifles was especially obvious.

Some Australians in the field knew that the M1 carbine was faster-firing, had a larger magazine, was smaller and weighed half as much as the Lee-Enfield, and they were recommending the adoption of the carbine early in 1943. A 9th Division infantryman given a chance to fire one in New Guinea was struck by the contrast between it and the Lee-Enfield, and says of the carbine: 'Any member of our rifle platoons would have stolen one of these without a moments thought had the opportunity ever presented itself.'[28]

Australian army authorities recognized as early as June 1942 that a semi-automatic rifle was 'a future army requirement', but, discouraged by the British army's determination to persist with the rifle to which it had committed many resources, and influenced also by unofficial criticism of the Garand rifle, they do not seem to have seriously considered the possibility of a wartime change.[29] Few, if any, front-line soldiers were aware of these deliberations, but in hindsight the army's efficiency in the matter of its basic weapon is questionable.

Another tactically pivotal Australian weapon, the Bren light machine-gun, was also criticized. It was not an unmitigated success when Australians used it in their early operations. In the week before the attack on Bardia, the fine dust of the area played havoc with these weapons: an inspection in one battalion revealed that just four days before the assault, only six of some 50 Brens would fire. More effective countermeasures to the dust were found, but Brens continued to jam, and it appears that some peeved 6th Division veterans passed on stories of problems to men in other formations. One of these articulated worries about the Bren's efficiency – or over-efficiency – immediately after a costly action in the defence of Tobruk:

> When the 6th Divvy made their advance to Benghase they complained of the failure of the Bren. Todays action, although a minor affair, they let us down again . . . One day someone will wake up and realise mens lives are being lost through official pigheadedness. It is a perfect gun, the bren, too perfect; but what is the use of a gun that needs cleaning after a few rounds . . . In action one can't stop to clean the gun.[30]

1941 saw various improvements in the Bren gun and in methods of cleaning it, although malfunctions continued to occur throughout the war, sometimes at crucial moments. Nevertheless, for all the occasions that it failed its gunners, the Bren was probably the best and most reliable light machine-gun then in use, and in part the users' remarkable attachment to it bears testimony to that fact.

One weapon that seems to have been disliked by all was the anti-tank rifle, which one of the official historians calls 'a so-called anti-tank rifle'.[31] Its notoriety was not entirely deserved in that there are many recorded instances of light tanks being knocked out or halted by these 'elephant' or 'bull' guns. However, there are also accounts of anti-tank rifles failing to stop larger tanks, and it seems that brave men died as a result of this failure.

Some of the most vehement accusations of inefficiency in a weapon, and incompetence in those behind its provision, concerned the Light, or Short, 25-pounder field gun designed for use in the S.W.P.A. In September 1943, the commanding officer of the 2/4th Field Regiment argued that the workmanship on a batch of Light 25-pounders sent to him for forthcoming operations was so poor as to indicate either 'suspicions of sabotage' or 'criminal neglect of duty' on the part of manufacturers and inspectors.[32]

On re-testing one of the criticized guns in Australia, inspectors rejected most of the criticisms as unfounded or trivial. However, one of the faults they conceded – false marking on a range cone – cropped up again a year later. Various improvements were made on the Light guns, and two Short 25-pounders used by the 2/4th Field Regiment in New Guinea operations during September and October 1943 drew praise from the men concerned. However, scepticism about the value of the gun persisted.

The prime reason that artillerymen were against the adoption of the Light 25-pounder was that they loved the standard 25-pounder. The latter was one of three key Australian weapons that proved very efficient. The other two were the 36M hand grenade and the Owen submachine-gun, although the latter was adopted only after General Blamey was dissuaded from his recommendation to adopt the inferior Austen submachine-gun. The army's highest authorities showed questionable judgement for more than two years, in their persistent failure to recognize the value and popularity of the Owen gun.

If attitudes to the quality of the available weapons were mixed but generally positive, clothing and footwear were regarded less favourably. Clothing proved adequate in the Middle East, but only a week after Bardia, half the men in certain companies of the 6th Division had to don Italian boots, which some wore in Greece, months later.

When one considers the uniforms that Australians wore in the various theatres of war, perhaps the difference that springs most readily to mind is that of colour – khaki in the desert, green in the jungle. Indeed, one of the army's wartime annuals was entitled *Khaki and Green*. Yet khaki actually gave way to green in the course of the Papuan campaign, rather than at its beginning, and this delay in the change to a suitably camouflaged colour probably cost lives. Even late in 1943, the dyeing of uniforms was a fairly haphazard affair, with the 9th Division units dyeing their own clothing only after arrival in New Guinea.

At the same time, Australian-based officialdom persisted in mucking Australian front-line troops about with a forlorn and half-hearted ban on American gaiters. These were worn in the S.W.P.A. by almost all Australian combat troops, who regarded them as far more efficient than the shorter Australian-issue cloth gaiters and web anklets as a source of ankle support and protection against mud, water, scratches and leeches.

Other Australian clothing drew loud criticism from its intended wearers. Although Australian uniforms were designed to be loose-fitting and comfortable, this was often not the case. In June 1943, an official report on clothing worn in operations in New Guinea criticized its quality, weight and fit. The report noted, for instance, that in trousers: 'Some crutches are so badly finished as to be unwearable and have caused a large number of chafes which have become infected . . . The manner in which buttons are put in position is disgraceful and

many button holes are very badly finished.'[33] Soldiers in the field
reported that buttons were liable to fall off, forcing men to use string or
wire to hold up their trousers. Socks were a common source of complaint, for in New Guinea they tended to shrink and creep under one's
heel.

Although by 1944 a new post of 'battalion tailor' had been created
for infantry units, an artilleryman could write home later that year:
'Honestly I am sure the clothes we get are cut out with an axe.'[34] In fact,
the clothing issued to front-line soldiery probably never drew louder
complaints than in the last year of the war. These concerned both quality and quantity, notably of trousers. For example:

> The clothing situation is still as atrocious as ever, most of the
> boys have only the one pair and if the situation remains
> unchanged I suppose we will have to emulate the boongs.

> For every five pairs of trousers made, another pair could be
> made out of the surplus. They must think we are superman.
> [During a recent visit by a politician, this] was demonstrated
> for his purpose. Some of the boys took their belts off and the
> trousers fell right to their ankles.[35]

Even if the soldier had a full set of comfortable clothes, he almost
certainly had inadequate protection against the rain that fell regularly
and heavily in the tropics. Men had to use their anti-gas cape as a rain-
cape throughout the war, despite attempts to obtain a replacement
designed for that important purpose.

Australians' boots received little credit for their performance in
the jungle. Canungra's training instructions described the standard
'Boots AB' (ankle brown) as 'among the best marching boots in the
world'.[36] However, those instructions did not recommend the boots for
patrol work – the basis of jungle fighting – and a 1945 report concluded
that this boot had performed well only 'until operations commenced in
S.W.P.A.'. On the boots' performance, the report noted that geographical and climatic conditions drastically reduced their life, that the
smooth soles gave no traction or grip, and that nails tended to rust and
fall out, taking heels with them.[37] A new boot, designed specifically for
jungle conditions, was issued from early 1945 onwards, but these too
were clearly not ideal. After obtaining his third pair in a month, a
chaplain with front-line troops in Bougainville fumed in May 1945:

Gosh I could spit blood when I see the stuff the manufacturers are putting out . . . I'm lucky because I can get away with a new pair when I want them, but the pte has to go on, without heels, without soles, until replaced and often he has only had the boots a week or two . . . Cross two rivers and what have you? A pair of uppers . . .[38]

To be fair, no footwear could have eliminated much of the discomfort suffered by feet, often over extended periods, in the jungle campaigns. Similarly, no clothing could long stand the rigours of operational conditions in the jungle. Nevertheless, Australians in the front line saw the deterioration of their clothing and boots as a sign of incompetence and inconsiderateness, and with some justification.

MEDICAL TREATMENT

In several respects, the efficiency of the medical treatment given to Australia's sick and wounded was dubious. During the 1942 New Guinea campaign two appalling errors were made in the struggle against sickness. One was an order, given to troops arriving at Milne Bay shortly before the Japanese attack, that they take no quinine – a vital malarial suppressant – until they had been in the area for a week. By the time the fighting concluded there, the malarial rate was already 33 cases per 1000 men per week (1716 per 1000 per year) and soon afterwards reached epidemic proportions.

The second example of incompetence occurred further north. During the trek over the mountainous Owen Stanleys to Kokoda, anopheles mosquitoes were not present to spread malarial infection, but as medical authorities on the trail realized, this would change on the lower ground that separated Kokoda and the north coast. However, their request for quinine and protective nets and cream to be landed at Kokoda in November met with no response for four to five weeks after troops entered the malarial region. Largely as a result of this oversight, within two to three weeks of arrival practically all soldiers in the area were infected by the disease, and dependent on a suppressant to keep going.[39]

Despite these blunders, the Australian Army Medical Corps' overall record against malaria was very creditable. The mortality rate of uncomplicated malaria in the Australian army was only 0.5 per 1000 soldiers. That this was due to the quality of the treatment rather than the intrinsic nature of the disease is well illustrated by the experience of 250 Australian soldiers who, in trying to escape from New Britain in 1942, suffered a 20 per cent death rate after their quinine supplies ran out.

The success rate of Australian treatment of its wounded does not seem to have been so distinguished. The Australian soldier's prospects of surviving a wound were statistically not much greater in World War II than in 1914–18 . While 7.48 per cent died of their injuries in World War II, 8.90 per cent is the corresponding figure for World War I.[40] This seems to indicate that Australian medical treatment was not much more effective in 1939–45, despite the great advances in chemotherapy and blood transfusion that had been made in the interval.

One might argue that various considerations make such comparisons facile: for instance, the relative lethality of weapons in the two wars, and the impossibility of knowing what proportion of men who officially 'died of wounds' were, like some abdominal casualties, virtually dead on arrival for treatment.

A plausible explanation of the small difference is that the chances of survival were more likely to be prejudiced by difficulties of evacuating the wounded during World War II. The official medical history points to this difference as a reason for not drawing comparisons between the respective success rates in the treatment of abdominal wounds, and certainly medical officers in the Kokoda campaign felt that the unique problems of evacuating the seriously wounded were costing lives. Moreover, those who did reach the rear area in this campaign, as in others, had excellent prospects of survival: of 750 casualties evacuated from the trail in August–September 1942, only four died subsequently in hospital. On the other hand, one piece of evidence suggests that, far from causing 'died of wounds' figures to be artificially increased, difficult terrain could lead to underestimates. A battalion historian says of Salamaua: 'Many of those listed as killed in fact died of wounds, which might not have proved fatal in a more accessible battle area.'[41]

A more important reason that the geographical explanation will not suffice is that the rate of death from wounds in the Middle East, where no unconquered evacuation problems existed, was only marginally lower than in South-East Asia and the Pacific, where the difficulties pertained: the respective died of wounds rates were 7.3 and 7.6 per cent.[42] It is also relevant that the mortality rate plummeted in the

American army during World War II. The American died of wounds
rate was half that of World War I, and at 3.5 per cent, less than half the
Australian rate in World War II.[43]

A thorough search for an explanation of the fact that the average
wounded Australian's chances of survival were not as good as those of
his American allies, and little better than those of his 'digger' prede-
cessor, is beyond the scope of this study. The soldiers themselves were
not aware of these statistics, and in fact wounded men being evacuated
for treatment usually were not in a favourable condition to comment
and especially to write about the important early stages of their treatment. The little available evidence of their attitudes is almost entirely
positive, although other sources hint that the severe organizational
headaches of the Kokoda and Finschhafen campaigns gave rise to criticism. A surgeon who had worked in the fortress hospital during the
Tobruk siege reported complaints about treatment given further forward, in the line: namely, of inadequate immobilization, bandaging
and morphine dosage.[44] The last-named was a recurring reproach, and
one possibly echoed by suffering patients.

The official medical history also implies that rumours about
wounded Australians lying unattended were usually current during
campaigns.[45] If so, these rather hysterical furphies did an injustice to
the stretcher bearers, who usually showed compassionate heroism in
performing one of the most stressful jobs in the army. Whether the
general quality of the treatment given to the dangerously wounded was
so high is less certain.

LEADERSHIP

A gunner who obviously regarded his military superiors as both a
source of frustrating boredom and the embodiment of inefficiency
noted in his Middle East diary:

> Had to stand around like a lot of apes as usual while the
> Officers gave us the usual baloney and give orders and
> immediately contradict them. Guarantee anyone of 80% of
> the gunners could have carried out things more efficiently.
> The more one sees of the Officers in charge of us, the more
> readily comes the explanation of the Malayan and Singapore
> disasters.[46]

Another Australian who doubted the competence of officers was a corporal who, after the disastrous Greek campaign, wrote of:

> ... that scarcest of things in the A.I.F. – brains ... I know I
> havent got many but unfortunately they function enough to
> get me into trouble with the nitwits above us – one would not
> employ them to cut the lawn at home they'd dig it up instead.
> Thank heavens they spend most of their time in action sweating in holes.[47]

That such striking criticisms were made is noteworthy, but most Australian front-line soldiers were not inclined to regard the majority of the officers of their acquaintance as fools or cowards. Even so, participants in several campaigns were at the very least annoyed by what they considered to be the ineptitude displayed by men in command, and particularly by those in high positions.

The campaigns that aroused the deepest emotions of this kind were the defeats in Greece and Crete in 1941 and at the hands of the Japanese early in 1942. An 8th Division artilleryman, whose World War I service put him in an unusually good position to assess the organization of the Malayan campaign, commented in the following way to his son in February 1942: 'I just can't give you all details of our fighting, as swearing is not good for sonny to read, or allowed by the censor, sufficient might be said when I say it was all plain hell, and Dad's experiences in the last war was just a lovely pic-nic in comparison to this frightful mix-up'.[48]

A feeling widespread in this campaign, as in Greece and Crete, was that the Australians had been failed, or 'let down', by people further back. During the fighting on Singapore, for example, a captain of the decimated 2/20th Battalion reported to General Bennett, the Australian commander: 'The men are very tired. Their rations have been irregular and inadequate, they have been constantly in contact with the enemy and they feel that they have been badly let down, I feel that too.'[49]

Another captain wrote soon after the Greek campaign of: 'the grand if savage spirit of our troops. They think they have been let down and have been made fools of.'[50] The Minister for the Army became concerned, soon after the Greek and Cretan campaigns, when he learnt that the American minister in Cairo had reported a widespread feeling

amongst Australians and New Zealanders in the Middle East 'that they
have been let down and that they have not received adequate material'.
General Blamey was asked to respond, and in doing so he said that
there was no evidence of any such dissatisfaction. He did concede,
however: 'Naturally after experience of Greece and Crete there is some
criticism of plans and arrangements by higher authorities that exposed
them to such superiority of force especially as regards air support'.[51]

Criticism of air support, or rather the lack of it, was indeed very
strong after these and the early South-East Asian campaigns: some
Australians went so far as to ascribe their defeats to its absence. This
issue of course had little to do with inefficiency in the Australian army,
but was the domain of air forces and especially of the most senior
commanders and politicians.

It is important to note that in each of the disastrous campaigns
Australian troops fought under British command, and as instruments
of controversial political decisions. Thus Australians' accusations of
incompetence tended to be directed at a broader group than just their
own army. An example of the soldiers' recognition of these causal links
is the following comment from an Australian in Singapore to a World
War I veteran in Australia:

> Andy you once said you hoped that this campaign would not
> turn out another Greece and Crete. I didn't think that Britain
> would allow it to be either, but Im sorry to say it is just that and
> it is inexcusable. We knew from the time we first met them
> and we had no plane support that we would have to fall back
> on the island . . .[52]

Immediately after the Greek campaign, the chief objects of cen-
sure were the British command and the air force, rather than the
Australian army, which won praise from its lower ranking members for
its organization of the withdrawal.[53]

Regardless of the sources of incompetent direction, as in every
army its effects on the front-line soldiers were grim. The momentous
blunders of 1941 and 1942 created an abiding resentment in many of
those Australians not killed as a result of them. For example, in a book
published in 1984, a survivor of the Malayan campaign and subsequent
imprisonment followed a definition of 'dereliction of duty' with these

Soldiers working together in the
perilous conditions of Buna,
December 1942.
(A.W.M. 013940)

Two Australians carry a
wounded mate to medical help
in appalling conditions near
Lae, in September 1943.
(A.W.M. 015787)

Soldiers sleep on the bench seats of the grandstand at the Adelaide Oval in 1942. Some of these then had to camp in the Botanical Gardens for more than a month, and then spent several weeks here. Conditions such as these led to complaints about army callousness and inefficiency. (A.W.M. P1568.022)

Tobruk, 1941: captured Italian anti-aircraft guns in use against bombardment by
German aircraft, one of the greatest sources of stress in the Middle East.
(A.W.M. 040689)

An infantryman's comment on the migration of front-line soldiers to base units.
(Red Platypus)

Making the most of it. John's Knoll, New Guinea, October 1943. In a front-line position under enemy bombardment, tired but cheerful infantrymen receive mail. (A.W.M. 059024)

Militiamen of the 61st Battalion patrolling at Milne Bay, in September 1942. The unit's performance in the battle there was later a source of dispute. Note the shorts and rolled up sleeves: clothing which contributed to the malaria epidemic in the area. (A.W.M. 026664)

September 1942. Militiamen of the 3rd Battalion prepare to go on patrol. Speaking to them is their C.O., Lt-Col Cameron, formerly of the A.I.F. 2/22 Battalion. The 3rd was later disbanded. (A.W.M. 027011)

In February 1945 an infantryman carries a cross to a forward position on Bougainville, where it will mark the burial place of a comrade killed in action. (A.W.M. 018176)

impassioned words: 'In my book inefficiency in command performance, as we witnessed in the Malayan and Singapore debacles ...
should come under the same heading. It is not the fortunes of war, it is
the criminal lunacy of people who think they can run a war ... who was
ever called to account for the destruction of the 8th Division?' The
author of that passage was bitter not only towards the British leadership, but also towards the Australian commanders who were 'very
brave with other men's lives.'[54]

There were at least two significant cases where the Australian
army, or more precisely, senior army officers, were the only obvious
human culprits for manifest errors. The drastic shortages of food that
plagued Australians on the Kokoda Trail had several major causes,
including the terrain and initial and inherent problems associated with
the use of air supply and native carriers. However, administrative
bungling, including a failure to build up reserves of supplies on the trail,
was also a major factor.

Poor preparation was the chief reason that many forward troops
also went hungry in the Lae campaign. When, two days after the fall of
Lae, Australians were still suffering shortages – of cigarettes and clean
clothing as well as food – Private Murphy recorded his unit's response:
'We are all disgusted with the way we are being treated and it is nothing
but a disgrace.'[55]

Despite accusations of bungling and callousness, the army's higher
command was not so inefficient as to prevent its formations from being
successful in the vast majority of their campaigns. Moreover, some
senior commanders – notably Morshead, Vasey, Allen, Savige and
Dougherty – won popularity with their troops, albeit mostly for their
obvious courage and humanity rather than their tactical ability.

It has been shown that in several vital aspects of front-line experience, inefficiency was non-existent or more apparent than real. Yet it is
clear that there were deficiencies that resulted in loss of life. Moreover,
in the day-to-day existence of every common soldier there were continual manifestations of 'the army way'. There must have been thousands of Australians who finished days with reflections such as that
penned by an artilleryman soon after he arrived with his unit on Crete:
'They mucked us about all day, and if ever the boys are jack of the Army
they are now. I am full to the ears of it.'[56]

CHAPTER EIGHT

RESENTMENT OF
INEQUALITY

*G*rievances about inequality weigh-
ed heavily on Australians in front-line units. Their anger focused on
civilian life, on non-fighting units and on the army's hierarchy. In
short, all Australians who were not sharing the front-line soldier's predicament were potential targets of his wrath.

FRONT-LINE TROOPS *VERSUS* CIVILIANS

'Equality of sacrifice' was a principle often touted in Australia early in
the war. To Australians in the front line, the disparity between their
own efforts and those of civilians at home represented an infuriating
violation of that ideal.

In particular, combat soldiers often reviled the civilian who had
not taken the opportunity to match their own sacrifice by enlisting. The
following angry declaration from the Middle East suggests the existence of a widespread antipathy towards the 346 000 to 500 000 men
aged 18–35 who never served: 'And how are all the nice little "essential
service" boys? By Jove, the 2nd AIF are bitter about the people who
won't enlist ... From officers down to the sanitation fatigue they've
nothing but contempt for them.'[1]

Many regarded such civilians as 'shirkers', cowards or men without feeling or decency. Some wrote resentfully or sarcastically of staying home in the next war so that, instead of making sacrifices, they
could make money like their civilian compatriots. An official report
written just after the war noted that a wartime argument heard
throughout Australia from deserters or soldiers asking for extensions of

leave was along these lines: 'Why shouldn't I, after four years service, go home to look after my sick wife and family when Jim Jones, who hasn't helped a cracker except to make big money for himself, is able to be at his home every night and every week-end[?]'[2]

Soldiers resented inequalities of leisure, as well as of financial opportunity. News of well-attended sports meetings angered some, including an officer who wrote to his wife from North Africa: 'I have just been reading some Australian papers . . . It makes me mad to see pictures of race meetings featuring fit and healthy looking little bastards in civilian clothes sitting in grand stands at home without even a look of shame on their faces . . . May their dirty little souls rot.'[3]

A witticism current at Tobruk was the suggestion that the garrison stand in two minutes' silence for the casualties on the sporting fields of Australia. This was a painful, if humorous, pointer to the unequal efforts being made by the two groups of Australian men. The anger, indignation and disappointment that gave rise to that quip were also responsible for the popularity of a poem, supposedly written by an Australian who was subsequently killed in action, and entitled 'My Friends Who Stayed at Home':

> I'm pulling off my colors, I'll fling away my web
> On going down to Cairo to draw my pay and get a bed,
> I'm tired of being a soldier so hel[p] – I am,
> Of chewing mauldy biscuits and eating bread and jam.
> Of fighting HUNS and DAGOES, out here all on my own,
> When I think of dear old AUSSIE,
> AND MY FRIENDS WHO STAYED AT HOME
>
> I'll bet they are walking down the street,
> Their chest puffed out with pride,
> And skiting with their cobbers,
> How they saved their worthless hides, while heres me in
>   the desert,
> afraid to show me head,
> For fear some HUN or DAGO will fill it full of lead,
> And when I told my mother, I had volunteered to fight,
> She said 'God Bless You Son and bring you back alright',
> They called me 'CHOCOLATE SOLDIER' and five bob
>   tourist too,
> They said you'll never see the front, or even get a view,
> They said you'll have a picnic, across the ocean blue,
> But they werent game to face it,
> MY FRIENDS WHO STAYED AT HOME.

And they were not bad shots either, on the rabbit track,
But there, they are in no danger, 'cos rabbits can't shoot back,
They shine before the barmaids, they brag, they are full of skite,
And at the corner of the street is where they have their fight,
The Billard Cue is their rifle, the Bar their fighting zone,
For their aint no bullets there, for
MY FRIENDS WHO STAYED AT HOME.

So I'll pick up my Lee Enfield, and buckle my web about,
Though I'm a flamin GUNNER, I'll see this business out,
If I stop a bullet I'll die without a moan,
'cos they've got me flamin' back up,
MY FRIENDS WHO STAYED AT HOME.[4]

The report that the author did 'stop a bullet' added to the pungency
of his criticism. A belief that all war dead had made the 'supreme sacrifice' heightened anger at the minimal self-denial being exercised in
Australia. Two Australians who wrote of the sacrifices that their dead
comrades had made for a higher cause added the following comments:

> ... I wonder if the people back home will ever realise what
> they owe to these men.

> ... I only hope that the people of Australia realise what they
> owe to men like your brother ...'[5]

A feeling, implied here, that the efforts of the fighting troops were not
receiving due attention at home was another source of grievance
among Australian soldiers. In the Middle East, for example, many
complained that Australia's government and general populace were
showing shamefully little interest in, or commitment to, the war.

As a consequence, when the Japanese entered the war some Australians in the Middle East actually expressed satisfaction, believing
that civilians at home would at last realize that there was a war on, and
that it threatened their way of life. A major factor in that attitude was
almost certainly a hope that the volunteer soldiers would now receive
the praise they deserved for their earlier perspicacity concerning the
war and their courage in going overseas to fight.

In fact, thousands of soldiers received not praise but blame after the Japanese entry into the war. A strong but groundless rumour among the Australian population suggested that the A.I.F. men who did not return to Australia in 1942, but instead stayed behind in the Middle East, had volunteered to do so. As a result, there were numerous reports of soldiers receiving letters containing white feathers or abuse, even from relatives or lovers.[6]

Similar acts of civilian tactlessness or ignorance had occurred in 1941, when letters and press reports alleged that Australian troops were having an easy time in Malaya and Tobruk. These allegations, like the 1942 rumour, were such bizarre and palpable falsehoods that some of the men they described considered them amusing. However, because the stories were genuinely believed by the civilians whose opinions and esteem meant much to the troops, most of the soldiers were deeply hurt.[7] Such misunderstandings added to their bitterness at bearing a disproportionate share of the war's burden.

The soldier's pain was also exacerbated by the manifest selfishness of certain civilian groups. He felt contempt for black marketeers and civilians who went on strike, especially miners and wharf labourers. A lieutenant writing from Tobruk said that he was inclined to write to the Australian press:

> ... expressing my view (and those of the majority if not all of the AIF) of that low scum that has the hypocrisy to call itself 'workers'. In my opinion, there is one quarter where the Nazi rule would really do some good – it would line the swine up and shoot them. Small wonder the world was not theirs after the last war – if the old AIF felt like this one about them.[8]

He and some others suggested that 'we' would like to shoot the strikers.[9] Wrathful criticism was directed at waterside workers for delaying troop movements with stoppages, and for stealing from the soldiers' supplies.

In the final year of the war against Japan, feeling against the Australian civilian population received a further spur from the fact that although more Australians were fighting the Japanese than ever before, they seemed to have been virtually forgotten at home. Some soldiers were outraged by the fact that in May 1945, while they remained in perilous forward positions in the jungle, the population celebrated the Allied victory in Europe. A typical criticism was:

Generous people these Australians, wave a few flags when you are leaving, then don't know you exist the next day. I can imagine all the people in Sydney shouting and shaking hands with each other, drinking beer and having a great time, a great victory for them no doubt, but I bet 75% of them don't even know what they are celebrating. I would like some of them up here for a while . . .[10]

When the combat soldiers took their periodic turns at home leave, many saw what they regarded as verification of their sense of injustice. Not only were they peeved or angered by the easy time being had by civilians, but they were also annoyed by those who had the gall to complain about their own relatively minor discomforts. Allan Jones recalls the period after his return from the Middle East, where he had been at Tobruk and Alamein:

Many people, some friends, some I knew slightly, and others who were total strangers, were all eager to talk about the war-time restrictions they had to endure, the shortages and even the lack of entertainments to keep them amused. About all I could do under the circumstances was listen politely and marvel at the divisions in opinion between service and civilian expectations . . . A few people asked me about the Middle East, listened for a few minutes, then told me heartbreaking tales about petrol rationing, the arrival of the Americans, the Kokoda Trail, and finally the greatest battle ever fought; the bombing of Darwin. If you were'nt there, you were nothing.[11]

There is an echo here of that sense of alienation from civilian life which featured in British and German writings of World War I. Indeed, Long states that in 1944 and 1945, Australian soldiers felt increasingly isolated from the civilian world, and that on home leave they tended to seek each other's company in order to reminisce and to complain about civilian Australia.[12]

This assessment is only partly true, however. The greatest attraction of home leave was the domestic circle of relatives and close friends, and the longing to be with its members, like the desire to receive mail from them, seldom waned. As Long acknowledges, these people were excluded from criticism of the population.[13] Soldiers might be disappointed or angered by the narrow-mindedness they encountered, but they still sought the company of families – and many of them sought new or additional loved ones. Home leave was desperately desired, and often overstayed, throughout the war, and while this was largely due to a longing for more congenial surroundings, generally it stemmed from a desire to meet civilians, and especially wives, mothers, girlfriends and prospective female companions. In sum, the deep sense of estrangement felt by European soldiers on leave in World War I was not usually the fate of their Australian counterparts in World War II.

Moreover, Australian troops did see signs of civilian support. Some members of the 6th Division felt that the public had originally snubbed and discouraged them – as the poem quoted earlier implies – but huge crowds turned out to see the formation's march through the streets of Sydney and Melbourne before it went overseas. Similar displays of appreciation, affection and interest were accorded to Australian units throughout the war, and although occasionally men were disappointed with their reception on arrival in Australia, these parades probably dispelled much ill-will.

Many soldiers were helped by Australians not previously known to them: their battalion might be adopted by a district, as was the 2/23rd Battalion by the citizens of Albury, who showed great generosity to the unit both before and after it went overseas; or they might receive donations from the public through the Comforts Fund, or hospitality from people with whom they were billeted. Thus it is clear that the soldiers' own families and closest friends would not have been the only civilians exempted from criticism.

In contrast to their anger at so-called 'friends' who stayed at home rather than go overseas, soldiers were often anxious that brothers or close friends should not join up, urging that at most they should enlist in home defence units. This solicitude derived largely from the fact that these potential volunteers, unlike the faceless or barely known 'shirkers', were valued by the soldiers, as were the women – mothers, sisters, sisters-in-law – whom the new recruits would leave at home suffering.

In John Barrett's postwar survey, civilian men of military age were said to have been regarded with contempt or 'some reservations' by just 54 per cent of the ex-soldiers who responded.[14] It is unfortunate that no distinction is made within that sample between front-line and non-combatant troops, for it seems likely that there was a difference in attitudes to those who stayed at home. Men seeing comrades killed around them were surely more inclined to be resentful towards 'shirkers' than were those soldiers further back. Whether or not this was so, it seems that during the war, whenever front-line troops expressed strong emotions concerning the vast majority of civilian workers, these were likely to be hostile emotions. The overwhelming impression from wartime evidence is that combat troops never considered the general population to be doing enough to match, support or recognize the fighting troops' own sacrifice.

FRONT-LINE TROOPS *VERSUS* BASE TROOPS

The comparative lack of sacrifice required of supporting troops was an enduring source of bitterness among front-line soldiers. Their resentment frequently expressed itself in contempt for base troops. More specifically, men in front-line areas argued that non-combatant troops were cowardly, lazy and not real soldiers. Their disdain is exemplified in Private Butler's record of a conversation between 9th Division infantry veterans and a base officer in Queensland:

> . . . an idiotic Major . . . with a few drinks in him abused us, called us the rabble and other cheap remarks, all because we did not make use of marquees but sat on the ground. He told us he saw as much service as us in the M.E. and I find he was Man Power Officer at Gaza [in the Palestine base area] – as a Sergeant said 'keeping the Hun at bay on Gaza Ridge.'[15]

Even officers in combat units engaged wholeheartedly in criticism of those further back. They seem to have reserved their greatest scorn for the most senior headquarters. Thus an infantry captain in the Middle East wrote of 'the Last Line of Defence Brigade, the famous Tail Sitters of AIF HQ which never moves more than five miles from a pub under any circumstances'. In the S.W.P.A., officers chose epithets such as 'those senile simpletons that repose at L.H.Q. for a few hours daily and imagine themselves soldiers'.[16]

The combat soldier generally directed his most passionate anger towards troops well behind the front: the 'base bludgers', 'base wallopers' and 'base wallahs', as he tended to call them. Indeed there seems to have been a figurative sliding-scale equating worthiness with proximity to the front. However, even men just behind the forward positions were castigated, including the foremost troops' own battalion headquarters and relatively safe 'B' echelon – the cooks, clerks and storemen who prepared meals and stores for daily transport up to the line.

Thus, although it has often been said that feelings between all members of the Tobruk garrison were exceptionally cordial, it is apparent in the soldiers' own writings that many on the fortress perimeter resented what they regarded as the comparatively easy time being had by those behind them. A relatively restrained expression of that feeling appears in a diary entry written on the Tobruk perimeter: 'In Tobruk . . . almost all the risk and hardship is assumed by a small fraction of the men, the front liners. If those further back did not hear the air raids from the depth of their shelters, life would be altogether too monotonous.' Another part of the same day's entry illuminates a second aspect of this sense of inequity:

> Back in Tobruk [town], Divisional Headquarters and all the other privileged sections are living like kings in deep shelters and consuming the best of food: home-made cakes, best jam etc. In the front line, where the hard unpleasant work is done, we have to subsist on bully beef, bread, possibly meat-and-vegetable ration, marmite and a very little cheap jam . . .[17]

Throughout the war, other Australian front-line soldiers echoed these envious references to the security and privileges of the rear-area troops.

The privileges were the main cause of resentment. Further insight into that attitude comes from remarks written by a combat soldier during the concluding stages of the Syrian campaign. Signalman Neeman commented on the decision to divert his infantry battalion around Beirut the day before various generals were to make a ceremonial entry: 'we were crook on that would have liked to have had a look at the place, but its the usual practice anything good-on the 'base walads' get the best, while the Inf[antry] goes ahead, looking for more trouble.'[18] Here there is not only a sense of muted anger at the greed of the 'base walads', but also an image of self as martyr, with all the moral superiority that image entails. These feelings emerge strongly in soldiers' writings, including an artilleryman's reflections on the selfish and callous inertia of base troops: 'it cant be expected that arm chair and desk soldiers would know what an army in the field requires. They are too concerned about holding down their nice comfortable jobs at Base to worry over the fighting man and most of the boys agree with me in that.'[19]

Sometimes the tone was one not of restrained self-pity or under-stated and cynical aggression, but of moral outrage. The following remarks, written by an infantry officer soon after he was evacuated sick from Tobruk, are a perfect example:

> No luxuries like tinned fruit, chocolate or anything is avail-able [in Tobruk] – that all goes down the throats of the 'soldiers' between base and the front. Why, I had not left the front for more than a few hours before someone casually offered me a plate of preserved peaches and tinned cream. God, it makes me boil to think of what our men are going through on next to nothing.[20]

A sense of moral superiority arose from the belief that the real 'soldiers' were making unequal sacrifices and were being materially disadvantaged. This feeling was heightened by a conviction that the base soldier's comforts and privileges were won largely by cheating the front-line men. Some complained that base troops chose for them-selves the best clothing and rations: 'I think all the "heroes" who are furthest from the front line positions pick the eyes out of the canteen consignments before we get the dregs', wrote one Tobruk defender.[21]

A belief that those further back stole items intended for troops at the front appears to have been widespread. For example, Private Keys wrote home concerning parcels sent to him in Libya: 'If they arrive where our Battalion is I am certain to get them, but [I], like others of the boys, think that some of the crowd well back, read on the labels what the parcels contain, and can't resist the temptation to eat the good things.' Two years later he chided his sister for trying to send him cigarettes: 'No doubt some base chap is smoking at your expense.'[22] An artillery officer in the desert found a neat metaphor to express the same message: 'tell Winnie not to worry about her sox at the bottom of the sea, they are probably being worn by some cold footed postal clerk back at base'.[23]

The front-line soldier's moral indignation was not without a basis in fact. Rations were poorer the closer one was to the front, and one reason for this was, that as the official medical history notes, 'the temp-tation to abstract the more popular and varied items and to pass the remainder on was not always resisted, despite the greater needs of the forward troops'. In New Guinea there were 'rackets' among some base troops, whose stock-in-trade included items intended for the front.[24]

Even when there was no illegality, men in rear areas might receive more rations than the troops they were supposed to be supplying at the front. The following diary entries, written by a sergeant in the Tobruk base area during the siege, reflect circumstances that if revealed to forward troops, would have provoked outrage about inequality:

> Fresh meat for tea, peas carrots and spuds – two bottles of beer between 3 and a can each. Wet the whistle a bit . . . Hectic night with spots last night. Had 4 cognacs for a kick off at 9 p.m. and then ran into 3 stiff whiskies from Major Fitz. Got home 1.30 a.m. and no raids but there was a corker at 4 a.m. Took my cig issue yesterday as QM not in. Received another lot this morning. OK with me. Also scrounged 16 packets last night but gave 10 away. Have my swim every day about 4 p.m. now.[25]

There is also some evidence that supports the front-line complaints about privileges accruing to men who were dodging their responsibilities at higher levels. In the last two years of the war, headquarters developed in such a way as to suggest that base officers were indeed engaged in the absorbing and self-centred task of empire-building. Although the Australian army decreased in size by 22 per cent between June 1943 and June 1945, Land Headquarters and Advanced Headquarters grew by 36 and 42 per cent respectively in that time. And while the number of men in the ranks fell by 20 per cent between June 1942 and May 1945, the number of officers rose by 14 per cent in that period.[26] One may safely assume that the new positions created were almost entirely in non-combatant areas.

There appear to have been two other practices among base officers that accorded entirely with front-line perceptions. One was that of reducing income tax by leaving one's base job in Australia for three months annually, to be spent in a 'forward area': this term could describe not just the front line, but also very safe parts of Bougainville or New Guinea. The term 'T.E.U.' – Tax Evasion Unit – was allegedly applied to practitioners.[27]

The other practice that raised the eyebrows of at least some front-line troops was that of officers leaving comfortable positions to take up posts in combat units only when the possibility of action and self-sacrifice diminished. For instance, on returning to Australia with the 6th Division in 1942, an officer temporarily in charge of a rifle company wrote: 'Maj X – took over command of D Coy as he has returned from Div – Fair dinkum wouldnt it. Just what I always go crook about – men do the job and when things get easy base wallahs come and take over'.[28]

'Base wallah' was a term that applied to all ranks, high and low, and the following delightfully frank outline of a day's work, written by a rear-area soldier, would have appealed to most front-line troops as the epitome of selfish and privileged 'Base wallahdom':

DAILY ROUTINE OF A SOLDIER BEHIND THE LINES

06.30	Reveille	17.00	Leave bar – bar closes at 17.00
07.25	Rise, bath, shave, dress, clean boots make bed	17.01	Start playing two-up.
07.30	Breakfast	17.30	Leave two-up broke.
08.30	Parade	17.31	Dinner.
08.35	Start work	18.30	Repair to bar
08.36	Finish work.	20.00	Stagger away from bar.
08.37	Hide somewhere, where no one can find you.	20.15	Enter local picture house
		22.15	Hop into bed.
12.30	Return to tent – look fatigued.	22.16	Start argument on war position.
12.45	Lunch	22.30 ⎫	
13.45	Parade	23.00 ⎬ still argueing about war	
13.50	Start work.	23.30	
13.51	Hide again	24.00 ⎭	
16.30	Return to tent.	01.01	Fall asleep after very heavy
16.31	Repair to bar		days work.[29]

Nevertheless, most of the antagonism towards rear area troops was mere prejudice. The Australian army followed the worldwide trend that saw an expansion in the supporting base of fighting troops between World War I and World War II. As in all western Allied armies, the Australian 'tail' grew in comparison to its 'teeth' in the course of the war. The Australian army was probably more economic in its provision of supporting troops than the American or the British, although the last provided most of Australia's base troops in the Middle East.

Of those Australians who were in base areas, many were making the biggest sacrifice they could, as they were ineligible for service at the front. For instance, of the 120 133 base and line-of-communications troops on mainland Australia in April 1945, 46.5 per cent were classified 'B' class medically, meaning they were physically unfit for front-line service. Most of these men were 'B' class when they enlisted – one-quarter of male reinforcements were, according to General Blamey in 1943 – but many were former 'A' class men.[30] No front-line veteran could have failed to know of men permanently invalided out of his unit for health reasons, while combat officers who reached the upper age limit for their rank – ranging from 30 for a lieutenant to 45 for a lieutenant-colonel – could not expect to avoid stepping backwards for long. Even when base troops met health and age requirements, transfers to the front were not necessarily available for those who wanted them.

Many support troops may have mustered little enthusiasm for their unglamorous jobs, in which the boredom tended to be unrelieved. Nevertheless, it seems that most showed commitment by working hard. Front-line soldiers noted the swift transformations that occurred in places developed as bases in New Guinea – Port Moresby, Milne Bay, Wau and Lae, for example – and although much of the credit belonged to American equipment, enterprise and labour, Australian base troops also contributed. And while lazy, pilfering and careless army dock workers grabbed most attention, there were others, as one veteran recalls in an account of his infantry battalion's travels in New Guinea:

> We called in at Buna, and tied up to the new wharf, while an Australian Docks Operating Company unloaded some cargo, and loaded other things in its place. With all the superiority of combat troops, who were not inclined to be particularly tolerant of troops who merely worked, we lined the rail to watch. Our disdain soon turned to pride and admiration, as these superbly trained experts . . . displayed such skill and speed as to be accorded a spontaneous and sustained round of applause.[31]

Enthusiasm often arose, too, in front-line troops who witnessed or experienced the skills of the army medical corps personnel who treated their wounds and illnesses.

At times, soldiers in supposed rear area units found themselves in the firing line. Support troops campaigning in the Middle East and

Malaya came under regular air attack and, in Tobruk and Singapore, under various degrees of artillery bombardment. In the S.W.P.A., support troops in most campaigns were in danger from Japanese ambushes. During amphibious operations, the distance between front and base was for a time small or negligible, and Japanese night attacks forced base troops into action. On one notable occasion, a docks operating company held off a large raiding party at Labuan.

Naturally, most support troops saw little or no action. To at least some of them this was a source not of satisfaction but of awed admiration for those who did fight, as well as guilt about their own role. When, for instance, a Bougainville provost described the state of two colleagues just returned from an ordeal of swimming several swollen rivers, the expression that seemed appropriate was 'looking like real soldiers'.[32] This was, of course, the terminology that appeared suitable to the front-line troops as well. Another example of the base soldiers' low self-esteem is that of a member of a railway construction company who confided to his diary: 'Ones Conscience troubles him a little at times being back here in a back line unit.' The diarist later joined the infantry, for similar reasons to those that motivated the transport driver who left his post and joined the attack at Bardia because he 'felt like a bludger sitting at battalion headquarters, and wanted to be in it'.[33]

No such choice faced men like the disappointed soldier who, invalided out of his combat unit before seeing action, reflected: 'I am now, what is termed a "B" class soldier, which to quote it bluntly is one hell of a position to be in.'[34] Such discomfort could only have been increased by public opinion, which was most interested in the fighting soldiers, and which expressed itself late in the war in a petition, signed by over 100 000 electors, asking that a pay increase – a 'battle bonus' – be given to servicemen in operational areas.

That proposal failed, but in general the government tried to ensure that front-line troops got preferential treatment over all other soldiers, and indeed over civilians. Thus the quartermaster-general stated in April 1944: 'At all times, preference is given to troops in operational and forward Areas to permit ample supplies to be made at forward locations. It will be recalled that tinned foods were completely withdrawn from sale in southern Areas so that supplies might be made available to troops in Northern climes.'[35]

Tobacco and cigarettes provide another example of this policy.

For Australian soldiers in Australia, cigarettes or tobacco – the latter was preferred by the majority – were generally available only if purchased as canteen goods. Those serving overseas could buy these goods, duty free, and also received a small amount of tobacco *gratis* from the Australian Comforts Fund. Australians actually at the front were entitled to purchase canteen goods, get the A.C.F. issue and receive free issues from the army. They were also given 'complete preference' in the best grades of tobacco and cigarettes.[36]

Clearly, then, supply was organized in such a way that the front-line soldiers, not the base troops, should have received the privileges, which were implicitly acknowledged as their just reward for the sacrifices they were making. In reality, the fruits of the policy of preferential treatment did not always, or even often, reach the front. Combat troops were not deluged with luxuries, or even necessities.

Yet the behaviour of selfish troops stationed between base and front is only a minor part of the explanation of the fact that the best-fed Australian soldiers lived behind the lines. The relative difficulty of transporting perishable food and storing it in operational areas was far more important. Access to Australian front-line zones was usually made difficult by geography and made dangerous by the enemy. Also, when troops were in action, the highest supply priorities had to be ammunition and military equipment rather than rations beyond the bare essentials. There was no good reason why troops further back should not enjoy the benefits of superior facilities – such as refrigeration – that could be made available there.

The often herculean task of supplying front-line troops was accomplished, despite occasional and dangerous lapses in planning and execution. Those at the front were entirely dependent on it being achieved, and the chief illogicality of their antagonism to Australian support troops lay in this fact. Yet as Holmes says of this bitterness, which affects all armies, it was not a matter of logic, but of belief: intense and natural belief.[37]

The contempt, envy and moral outrage that the front-line soldier harboured towards those further back made for a powerful stereotype, the existence of which helped the combatant to see himself as a morally upright stoic. The image of the grasping and cowardly base soldier helped the front-line soldier to regard himself as a man 'taking' the missiles of outrageous fortune with courage and altruism. Because the Australian combat soldiers' experience was unlike anything undergone behind the lines, they developed a sense of exclusiveness similar, though not identical, to that of combatants in other armies. The concept of the cold-footed 'base bludger' allowed the soldier who negotiated the trials of the front to consider himself not just as different, but as superior. In this sense, inequality suited the combatant.

This negative counter-image created a dilemma for those who were forced, or eventually chose, to leave their front-line units permanently. As the war progressed, there must have been an increasingly large number of uncomfortable base troops who had themselves once criticized those further back.

INEQUALITY AND THE HIERARCHICAL ARMY

The Australian front-line soldier's primary complaint against officers was that they were recipients of privilege. There was deep resentment of the fact that the army conferred upon its higher ranks advantages that were denied to the majority. These advantages included better pay, accommodation and food, and greater access to alcohol and information.

Thus, on a ship in Cairns harbour, Lance-Corporal Clothier angrily painted a stark contrast between conditions on board: 'We had a sloppy stew for breakfast and sat on a dirty floor to eat it. As usual, the officers are in cabins and eat like civilised beings.'[38] In a diary entry written in the Middle East, Gunner Birney presented a more overtly political and aggressive stance, asserting that the officers' privileges were undeserved:

> There has been far too much of that rank distinction over here. The whole business stinks. There are many in the ranks who could buy and sell the majority of the officers, over and over again. Just fancy special places for officers to eat and drink and special places for sergeants as if the ones in the ranks who really do all the fighting are not good enough to associate with the above ... Over here we would do little about it but we will at home.[39]

A feeling of outrage spurred the usually laconic Private Berry to write a similarly political comment while on a ship taking 7th Division men back to Australia:

> As regards to conditions on this boat and the distinctions between ranks is very pronounced. The men get the usual

meals, while officers and Sergants have as much as a seven course meal. They also have beer and spirits, these being denied to the man in the ranks. These conditions were the same in Palestine and Syria. What is good enough for the men should be good enough in the higher ranks. I only hope that the men in the ranks open the peoples eyes as to what went on. It is costing the people a lot more to keep the officers and Sergants in rations than what it does to feed the men. We are led to believe that we are fighting for democracy.[40]

Other Australian soldiers expressed resentment at the obvious presence in the ranks of 'Old School Tie Merchants': members of the civilian upper class. Two lighthearted discussions of the Soviet Union also seem to reflect a conception of the officers as a separate, and by implication privileged, class. Soon after the German invasion of the U.S.S.R., an Australian sergeant wrote home: 'We . . . have gone dreadfully Communistic as a tribute to our newest glorious ally, Russia . . . the singing of the [R]ed Flag is now a normal part of our mess routine. The officers are a little perturbed about it all but hold their peace for fear of international complications.'[41]

Similarly, Medcalf tells of an incident four years later, when at a film screening for officers and men on Bougainville, the soldiers in the ranks called for a photograph of Stalin to be shown after that of the King. When the projectionist obliged: 'We cheered lustily and resumed our seats. Nobody was really interested in Uncle Joe, but it annoyed the officers.'[42] There was also some evidence of a form of class solidarity among the lower ranks. A common saying was 'No names, no pack-drill': do not inform, and there will be no punishment.

Birney's and Berry's statements were both unfair in certain respects. The notion that 'the ones in the ranks . . . really do all the fighting' was incorrect in that officers died in action at a greater rate than their subordinates, and, when at the front, officers 'enjoyed' the same type and quantity of rations as the lower ranks. Even in camps, food and drink additional to that available to the troops tended to be paid for by the sergeants and officers who received it.

Moreover, within the Australian army the social backgrounds of its men fostered what the official historian calls an 'equalitarian outlook'.[43] Complaints about inequality stemmed mainly from a belief, brought into the army from civilian life, that equality was desirable and practicable. Yet that ideology also influenced those in the positions of advantage, and the informality that characterized relations between Australian officers and men would not have existed if not for the leaders' subscription – or rather, their partial subscription – to that philosophy.

Even if one can talk of an 'equalitarian outlook' and a 'team spirit', the team was one with limited membership.[44] As far as the numerous men in the ranks were concerned, their team contained, in addition to themselves, only the officers within front-line units: certainly not men in base units, and none but the most charismatic higher officers. Some would not have included any officers in their side, for although the common soldier's immediate, face-to-face superiors were much closer to him in lifestyle and perspective than high-ranking officers, the structure of the Australian army provided plenty of evidence for those who regarded everyone as either a privileged leader or an underprivileged follower.

The relative informality of Australian civilian life made relations between ranks friendlier than in the British army, but the latter was the model for the structure of Australia's army. This hierarchical edifice had an inescapable logic. It ensured that however friendly officers were, they were manifestly privileged. Perhaps the best example of this class distinction was the institution of the batman.

Each officer was entitled to a batman, whose tasks were essentially those of a private servant: preparing the officer's bath, washing and mending his clothes, bringing him food and drink, digging his dugout, and in battle sometimes acting as a runner. Perhaps, as in World War I, there was a specious notion of Australian batmen being 'guardians and helpers' to the officers. Certainly a sergeant in Tobruk noted and shared the amusement caused at an Australian R.A.P. when an Englishman referred to the Australian batmen there as 'servants'.[45]

However, the language used by Australian officers to describe their batmen was not merely friendly, but condescending, and even redolent of the British upper class. They employed phrases such as 'my faithful old batman', 'my poor little batman', 'dear old R. my trusty batman', or this passage: 'my new batman – Kavanagh – is proving most satisfactory, and if the present standard of his work is maintained, I shall consider myself most fortunate.'[46]

Such attitudes and, more importantly, the mere existence of servants were hardly the stuff of an 'equalitarian outlook'. Neither was the exclusiveness of the officers' mess: a condition well illustrated by one battalion history's reference to the farewelling of even a regimental sergeant major from the officers' mess as a 'unique ... distinction'.[47] These privileges were just two of numerous divisive advantages accruing solely to those in authority.

The officers' privileges would not have been so contrary to the spirit of equality if the other ranks had enjoyed reasonable prospects of sharing them. The available evidence, which admittedly is far from conclusive, suggests a strong correlation between military rank, on the one hand, and educational and socio-economic background on the other.[48] What is more certain is that promotion in front-line units was organized in such a way that for most of the war, and particularly the second half, it was difficult for men who had joined those units in the other ranks to become officers. In the final year of the war, there arose a bizarre situation where many experienced soldiers were led into action by officers who had never previously experienced battle, let alone led men in it.

Proven soldiers often did rise through the ranks of fighting units, and this was a factor which made for good officer/men relations. However, numerous obstacles littered the path of aspirants. In the Middle East in 1940 and 1941, a plethora of reinforcement officers from Australia, and the A.I.F.'s parsimonious attitude towards sending candidates to the British officer cadet training units (O.C.T.U.s), made things difficult for potential officers in fighting units. In 1941, N.C.O.s were taken into O.C.T.U.s at the rate of just three from each battalion. This was in stark contrast to the World War I practice of promoting nearly all Australian officers from the ranks in the field.

The subsequent expansion of the army created greater opportunities for promotion, especially for A.I.F. men. However, from 1943, a reduction in the size of the army brought the dissolution of many units with little or no front-line experience. The result was a surplus of officers and N.C.O.s. Many of the surplus leaders underwent 'conversion' training and became eligible for posting to combat units. As a result, an N.C.O. who had for months held temporary command of a platoon at the front might find himself suddenly replaced by an inexperienced officer, who might well depend on the N.C.O. to help him settle in.

This second glut of reinforcement officers again made it difficult for eligible veterans to reach O.C.T.U.s. In September 1943, the monthly intake of Australia's O.C.T.U. was reduced from 300 to 200, and by July 1945 it was ninety.[49] To give an example of the effect this reduction had on combat units, the 2/28th Battalion was unable to send a single candidate after January 1944.

Ironically, some campaigning units became very short of officers in 1945. For instance, 55 officers were promoted from the ranks to fill half the shortage that existed on Bougainville in April 1945. It was always possible to win a commission in that manner – 'in the field' – rather than at a school, but apart from the 55 Bougainville officers and a large number late in 1942, this was a distinction seldom bestowed. Thus, although the officer/men ratio fell in the course of the war, the other ranks of fighting units did not receive a proportionate benefit in terms of promotion.

From 1943 onwards, even if one reached an O.C.T.U. one had almost no hope of gaining a position with one's old unit, for this ran counter to official policy. Again, the opposite had been the case in World War I, and Bean regarded the earlier practice of returning pro- moted men to their units as a key factor in the success of what he saw as the highly disciplined First A.I.F.[50] In World War II, the consequence of the changed policy was that some potential leaders refused the possi- bility of promotion because it meant leaving their beloved units. The reluctance of commanding officers to relinquish their best N.C.O.s may also have blocked avenues for the advancement of some potential officers.

Many soldiers had no desire for promotion, although the financial rewards for being even an N.C.O. were strong inducement, and most imported leaders eventually won acceptance. Despite this, the diffi- culties attending promotion served to maintain a gap between officers and men, and presumably a lesser degree of enthusiasm for authority than might otherwise have prevailed. Officer training also perpetuated this gap, for, like rites of passage, it forced footsloggers to re-evaluate the world of soldiering.

Thus, the mateship of Australian soldiers rarely cut across the dividing line between those with commissions and those without. The relative informality of Australian officer/men relationships does suggest an unusual degree of fellow-feeling between ranks. However, true mateship implies equality, and even the warm relations that often existed between junior officers and their men followed vertical rather than horizontal lines: friendship with 'the Boss' or 'Mr Jones' rather than with 'Fred' or 'John'.

Relationships within fighting units usually became closer in battle, but although this left a residue in the combatants, the gap between the ranks widened again after action. This is exemplified in an N.C.O.'s description of a parade held immediately after a New Guinea campaign:

> [The captain] gave a little speech of thanks to the men and then explained that discipline in such matters of saluting, dress, etc would commence again right away. The dirty cows, their only too willing to hobnob with the lads and be one of them when it helps to save their hides but now they must climb back to their supsrior plane once again.[51]

A crucial question about resentment towards inequality, and indeed towards the other burdens described in previous chapters, is how the complaints men wrote in letters and diaries translated into action. The answer must include a discussion of discipline, for any protests against annoyances or perceived injuries were bound to bring confrontation with military law. In a sense, all the problems discussed in this and the previous two chapters depended on the legal bonds that tied Australians to the army. Without the discipline to which soldiers became subject on entering the Australian army, they need not have put up with, and many would not have put up with, the boredom, inequality, inefficiency and so on. In this discussion of 'the army way', discipline's presence has largely been taken for granted, as the existence of an army presupposes it. What challenges discipline and brings it into the light is the behaviour of men dissatisfied with their treatment.

CHAPTER NINE

DISCIPLINE AND MAKING THE MOST OF ARMY LIFE

*T*he most natural reaction to the burdens inseparable from membership of the army was to escape them. Substantial discharge and desertion rates reflected a desire to do so. For moral or practical reasons, neither discharge nor desertion was a viable course for most Australian soldiers, but the wider prevalence of the crime of absence without leave (A.W.L.) owed much to an urge to undo the chains that tied men to the military life. This form of temporary escape was the most common breach of discipline in Australia's wartime army. Yet the vast majority of soldiers were absent without leave for a minute proportion of their army lives, if at all, so that their remaining periods of service offer the most clues as to how or whether resentments recorded on paper were turned into action.

INDISCIPLINE: THE EXPECTATION AND REPUTATION

There is good reason to expect that Australians would have expressed their frustrations, anger and bitterness in behaviour more aggressive, antagonistic and rebellious than that of going A.W.L. or leaving the army. The trials examined in the previous chapters were enough to test the patience of any man, and the officers whom Australians saw around them were personifications of the army responsible for those vexations and injustices. One might expect many face-to-face confrontations to have occurred. Furthermore, Australians entered World War II bearing a mental image of the 'dinkum Aussie' soldier who showed scant respect for authority, and who engaged in 'drunkenness, thieving and hooliganism'.[1] Clearly many could have been expected to see this undisciplined image, derived from World War I, as a standard that must be upheld. Even those with the least reason to see themselves as successors to the First A.I.F. – namely, those conscripted into the C.M.F. – had strong reasons to show open hostility to the army. The grating, infuriating practices of military life must have had an unusual sharpness for them.

The topic of discipline can hardly be avoided in discussions of Australian soldiers. It should not be omitted in an examination of any nation's soldiers, for the very notion of 'soldier' implies some discipline and no army is free of discipline problems. Where Australian soldiers are concerned, the crucial question is one of degree: whether undisciplined behaviour and attitudes that were present in, say, the British and German armies, but were regarded as unusual and atypical there, were commonplace in the Australian army. There was some exercise and acceptance of authority – the army's existence and its battlefield successes testify to that – but this does not necessarily mean that there was sufficient discipline to refute a charge that indiscipline was characteristic of the Australian soldier, with all his resentments.

Wartime misbehaviour was characteristically Australian in the sense that much of it was clearly related to prewar Australian life, despite the fact that men with criminal records were barred from enlistment. For example, Bentley tells of a group of new recruits returning from receiving kit at Caulfield Racecourse in Victoria who, on finding a man going through their civilian belongings, threw him from high in the grandstand. Another indication that the civilian background may have made military indiscipline likely was this note from a soldier to his father: 'I would have liked to have taken part in the beer brawl at Uncle Jim's place, she must have been some turno-out.'[2]

Yet there was, and probably still is, a belief that indiscipline in the army was 'typically Australian' not merely in that its character had roots in prewar Australia, but in the wider sense that the average Australian soldier was undisciplined. In the Middle East, for instance, although Australians enjoyed high standing as combat soldiers amongst the many national groups present, they also bore a poor reputation for behaviour out of battle.

This reputation related largely to theft. Thus, when Australians unloading a truck at Alamein asked a watching British soldier to

remove his coat and lend a hand, the reply was: 'We have been told not
to take our overcoats off while the Austs are here.' Jack Craig reported
on the pilot of an American bomber that crashed nearby at Alamein:
'He said he cant remember bailing out, but on landing said. "Dont let
the Aussies get at my parashute." '[3] That this reputation had spread
even further is indicated by the fact that German radio dubbed
the 9th Division 'Ali Baba's twenty thousand thieves', a title happily
accepted.

It is more relevant to our examination of reactions to the annoyances of army life that many members of the allied armies in the
Middle East regarded Australians – and not just, or especially, the 9th
Division – as outrageously defiant of authority. In large part, this criticism sprang from British attachment to a prewar image of the 'digger'
similar to that held by many Australians. Indeed, one assumes that in
incidents such as the following, the British and Australian participants
believed that they were filling roles first played a quarter of a century
earlier: 'The mob had a laugh at me the other day, we were walking
through a town on leave and came across a Pommy Brigadier looking at
some horses and a couple saluted but 4 or 5 didn't and catching my
eye he beckoned me over and gave me a great lecture on Aussies and
saluting in general.'[4]

In other cases, the defiance of British authority was much more
aggressive. For instance, Eric Lambert wrote of fishing with mates in
Palestine:

> I got some gelignite and we blew some fish up. An English
> officer, Woods by name, came up and told us to stop – Faint
> said we were not interested in his notice board and it was no
> business of his. It was plainly the first time a man had ever
> answered him back. He talked of insubordination and arrest
> . . . Blasted more fish. Woods came down and took our names.
> Hawkins asked for his paybook. Woods was white with
> rage.[5]

In a variation on the saluting story, Sergeant Lovegrove wrote of an
incident that occurred during leave in Jerusalem: 'At one point we had
a difference of opinion with a British Army captain who had taken
exception to us not saluting him! he of course received a good mouthful
of back-country Aussie retaliation.'[6] No doubt the motives here
included a longstanding Australian dislike of pomposity, and a desire

to uphold World War I tradition. However, the 'Aussie retaliation' may also have been against a perceived lack of competence and compassion in the British treatment of Australians in the Middle East.

Examples of defiance towards Australian authorities can also be interpreted as responses to inefficiency, callousness and the other features that men in the Australian Army resented. The following incident, concerning an A.I.F. infantry battalion during training in Australia, is a remarkable example:

> ... today we have sure been fighting for our rights ... They started giving us drill this morning We were not in a very good mood. So we went as slow as possible. The Sargent was calling out Left-right but no body was takeing any notice of him at all. The Lieut ... tryed to march us about but we only moved at a crawl ... he tried giveing us some rifle excises but he soon found we would do anything but what he was trying to make us do. [The Lieutenant marched the group almost to their camp, then headed them away from 'home'. He then tried to repeat the manoeuvre.] So he gave the about turn to head us back from Camp again. But this time we had him in a good place to make a fool of him and we did. Instead of turning round and going where he wanted us to go. we broke off and headed in all derections. For our own huts ... He said alright fall in and we will go back to Camp. We were going there whether or not So it made no differences at all to us.[7]

It was not unknown for Australians to create disturbances, including strikes, when inefficiency led to them receiving poor meals. The best example of indiscipline resulting from resentment of inequality, or 'class distinctions', took place in Palestine in May 1940, when Australians staged a 'rowdy demonstration' concerning a new theatre supposedly offering the best seats to officers.[8]

Australian soldiers became especially rancorous when they felt that they were callously being denied their leave entitlement. For example, the anger of a large group who were told in Perth of unexpected travelling deductions from their leave was clear in the fact that they 'were heard to say "they'd ----- well take it anyhow"'.[9] When 7th Division units that had fought in Papua received 'special leave', this gave rise to a belief in the 9th Division that it had received unfair treatment. The upshot was complaints to politicians and sit-down strikes by several battalions that had been ordered into camp.[10]

No other incidents were quite as dramatic as the 9th Division one, but an occurrence involving the 6th Division was on a similar scale: the large number of its members who were not granted leave on returning to Egypt from the Libyan campaign seem to have almost unanimously given themselves unsanctioned leave.

Individual Australians were quite often argumentative or openly defiant towards those in authority. Some men made a point of doing forbidden things, such as going into restricted areas, precisely because they were prohibited. At times, defiance even expressed itself in threats or actual violence.

Resentment of the army way expressed itself not only in open insubordination, but also in a slack approach to military duty. The following comment provides an example of this reaction, and also supports the traditional notion that the Australian male is not amenable to military discipline because it offends his principle of antagonism to authority in general and policemen in particular: 'This job of Picquet is a swine of a job Darling, keeping the boys out of the pubs. Just like a dam copper. I just stand about like a dummy and let the officers do their own dirty work. They dont get me stoping the boys from haveing a drink.'[11] Australian soldiers' wartime writings and reminiscences contain stories of piquets themselves being drunk, of working parties stealing the stores they were handling, of guards permitting the theft of equipment and even the escape of their prisoners.

This laxity derived mainly from lack of commitment to the army or, more precisely, to its structure; a feeling which in turn originated from the prewar culture and was heightened by experience of the army's treatment. The same emotions were presumably a cause of the widespread theft of army supplies. However, both the slackness and the stealing also occurred because of the faulty exercise of authority: officers and N.C.O.s did not prevent these incidents from occurring. Throughout the war, various transgressors against military law were given lenient treatment by their officers. This was particularly the case with A.W.L. and offences committed on leave. The latter were commonly reported by provosts, who were often as unpopular with officers as with their men. The negative effect that a nonchalant official attitude to A.W.L. could have is well illustrated in a diary entry written some weeks after the 2/13th Battalion was supposed to reassemble at Ravenshoe: 'The Bn strength is only 370, which is about 40 per cent.

The camp has an air of hopelessness about it, possibly because the officers aren't worried, and so it comes down.'[12]

An ex-officer, Cam Bennett, says of Australian military officialdom's attitude towards misbehaviour: 'the sheer impudence and science of bucking the system was ingrained in all of us. As an officer I often had to take some action against the culprits, but I fear that fellow-feeling usually affected decisions, resulting in penalties less harsh than they should have been.'[13] Australian officers were regularly chastised by British commanders in the Middle East for their lack of control over troublesome men.

DISCIPLINE IN BATTLE

Leaving aside for now the question of the degree to which leniency was typical, it is important to recall that most combat troops had confidence in the men who led them into battle. Whatever faults there were in Australian officer/men relationships, these relationships were clearly a help rather than a hindrance in the army's quest to fulfil its overriding purpose, namely, winning victories on the battlefield. In reading about Australian combat officers' feelings for their men, one can see a potential explanation of their leniency, which adds to Bennett's notion of 'fellow-feeling'. For example, after leading his platoon in the famous 2/43rd Battalion raid at Alamein, Lieutenant Gordon Combe wrote of his subordinates with pride and warmth: 'There were only a few casualties in the company and fortunately I had none at all in my platoon, thank God. One certainly becomes attached to one's men. I was immensely proud of them, most of them are just plain common people it might be said, but they were gallant and heroic in this action.'[14] Similar solicitude emerges in Warrant Officer 'Cobber' Craig's poignant description of a young officer's actions immediately before the battle of El Alamein:

> My skipper then Capt. Sanderson . . . was just as loyal to his superiors as the men under him was to him, we all loved him, and followed him with every confidence. At the last minute he told me to go around with him to the P/S [platoons] as he wanted to speak to his men on the eve of the big show. We went around and he spoke beautifully then shook hands with each P/Commander and wished him luck. Then we went back to our H.Q. and he shed a few tear and said Cobber we have a

grand lot of boys here, I wonder just how many of these faces we will see this time to-morrow. He really and truly loved every man under him.[15]

Sanderson was killed under tragic circumstances the following day. The deaths of subordinates, a prospect that he and Combe dreaded, had become a reality for another officer, Lieutenant Lance Heffron, when he wrote after the Tobruk campaign: 'I left a few men in Libya in their last resting places and I managed to visit the cemetery before I left. I never spent a more miserable hour I can assure you and it was hard to leave them there – but I know that they shall ever be remembered.'[16]

There is no reason to believe that any of these three officers was excessively lenient, but their attitudes are noted here to suggest that while the fatherly concern (rather than a more egalitarian 'fellow-feeling') that many officers felt for their men may have made for less than perfect discipline behind the lines, it probably also promoted trust and effectiveness in battle. At the same time, one must bear in mind the evidence noted in the previous chapter that although the closeness created by combat left some residue in relations between the ranks, those relations tended to become more formal and, possibly, cooler after action.

The argument that leniency was associated with the growth of an emotional bond in battle comes close to supporting the traditional belief that the typical Australian was undisciplined behind the lines, and disciplined where it counted, in battle. This would seem to be a logical corollary if officers were lenient behind the front, but true leaders in action. On the other hand, according to the stereotype the discipline of the Australian in combat is essentially self-imposed, and his success on the battlefield is chiefly attributable to the independence and individualism that also give rise to his larrikinism off it. That image of a soldier who combines discipline and indiscipline has some support in wartime writings. After El Alamein, for instance, 'Cobber' Craig wrote of the wonderful 'team work' and 'disaplin' of his company, adding: 'Back in camp some of these fellows may be a bit troublesome, but here where the fighting is done, they are troublesome to the enemy in many ways and 100% soldiers for their Officer and [N.]C.O's.'[17]

Nevertheless, larrikinism and military effectiveness were generally not complementary in the Australian army of World War II.

Inevitably, many miscreants failed in combat. Unless a man received and imbibed a certain amount of technical and tactical training, he simply could not function effectively in a World War II army; a fact not lost on authorities concerned about A.W.L. It is surely no coincidence that the battalion which became infamous for its disastrous baptism of fire on the Kokoda Trail had previously been notoriously ill-disciplined. As one of the most respected and successful battalion commanders in the Second A.I.F. said in a wartime training memorandum: 'An ill-disciplined unit out of the line will be an armed mob in battle. There will be no sudden magical change.'[18]

More importantly, the supposition that most Australians were undisciplined behind the lines is not justified. It was not true largely because, although some men may have been 'a bit troublesome' in camp, and although certain officers may have been lenient, the man in charge of the unit usually set very strict limits to misbehaviour.

THE INFLUENCE OF COMMANDING OFFICERS

The commanding officer seems in the overwhelming majority of cases to have been regarded by his men as a strict disciplinarian. A published wartime discussion of the 'lieutenant-colonel', the typical C.O., said of him: 'He is held in respect by majors, awe by captains, fear by lieutenants and fear and trembling by other ranks.'[19] Some commanding officers showed an inclination to be lenient or sympathetic to any of their own men accused of misdemeanours by outsiders, but within his own 'home', the C.O. was a stern family head.

The chief consequence of the C.O.'s presence was, that regardless of any tendency to misbehave on leave, men were generally well behaved while within their unit lines. Every soldier knew that barring unusual good fortune, he could expect strong punishment if he struck or abused an officer, or failed to perform guard duty, or, in short, if he committed any offence within the camp boundary that normally set limits to his everyday activity.

C.O.s were men who insisted on the value of instinctive discipline. As Hay points out, 'Discipline was always something of a preoccupation with commanding officers.'[20] Indeed, C.O.s' lectures on discipline feature in soldiers' writings, as do commanding officers' punishments. These sometimes brought resentment towards the commander's supposed inflexibility, but seem generally to have been

accepted with good grace. Far from adding to the grievances associated
with army membership, the reserved and austere demeanour of commanding officers seems often to have been approved. C.O.s and their
headquarters certainly did not escape criticism, but it is remarkable
how many men regarded as stern disciplinarians were popular. This
phenomenon is also hardly consonant with an undisciplined army.

Australian commanding officers enjoyed strong coercive powers –
stronger, for instance, than those of their British counterparts – and
this probably tended to counteract any relative leniency on the part of
their subordinate officers. The C.O. could impose summary and minor
punishments for many offences, although the most serious went to
courts martial.[21] Significantly, there was a general feeling that these
courts, like C.O.s, offered justice tempered with common sense. This
perception, and the general attitude to commanding officers, had a
restraining influence on Australian responses to 'the army way'.

Many humorous anecdotes told in the Australian army revolved
around the C.O. or other high-ranking officers, and more particularly
around the possibility of those officers receiving undisciplined treatment from their subordinates. The stories offer some insight into the
soldiers' reactions to their grievances about the army, and to discipline
in general.

Anonymity was a feature of one type of anecdote. A good example
is Medcalf's story of 'Johnny', a soldier who had the ability to 'break
wind loudly at will', and who did so when the C.O. was haranguing the
battalion regarding its discipline.[22] Similar stories concerned remarks
called out from the ranks, a smoke bomb dropped into a general's car as
he drove past tired footsloggers, and Australians in Greece 'helping' to
push a brigadier's car out of the mud with hands caked in as much slime
as they could carry.[23] Such tales showed men having a measure of
revenge, but they were funny largely because the events they described
were atypical. The average Australian would never have dared to do
what Johnny did, let alone anything more direct or articulate.

Another type of anecdote concerning insubordination depended
on mistaken identities, as here at the beach near El Agheila:

> While there two chaps came along. One chap looked every bit
> as disreputable as we were, if not more so. He pulled up and
> was talking to us and about different things, we didn't know
> his name and called him 'Dig'. Imagine our surprise when we

found out after he left us that he was our Brigadier, Brigadier Murray.[24]

Or in Tobruk:

> A funny incident occurred the other day – during the height of an air-raid a private was cowering in his slit trench when a human body landed on him with some force. The human body immediately stuck it's head up to see what was going on, with the growing sense of having reached a comparative haven, so the digger, recovering, said in his own peculiar style 'Put yer head down yer silly bastard before yer get the bloody thing knocked off.' The body complied and then identified itself as our C.O. and the digger began apologizing profusely – however the Colonel thanked him instead of going off the handle as the advice, if somewhat terse, had proved extremely timely.[25]

Here the humour depended largely on acknowledgement of the fact that no private in his senses would abuse a high-ranking officer, or call him 'Dig'.

There was a similar theme in a third type of story, wherein the common soldier was too familiar with his superiors: offering to shake hands, or swearing in conversation, for instance. Again, such stories tended to be told because there was humour in individual privates acting in a way the average soldier never would. A far more typical response to high-ranking authority emerges in Major Dunkley's account of a visit to his battalion by a general and three brigadiers: 'My blokes were so stunned at the flash of scarlet and gold that they were inclined to jump and salute when a stick broke near them for hours after.'[26]

Although most of the anecdotes suggesting that insubordination was exceptional concern high-ranking officers, the point that open defiance was unusual applies at all levels. The main form of insubordination, and the prime means of protest against the army, was 'grizzling', 'growling' or 'grumbling'. So prevalent did this habit appear to a chaplain in one veteran infantry battalion that he chose to list it first in his affectionate description of the traits which made the unit typically Australian: 'a body of men who could grumble, curse, fight and generally play the big game of life as well as any who ever left the shores of Australia'.[27]

In a life where the essential, inescapable daily routine was seldom without frustrations and onerous duties, the simple and almost automatic response of swearing and complaining could have been a dangerously defiant practice. In reality, this generally indiscriminate and anonymous grizzling seems to have helped men to cope by letting off steam, rather than to have seriously threatened the authority of their superiors. Its role as a safety valve, protecting both the existing order and the individuals within it, is indicated by the fact that two battalion historians, both former officers, depict grumbling as 'the soldier's privilege' or 'the soldier's right'.[28]

THE TRUTH ABOUT INDISCIPLINE

The impression that the vast majority of Australian soldiers did nothing more against their army than grizzle timidly is borne out by statistical evidence. Thus, although fights with military policemen are often regarded as inseparable from the archetypal Australian soldier's behaviour, and as the ultimate sign of his refusal to accept the army's authority, the Provost Marshal reported in November 1942 that only 89 assaults had been made on M.P.s in the course of some 33,000 arrests made in Australia between April and September. Similarly small ratios of violence were recorded in the Middle East, while outside Port Moresby and Australia there was very little scope for larrikin behaviour in the S.W.P.A.[29] As to other forms of indiscipline, theft and drunkenness do not appear to have been so much more prevalent in the Australian army than in other armies as to render those crimes typical of the Australian and atypical of the others.[30]

And though A.W.L. was of major concern to Australian authorities, men who committed it or any other offences were always a minority. On occasion, the majority in returned combat units overstayed their leave, but in January 1943 only one per cent of those who had joined the A.I.F. to that point were in gaol, on leave without pay, unaccounted for or 'illegal absentees' – that is, A.W.L. for over 21 days and unlikely to return. At any one time between 1943 and 1945, the number of men who had in the course of the war become 'illegally absent' – that is, deserters – never exceeded 2.5 per cent of army strength. The number of short-term absentees was probably always considerably larger – it was nearly twice this number in the three months to September 1942 – but the great majority of these absentees without leave returned to their units voluntarily, rather than after arrest. Their crime constituted a lesser threat to discipline than desertion, with which it did share the quality of being very much a minority offence.[31]

The total in detention was always considerably smaller. Available figures for the Middle East, covering the period October 1940–February 1941, show no more than 172 Australians in Australian and British detention barracks at any one time there. In Australia between 1943 and 1945, the maximum number in detention, military prisons or civil gaols was 4031, during September 1943, which represented less than one per cent of the army's strength. At any one time, most prisoners were probably incarcerated for being A.W.L.[32]

Considering the dismal regimentation and the strain of army life, it is surprising that when on leave, more Australian soldiers did not take the opportunity to find release in misbehaviour. After seeing troops throw bottles around a Cairo nightclub, an Australian artilleryman asserted that the soldiers' 'main source of relaxation seems to be to get drunk and break things'.[33] Yet while this was not an isolated incident, misconduct of this or any kind was not the form of catharsis chosen by most Australians.

Lieutenant-General Blamey went so far as to suggest in a report in April 1940 that just 40 Australians were 'solely responsible for the breaches of discipline and other misconduct reported from abroad'. Needless to say, this understated the problem, but he was closer to the mark several months later, when he asserted: 'In any collection of Australians it may be stated that the overwhelming majority are decent men.'[34] Certainly the average Australian front-line soldier was not an undisciplined man, and his reputation to the contrary was due to the work of a conspicuous minority. To the extent that the postwar Australian self-image has included a notion of the typical World War II digger as a larrikin, it has been a delusion.

There is some evidence that discipline in the Australian army even deserved the sought-after adjective 'good'. Undoubtedly there was an improvement in discipline within units intended for battle: at the end of training, soldiers had a sense of *esprit de corps* and were far more disciplined than at recruitment; the next watershed for most original members of the A.I.F. came with arrival in the Middle East, where discipline, like training, became markedly harder. A further stage in improving discipline occurred in many combat veterans, who were said to lose some of their boisterousness after experiencing battle.

Fearnside uses this changed outlook to explain one piece of evidence that indicates a high standard of Australian discipline, namely the fact that late in 1942, after Alamein, the British major-general in command of the Cairo area lavished praise on the 9th Division's men for their recent exemplary behaviour on leave. This made a change from the British accusations of Australian indiscipline, most of which seem to have been at best exaggerated, at worst completely unjustified.[35]

Further evidence for good Australian discipline is Allan Jones' reflection in his memoirs that from his experience in the 9th Division, Australians in the Middle East were 'disciplined, comparatively sober, and generally better behaved than some troops of other nationalities'.[36] The Australian Archives contain another most interesting piece of evidence in the form of a letter written to the Australian government in 1941 by Fouad Bushakra, an American ex-serviceman living in Syria. Of the several hundred Australian soldiers who had camped on his estate during the Syrian campaign, he wrote:

> ... it gives me genuine satisfaction to testify to the courtesy, thoughtfulness and respect for our property, shown by the officers and men ... Even our Druse maid, by custom shy and fearful of strangers, shared in our confidence and liking for the boys ... It was with real regret that I learned in general a different opinion was held in the cities concerning the conduct of the boys. I cannot help but feel that it is due to the magnification of small incidents, a lack of understanding of their good humour, and a desire to do the boys, at which they retaliate. Only a few weeks ago my wife and I were on the coast and found the cities filled with soldiers but wherever we talked with them, we were accorded the same friendliness that we experienced up on the mountain ...

Included in his letter was the comment: 'We all noted the fine spirit between officers and men.'[37]

Yet it would be an exaggeration to say that the standard of discipline in the Australian army was unusually high. The disgraceful behaviour of a minority of Australian troops in every leave centre they visited in their wartime travels has ensured that few from other countries would believe such a description, but this is not the fundamental reason that it is unconvincing. Rather, it is because 'well disciplined', as applied to an army's general disposition – behind as well as in the line – implies an enthusiasm for discipline that simply was not present in force in the Australian army. Australian soldiers reveal too much pride in themselves as individuals to be members of a 'well' or 'highly' disciplined army, at least off the battlefield.

This is not to say that Australians were unenthusiastic about all aspects of soldiering. The reluctance of most to protest openly about conditions in their early training days was probably due largely to their eagerness for action. As mentioned, this enthusiasm usually persisted beyond the first campaign, albeit in attenuated form. One of the most surprising features of Australia's war was the willingness of huge numbers of men in the C.M.F. battalions to forego the greater security of militia status by volunteering for unrestricted overseas service within their units. More than 200 000 men – many of them conscripts – made this change between November 1942 and the end of the war.[38]

Yet the zeal of the volunteer was alien to a sizeable minority of members of C.M.F. combat units who chose not to transfer. According to one diarist, conscripts who made this choice did so essentially because 'it was one matter on which the army couldn't order them about'.[39]

The implication here was that in most things the army could order them about. Nearly all Australian soldiers seem to have regarded army membership in this way. Their response to its unpleasant lifestyle was not rebellion, but resignation. Many may have agreed with the trainee we have already mentioned in Chapter 6 who wrote that 'If there were no war on I wouldn't put up with a lot we do here', but the conditional 'if' was crucial. There was a war on.

The essential point is that the norm was fatalistic submission, not enthusiasm or insubordination. Most Australians recognized the folly of trying to protest vigorously about the tedium, inequalities and injustices that pressed upon them. This attitude extended to the battlefront, where even inept, callous or suicidal orders were almost invariably obeyed without question. Soon after joining the army, many learnt to supplant exasperation with 'stupefied resignation'.[40]

The majority probably never seriously considered protesting. For instance, it is clear that despite all the resentment of the inequalities associated with hierarchy, most accepted the system not only without open insubordination, but often without even private demur. For example, in their personal diaries common soldiers regularly followed the official army practice of giving the lieutenants the title 'Mr'. Soldiers' writings also contain surprisingly little criticism of the concept of batmen. The official historian states that Australians only resented the distinctions between officers and men if these were 'above what efficiency demanded', and possibly most soldiers felt that batmen did not fall into that 'inefficiency' category.[41] Perhaps batmen were considered a corollary of the general and unfortunate truth that armies have to be hierarchical.

Yet if the resigned acceptance of inequality and the other burdens of army life was built partly on philosophical reflection, the basic foundation was fear of punishment. Even in the matter in which men were most likely to forget their fear – namely, leave – dread of losing one's entitlement probably prevented many from engaging in punishable behaviour. Fear was clearly fundamental to the admiration, and even the humour, surrounding the strict C.O. To the extent that fear of punishment stopped men from behaving as they would have in civilian life, discipline was a burden like those discussed in the previous chapters.

Nevertheless, it would be unfair and inaccurate to portray Australian troops as constantly troubled by fear of punishment. Most kept to a middle road, neither being insubordinate nor enthusiastic. Some actually took comfort in not having to think for themselves. The majority seem to have thought enough to be irked by much of what they experienced. Many complained of being sick of the army, and at times whole units appear to have become unhappy with army life.

MAKING THE MOST OF ARMY LIFE

The average Australian soldier was not a larrikin, but neither was he entirely a victim, powerless against the stress of the front line and the afflictions imposed from further back. He was occupied not only with 'taking it' – and particularly holding off the threat of death – but also with making a worthwhile life. On leave he tried to satisfy the needs and desires, especially sexual ones, that the army routine denied him. Yet leave represented a minority of his service. He sought also to obtain some pleasure from the long hours of inactivity in camp and in transit, and he searched eagerly for some diversion from the intensity of the front line.

The most appealing diversion was contact with the outside world. Through radio broadcasts and newspapers, many maintained an interest in the progress of the war. There was even stronger interest in Australian news, national and local. The best source of detailed news from home was Australian newspapers, which were always in great demand overseas, as indeed was any reading matter that could deliver men's minds from their current situation. Magazines and books were highly sought after. Again, the problem for men at the front was scarcity. Travelling libraries went to the front in certain areas of New Guinea, and American army paperbacks reached some in 1943 and 1944, but books were generally scarce indeed in that firing line. Even at Alamein, where the front was unusually close to a well-stocked base, reading matter could be 'as scarce as gold'. As late as 1945, a C.O. could write of papers and magazines he had received from Australia being circulated throughout his battalion on Bougainville.[42]

In time, the inability of the mail service to meet demands for news on the S.W.P.A. front was partially overcome by the local production of a small newspaper, *Guinea Gold*, which was frequently taken forward and which became popular. Prior to that, the men in the combat zone had to depend almost entirely on cuttings sent from home, for newspapers sent from Australia were apparently never delivered to the front. Colin Kennedy recalls that when his unit was at Imita Ridge, during the Kokoda campaign: 'With time to relax, everyone resumed an interest in the outside world. Those few who received news cuttings of the progress of the war elsewhere were very popular.' Another soldier on the Kokoda Trail asked his mother to send newspaper cuttings, adding: 'We have absolutely nothing to read and nobody knows what is going on at home unless it is in letters.'[43]

Letters were generally desired for much more than the printed news they might contain. Apart from leave, the handwritten words from family and friends were the form of contact with the outside world that was most desired by Australian soldiers. A battalion periodical in Tobruk described perfectly the way mail could transport soldiers from the trials of service, at or behind the front: 'There's no doubt about it, when a mail arrives our whole outlook changes; no beer, no fresh food; dust; heat; flies; what do all these matter so long as our letters come to hand.' This attitude persisted throughout the war, as the following Tarakan diary note implies: 'Got 12 letters. 6 from Jeanne. Gosh but those letters were better than food and rest.'[44]

The mail was significant to Australian soldiers because it provided contact with the outside world, which was the focus of their deepest nostalgia and hopes. It also permitted reciprocal relationships, in which the soldier could participate, and thereby see himself in the role of father, husband, boyfriend and the like, rather than merely as a lowly soldier. Moreover, the mail kept him in touch with people who cared about him personally, and who often wanted to give him emotional support.

Of course, there were strict limits to the participation any civilian correspondent in Australia could have in the life of a member of a combat unit in the Middle East, Malaya, New Guinea or even in most training areas at home. Apart from the fact that mail was irregular on some fronts, the man in the line was worlds away from the people and institutions that had provided support and fulfilment in Australia. Civilian writers could not speak directly to the soldier's situation. Even old Diggers at home knew nothing of dive-bombing, tank attacks or jungle warfare.

As mentioned, the role of 'home' for the combat soldier came to be filled by his unit, and that of 'family' – the people who turned house into home – was taken by his comrades. The Australian's opportunities for privacy and individual choice in his prewar life were so much greater than after enlistment that his individual 'space' had diminished almost to vanishing point. Almost everything he made of that life he did in interaction with the men around him. For example, in seeking to maintain contact with the outside world, he frequently had to share the available resources. John Butler's evocative portrayal of a typical radio 'listen-in' revealed the communal nature of news gathering and dissemination – as well as the competing claims that could be made on scarce means:

> . . . a crowd of blokes sitting in the dust or standing in the rain. Someone fiddles with the dial, 'arr, dyer own the b . . . thing?' says one, 'Leave the damn thing where it was' says another . . . and then a chorus 'For Christs sake shut up you winging b . . . lets hear whats being said' complete silence then the breaking into groups some squat and discuss political and military. Some stand, some are eloquent, some quarrelsome, many walk away; from a tent someone sings out 'What's the news Buzz' 'Sweet Felicity Arbuckle' says I . . . [45]

Sharing rather than arguing seems to have been the theme in the use of reading material. For example, an Australian wrote to his sister from Tobruk. 'If you get any stray reading matter I'd like you to send it along. All the reading matter we got is usually read by the whole platoon, so it does good work.' In thanking a friend who had sent such material to his platoon at Tobruk, another Australian claimed that thousands of soldiers had read them. One veteran asserts: 'Reading matter in Tobruk was shared like nothing else.' Fellow-feeling at a time of shortage prompted this behaviour. It was also present in an instance of cooperation cited by Steward, who recalls troops in New Guinea tearing out pages as they read and passing them on, relay fashion, to the next man.[46]

Letters to and from home remained essentially private, but even here there was scope for sharing. A combat officer recollected times shared in Tobruk thus: 'More often than not . . . it was just a matter of lounging about the dug-out, recounting experiences, airing grievances, swapping stories, looking at each other's photographs, and on those few never-to-be-forgotten days – reading aloud, pieces from our letters.'[47]

At the front and in camp, Australians shared certain satisfying things that were more immediate than their rather sterile communications with the outside world: when possible they smoked, drank, and gambled. Above all, as the previous quotation implies, they talked.

The subject-matter of conversation varied enormously. Sometimes broad political and philosophical issues were discussed. For example, Eric Lambert wrote in his diary during the Alamein battle: '. . . we dug by moonlight and I drank Mahoneys whisky and discussed La Bruyere and Communism'.[48] Sergeant Edwards wrote from New Guinea of both the content and the value of his intellectual conversations: 'We have been passing the time of day quite a bit with friendly arguments which chiefly centre around post war problems in Australia, politics, Britain's share in Aust's past present and future etc. and we get a lot of good out of them. At least it keeps one mentally alive.'[49] This metaphor of staying alive was an apt one for soldiers.

Discussions between Australian troops appear usually to have concentrated on less abstract and more personal, mundane matters. For instance, a private noted in Tobruk: 'we spend our leisure largely in endlessly talking of home, the merits of our superlative girl friends and other dear intimate topics'. The often connected subjects of home and women do seem to have been especially popular. Outside Bardia, one diarist recorded that when he and some friends had yarned, 'talk followed the usual channels, first horses, then beer or the lack of it, and finally the inevitable, – Women!' Another Australian noted that amongst his group: 'Sometimes we argue and discuss the current situation but the talk inevitably drifts to "home".'[50]

In fact, most conversation about home and women apparently did not go into 'dear intimate' detail. And the deep emotions aroused by the more immediate issues of the front seem generally to have been a taboo subject, placed off-limits by the demands of masculine self-esteem and by a desire to forget. Nevertheless, even when discussions were banal and frivolous, the mere act of talking helped to build up a sense of shared experience, and cemented the bonds that enlistment and allocation had created between soldiers. The powerful uniting and homogenizing effect of shared language is suggested by a diary passage concerning a chaplain at Sanananda: 'A friend of Frank's, Padre W-popped in this afternoon – only young chap, he has seen lots of fighting in N.G. . . . . He is quite the regular soldier in manner and use of choice adjectives Frank said later he was amazed at the change in his outlook and speech. Seems even ministers are effected by environment and companionship.'[51]

A touching example of that companionship – and the language at its heart – helping men to make the most of miserable circumstances is this diary entry, written during the siege of Tobruk:

> Ron's birthday, and we stage a hilarious party for his day. The cake was half a loaf with 25 matches stuck into it, which Ron duly and solemnly lit and blew out. We drank his health in very strong black tea, toasts mostly hair-raising or uncomplimentary and a parody on 'Happy Birthday to you' was sung. The affair was side-splitting.[52]

Such shared experiences, as well as the terrible ones that occurred under fire, gave men a sense of self-esteem and purpose.

Thus although the average Australian eventually wanted to escape the herd existence of the army, with its lack of privacy and of individual scope, that life also had positive features, which helped him to endure the strains inherent in soldiering. His interaction with others, and more particularly with his friends, provided enjoyable activities when he was not in action, and in battle gave him a preparedness to risk all – both to save those friends and to maintain their respect.

The evidence indicates that mateship did not really extend between ranks; even the reciprocal warmth between common soldiers and junior officers was, to use the family metaphor, less like one between brothers than between generations. Those in authority had a significant part to play in the struggle against boredom, for theirs was the responsibility of organizing recreation, especially sport. However, important as such activities were to the quality of the soldier's life, the prime sources of whatever comfort and pleasure he obtained in that existence were the mates with whom he shared it.

The front-line soldier's sense of comradeship also virtually excluded the men at base, and the division between front and base strengthened the bond between combat troops. Nevertheless, as well as the mateship, there was often a surprising degree of unfriendliness between front-line troops. It is to this unfriendliness, another strain on many combat soldiers, that we now turn.

PART THREE

MATES

CHAPTER TEN

A BAND OF BROTHERS?

*W*e have seen that because of their status, officers and base troops were virtually excluded from mateship – personal or theoretical – with the ordinary front-line soldier in the Australian army. Status differences were also the basis of emotional chasms within the front-line rank and file itself.

However, there were other sources and forms of ill-feeling between combat troops. Personality clashes are inevitable in a group as heterogeneous as a twentieth-century army, and naturally there were quarrels among men forced to share each other's company over the long periods of inactivity in the Australian soldier's life. The Australian army also had its share of bullies: men whose character was inimical to friendship. For example, Bellair tells of a man driven to suicide by the jibes of 'insensitive barbarians' concerning the size of his genital organ.[1]

Men who showed signs of weakness in combat sometimes received intolerant and unfriendly treatment. For instance, one sergeant wrote of another in the desert: 'Am sharing a dingus [or dugout] with S– he gets on my nerves, he's just a plain chocolate soldier, not worth a damn when things get tough, he wouldn't even make a good private let alone a sergeant.'[2]

Similarly, on Tarakan in 1945, a private commented in his diary about one of the men sharing his post: 'Nerves are getting W–. – not much of a chap.' Corporal Campbell referred to such attitudes when he wrote to his parents about the role of an N.C.O.: 'there are hundreds of things a fellow can do for the men. Some of them are helpless and the ones who are not havent much time for them.'[3]

TREATMENT OF REINFORCEMENTS

The most helpless men in any front-line unit were, as a rule, the untried reinforcements. The distinction between them and the more experienced soldiers is one of the major status differences that adversely affected relations within the front-line ranks.

An unfriendly reception often awaited the reinforcement. Private Ayling wrote of his introduction to the 2/18th Battalion, in Malaya: 'Being in a unit, now, I found things very different. We reinforcements had to take a very lowly place, and were hardly spoken to for awhile.'[4] A remorseful former sergeant-major recalls that he and the other original members of the 2/2nd Battalion gave inhospitable treatment to every group of the unit's reinforcements, from as early as December 1939. He depicts a group that arrived in Palestine in 1942 as being 'paraded, tiraded, promulgated, investigated and castigated, inspected like cattle and then tolerated only until they could "prove" themselves.'[5]

Some Australian soldiers fell victim to 'old soldiering', being imposed upon or belittled by those with greater experience. In 1942, reinforcements to the 9th Division sometimes found themselves treated to constant reminders of how good their predecessors had been at Tobruk; indeed, the term 'Tobruk happy', a variation on 'bomb happy', was used by 9th Division reinforcements to describe those old soldiers who did little else but praise the old hands at the expense of their replacements. During the siege itself, John Butler was in one of the perimeter posts when he noted an example of the treatment given to some reinforcements:

A few [reinforcements] came in two days ago and one – well can you blame us, he was simply asking for it – We were talking at tea-time about the forth-coming band concert at B.H.Q. and the wag suggested the dance in Tobruk would be better: (the only dancing in Tobruk is when the bombs are dropping and females are conspicuous by their absence) The Dope intends to visit a few (I pity his hike – Tobruk looks near but aint). Of course he was told where the Dance Hall was situated. One of his questions was 'Are we allowed to shoot at anything?' 'Yes' was the reply 'There is much competition

amongst the boys to see who can hit the R.S.M. at 2,000 yards
...' ... We then solemnly discussed a gazelle hunting party,
who would be the beaters and who the waiters – Dopey said
'I'm in on that' and was up bright and early for it.[6]

Some reinforcements were 'asking for it' in that their inexperience
or early nerves led them to endanger the lives of more experienced men.
In describing an advance at Buna, one veteran recalled: 'The Reo's
were giving us a lot of trouble by hanging back and that is one of the
reasons why I think so many of the old hands are getting bumped off.'[7]
During the fighting on Singapore, an officer wrote of one night: 'We
heard odd firing in all directions and the men, mainly reinforcements,
did not seem to know enough to be quiet and not light cigarettes.'[8]

Such behaviour was unlikely to endear 'reos' to those doing what
was prescribed by experience and training. And it was not only lack of
battle experience but also insufficient training that in the early years of
the war were largely responsible for the gulf that separated newcomers
and veterans. The burden of that insufficiency, and of the consequent
lack of coordination between veterans and 'new chums', seems generally not to have fallen on the old hands, as in the Buna example, but on
the reinforcements. Again and again, newcomers were killed or
wounded in their first actions, sometimes before they had even been
introduced to their new 'mates'.

Many suffered emotional pain in their dealings with their new
colleagues. For instance, a poem called 'I'm just a reinforcement'
expressed the disappointment and indignation of a newcomer who was
sick of being ridiculed as 'just a flaming "reo"'. On being badly
wounded in May 1945, a reinforcement officer in the proud 2/6th Battalion told his commanding officer: 'Now they won't be able to call me a
reo.'[9]

Officer and N.C.O. reinforcements, even if they were experienced,
were far more likely than the other ranks to be accorded by their peers a
reception that had no hint of 'mateship' about it. There were several
reasons for this. One was concern that these unknown, often untried,
men could bring catastrophe upon those put under their command.
Another may have been a rather exalted self-image amongst the established officers of some veteran units.

Most importantly, peers and subordinates resented newcomers
who, by filling vacancies in the unit, had denied promotions to men

with a proven record of achievement and with the supposed virtue of familiarity. Rather than permit this to happen, some unit commanders refused to accept reinforcement officers, and insisted that reinforcement N.C.O.s revert to the ranks.

Indeed, reverting these N.C.O.s to the ranks seems to have been a matter of course in the Middle East, and also occurred in the S.W.P.A. In October 1942, a group of C.M.F. and A.I.F. non-commissioned officers sent among reinforcements to the 2/5th Battalion complained of being told that unless they applied to be reverted to the ranks, 'a charge would be prepared on which they could be reverted'. By this time, higher authorities appear to have been far less amenable to the practice than previously, and orders were given that the group concerned be reinstated.[10] One can easily imagine that such incidents created ill-feeling in those who perceived themselves as victims.

It seems that demoted N.C.O. reinforcements often regained their rank eventually. Moreover, officer reinforcements came to be accepted as comrades by equals, especially if they showed themselves capable of leadership in battle. Even more quickly did 'reo' privates tend to be regarded by their peers as 'mates'. Various factors ensured this.

Throughout the war, units in the line were generally under-manned, sometimes desperately so. In such circumstances, the arrival of reinforcements was usually welcome, if for no other reason than the consequent easing of the veterans' burden. Of course, satisfaction at the arrival of reinforcements did not necessarily translate into friend-liness towards the newcomers. However, as Private Butler suggested, reinforcements were not automatically treated with disdain:

> . . . apropos this Reo business, the only one who has a complex is the reo himself. He thinks erroneously that the originals look down on him, but speaking as an original when a reo comes in he is sized up not as a reo but as a man, if the con-sensus of opinion is 'he doesn't seem a bad sort of bloke' well as far as we are concerned he's an original, but heaven help the windbag.[11]

Some originals certainly did have a 'complex'; nevertheless, most vet-erans clearly were prepared to accept reinforcements as comrades.

At the personal level, the naive enthusiasm of reinforcements was probably a morale booster to tired and often jaded men – certainly commanding officers considered it so. In the midst of the 9th

Division's draining New Guinea campaign, a veteran N.C.O. reflected: 'All our reinforcements seem to be good blokes and should make good soldiers. All of them are young and fresh and full of fun and laughter which is good to hear again.'[12]

As in the originals before them, the reinforcements' enthusiasm was largely directed towards going into action. Lack of training did not imply lack of courage. Thus, despite finding themselves embroiled in one of the ghastliest and most hopeless battles of Australia's war, the reinforcements sent to the 2/29th Battalion in Singapore 'stuck to their job', as did their counterparts on every front.[13] In so doing, they gained the respect and friendship of their more experienced peers.

Undoubtedly the reinforcements' enthusiasm was endearing when accompanied by respect for the old-timers. While working at the 24th Infantry Training Battalion in Palestine, Tobruk veteran Will Taylor commented: 'Took charge of 1 pln of new troops on route march and got one big thrill at the way the boys look up to an X man. One is constantly being questioned by them and it is a pleasure to explain things.'[14] Some veterans were very sympathetic to the youngest recruits, while others made a point of setting an inspiring example of cool courage under fire.

Yet another factor making for friendly treatment of new arrivals was that as the war progressed, the vast majority of old stagers in the fighting units were themselves former reinforcements. Even originals, if they had ever been evacuated wounded or sick, would have known the experience of returning to the unit from a replacement pool. The degree to which operations made units dependent on reinforcements emerges in Jack Craig's diary entry 76 days after the beginning of his battalion's New Guinea campaign: 'Nearly all our men are new . . . only 4 of the original platoon that landed at Lay still left'.[15]

By 1945, there were very few originals left in combat units, and the drive and enthusiasm necessary in that year's futile campaigns came largely from eager, unblooded reinforcements. One unit historian describes their contribution to the last campaigns of the war:

> . . . these young men were the cutting edge of the army, and nobly took the strain . . . For their leaders within our battalion, as in others, they provided a source of inspiration in their cheerful spirits, their unfailing enthusiasm, their eagerness to tackle the allotted task, and to prove themselves the equal of their predecessors in their units.[16]

Clearly these men won acceptance as worthy members of their units. It was the veterans' pride in those units which had generally been responsible for any initial reservations about reinforcements. Throughout the war, newcomers faced the challenge of winning admission into the cliquish mateship of section, platoon, company and battalion. Barring accident or failure in action soon after arrival, the 'reo' quickly became a 'mate' in most units. The period before that transformation was uncomfortable.

INTER-UNIT RIVALRY

For the reinforcement, mateship came with integration into the unit. So too did loyalty to that unit. This emotion was the basis of a second status distinction that presented a barrier to fellow-feeling within the army. More precisely, it worked against a spirit of comradeship extending beyond one's own unit, especially one's battalion or division. For unit pride and loyalty derived not only from good relations between members – if they did, *esprit de corps* would be synonymous with mateship – but also from pride in achievement, and particularly a belief that one's own was the best of all such units. The logical corollary of this notion was that other units were inferior. Thus when such units were discussed or, more pertinently, when members of other units were encountered, there could be a presumption that the other deserved to be disparaged.

Because men were usually identified with their unit, the misbehaviour of isolated individuals was described as the work of, say, '7 Div coves'.[17] That this practice fostered uncomradely prejudice seems likely; certainly some troops ascribed poor behaviour to whole units. For instance, Griffiths-Marsh tells that his entire battalion (the 2/8th) was stigmatized after the discharge of two members for homosexual behaviour. 'Backs to the wall! Here comes the second-eight' was supposedly the provocative greeting extended indiscriminately to battalion members for some time.[18] Another example of the conflation of individual and unit is this note by an artilleryman: 'Walls was our regimental mascot a small dog of indefinite breed and beloved by all. He has been through all our campaigns and last week was shot by an officer of the 2/1 Batt. It caused a terrific stir in the regiment and relations with the 2/1 have been very strained since.'[19]

A noticeable feature of soldiers' diaries was a tendency to criticize the efforts of the previous occupants of any living area being taken over by the writers' unit. This occurred so often that it appears to have been an automatic response, drawn from a sense of superiority. An illuminating example of this tendency, and of the manner in which unit pride was often inimical to comradeship, appears in Lieutenant-Colonel Field's diary entry after the occupation by his battalion of a sector of Tobruk: 'The administrative state of this area is too pitiful for words. All my officers and the majority of the men are scornful about the poor housekeeping of their predecessors . . . A good sign of esprit de corps when there is a healthy scorn like this.'[20]

All that the average soldier was likely to know of another unit, especially outside his own battalion and brigade, was something about its military record and its state of origin. Although the state identity of battalions became increasingly diluted and was rarely a cause of animosity, it helped to preserve their mutually foreign status, and cut against army-wide fellow-feeling.[21]

More importantly, the experiences of their respective units in action often formed the starting point for conversations between men thrown together from different military backgrounds: for instance, in hospital or on leave. Unit pride could easily turn these conversations into confrontations. A discussion reported in some detail to John Butler was certainly friendlier than others along similar lines, but it indicates well the sort of arguments used:

> [A mate] relates a conversation he had with 6th and 7th Divvy blokes. 6th won the war in Greece, and Crete, 7th won it in Syria, 9th won it at Tobruk. The 6th said 'you let us down at Barce' [The 9th] replied with 'You're the Grecian Harriers'. The 7th said 'our divvy hasn't lost a battle yet.' 6th and 9th in unison 'You've only met French civvies and wogs, you don't know what fighting is yet.' No rancour, all in fun . . .[22]

Original members of the 6th Division seem to have been inclined to harbour uncomradely thoughts about those who joined the later formed divisions. The latter men were often labelled 'deep thinkers', or 'rainbows' – men who supposedly came after the storm. This resentment arose partly from anger at the 9th's retreat, in April 1941, from the territory won by the 6th Division: hence the comment about Barce, one of the places the 9th Division abandoned, in the previous quotation. While the 6th Division was sent on the forlorn expedition to

Greece, the vital and more viable task of defending Tobruk was given to the 9th Division, which was thereafter envied its publicity and 'glamour' by the other divisions. Even in 1945, some 6th Division men wrote resentfully of the fact that the 9th Division operations in Borneo were receiving swifter and greater coverage than their own efforts in the Aitape-Wewak region.[23]

Men of the 9th Division were not above holding similar resentments. An example is this bitter reference, written by an officer in Tobruk, to the publicity given the 6th Division after the Greek and Cretan campaigns: 'I notice a decided tendency to over-exaggerate their hardships and bash in as much glory as possible – particularly the guards of prisoners (A.I.F. from Crete) who had to pay to wash the "mud and blood of Crete from their uniforms" – utter tripe and just a dodge to get the maximum sympathy.'[24] The same officer was able to give the 6th Division a compliment, albeit a backhanded one: 'Most of my [command] was originally 6 Division, but are a very fine lot. None of the type which has made 6 Div. famous (or infamous) in leave towns.'[25]

The 8th Division came under criticism for supposedly complaining about conditions in peacetime Malaya. A 6th Division officer wrote after the Libyan campaign:

> We were not amused to read that the 8th Div. had a riot because they had to have cold meat for one meal . . . I wish the cold footed bastards were out here living on dry biscuits and bully beef for weeks at a time . . . They would probably die at the thought and yet the men out here thrive on it.

Further adverse comment resulted when the 8th Division was defeated in Malaya and Singapore.[26] The 7th Division received its share of criticism from 6th and 9th division troops for the early departure of its units from the Middle East. For example, a 9th Division soldier wrote home: 'we . . . have done more continuous fighting than any other division in the A.I.F. and feel we should have been given preference over another division who fought for three weeks in the Syrian campaign, a half-hearted affair.'[27]

Members of the 7th Division, sometimes dubbed 'The Silent Seventh', were in part united by dissatisfaction and resentment over the relative lack of attention given to its exploits. Some degree of unfriendly rivalry also existed between certain C.M.F. formations.[28]

The *esprit de corps* of battalions and divisions was obviously a source of unpleasantness, but one must be careful not to go too far in asserting the unfriendliness of men in front-line units, particularly the A.I.F. On their introductions to the Middle East and New Guinea, battalions and regiments usually made friendly and humanizing, if fleeting contact with other units allocated to foster them into new surroundings. As to combat, Australians were not always blind to the ordeals undergone by other units. Again Private Butler recorded a pertinent conversation, this time at a convalescent depot in Palestine:

> ... one [soldier] was talking of Greece and Crete. I said 'You were there were you mate?' 'Yes' me: 'Glad I wasn't there, you fellows had a bad time' 'Oh I don't know, I wouldn't have liked to be in the position of those poor blighters in Tobruk, they went through seven months of hell.' I laughed and said 'I was at Tobruk and the boys were of the opinion that they wouldn't like to change places with the sixth Divvy' – and so it is with human nature, minimising its dangers and sympathising and lauding the other bloke.[29]

Within brigades and divisions, men above the rank of corporal tended to know personally at least some of their counterparts in other units, through social functions, convalescence and training exercises. Thus, ironically, unit membership was probably a smaller mental block to a more universal mateship amongst the men who vehemently promoted *esprit de corps* than amongst the other ranks.

However, within the ranks, too, the growth of ignorant and negative attitudes may have been largely prevented by personal knowledge of individual members of other units, especially from the prewar period or prior to allocation or transfers. Many members of fighting units had previously been in other battalions or regiments and, like most reinforcements, they were usually quickly accepted. These men must often have made a case, by example or argument, for the value of other units. An illustration of this process, and an indication of the other ranks' ability to recognize that what passed for *esprit de corps* could be mere prejudice, appears in the 2/23rd Battalion's history, *Mud and Blood*. This contains an account of the C.O.'s address before Alamein, and of the response:

> 'The old "muds and bloods" won't let the division down [said Lieutenant-Colonel Evans]. There are a number of men in the

boob who won't be with us in the attack, the usual broken
reeds who committed self-inflicted wounds, and a percentage
of anxiety neurosis cases. I am pleased though, that for the
most part they are cast offs from other units and came to us
with a bad record.'

The whole battalion was quiet at the conclusion of Evans'
address. 'Pay-day' Cleary rose to his feet. He had been cross-
posted from the 2/5th Battalion . . . In a few short and well
chosen words Private Cleary reminded the Colonel that there
were many cross-posted men in his battalion, men as good as
any the 2/23rd could produce . . . 'Undoubtedly they will do a
good job in the coming show, even though circumstances have
attached them to a battalion to which they had no wish to
belong!' 'Pay day' was cheered as he finished his outburst,
and Evans, equal to the occasion, was man enough to
apologise.[30]

The value of other units was often demonstrated on the battlefield,
particularly within brigades and divisions. For instance, the historian
of the 2/16th Battalion says of its relations with the 2/14th Battalion:
'Rivalry between the units was always keen – sometimes brittle early –
but in the stress of battles an enduring bond of comradeship was
formed.'[31] Pride in the record established by one's brigade or division
in combat created some degree of fellow-feeling with all men who
composed it.

In 1943, members of the recently-returned 9th Division were
given insight into the quality of soldiers in the 6th and 7th divisions
when some of the last two were assigned to pass on the lessons of their
experience in jungle warfare. Yet recognition of this high quality must
generally have come some two years earlier. For even without eyewitness evidence, no thinking soldier in any of the three most experienced
A.I.F. divisions could, after 1941, have seriously doubted the proven
quality of the other two. Thus, while 9th Division troops boasted in the
Middle East in 1942 that they were the best A.I.F. soldiers, they also
reportedly expressed great faith in the ability of the other A.I.F. divisions to defeat the Japanese.[32]

Moreover, as part of a huge multinational force in the Middle East,
members of the 6th, 7th and 9th divisions had good reason for a strong
sense of national identity, and consequently of fellow-feeling. We have
seen that feeling was not strong between front-line and base troops or

between ranks, but when the surviving Australian Imperial Force divisions returned home in 1942 and 1943, they did so with a perception of themselves as having a combined identity. Part of this identity was a contrast with the Citizen Military Forces. That contrast, the third major status distinction, was at the centre of the best, or perhaps worst, example of a lack of mateship in Australia's wartime army.[33]

A.I.F. PREJUDICES

The seeds of trouble lay in the initial organization of the two forces: one raised especially to fight the war and based on voluntary enlistment for service overseas (A.I.F.); the other already existing before the war and revolving around conscription and voluntary service on Australian territory only (C.M.F. or militia). If the Australian army had followed the British in its methods of raising units, as it did in so many other military matters, this unfortunate system would have been avoided.[34]

As has been argued, the *esprit de corps* of front-line battalions and regiments led some members to presume automatically the inferiority of other such units. If this could happen among units in which differences were nominal rather than real, then where there were substantial dissimilarities *esprit de corps* could be expected to create great friction.

As early as 1939, when the A.I.F. consisted essentially of the 6th Division alone, relations between its members and militiamen were at best cool, at worst violent, with fights occurring between soldiers in leave towns and camps. Similar incidents occurred after the raising of the subsequent divisions.

In the early days, enthusiasts for the A.I.F. had some reason to feel aggrieved about the C.M.F., for less than half the anticipated number of militiamen volunteered for the 6th Division. Moreover, it was clear that some C.M.F. commanders had actively discouraged militiamen from enlisting in the A.I.F.[35] Yet the issue was not a simple one.

At the time of the creation of the A.I.F., there was no certainty that it would be sent overseas. Thus many militiamen hesitated to leave their established units and positions, and to forego better pay. Reasons of conscience almost certainly prevented many from volunteering for the A.I.F. and unrestricted overseas service, as the thousands who had flocked to join the C.M.F. in the year preceding the outbreak of war had done so amidst a recruiting campaign that stressed the importance of

protecting Australia against invasion.[36] Numerous militiamen were
too young, or otherwise ineligible, for the A.I.F and later, between
January and June 1942, cross-enlistment from C.M.F. to A.I.F. was
forbidden. Twenty to twenty-five per cent of the 6th Division originals,
and most of the senior officers in each of the four A.I.F. divisions, were
in fact former militiamen. Some of the officers who joined the A.I.F.
only after the 6th Division was formed did so, as recommended by their
superiors, in order to retain their rank.[37]

Despite these complications, many A.I.F. men poured unmitigated scorn on the C.M.F. From the early days, they dubbed militiamen 'chocos', or 'chocolate soldiers', because of their supposed
unwillingness to fight. The message that militiamen were cowards also
informed most of the numerous other nicknames given to them in the
course of the war, for example, 'wheelbarrows' (having to be pushed),
the 'F.I.A.' (forced into action), 'dingos', and 'Koalas' (could not be
shot at or exported).

A similar sentiment emerged in two lines of a poem popular in the
A.I.F. of the early period:

We'll do all the work and all the killing:
Scum, scum, the militia may kiss my bum.[38]

The 6th Division left Australia in January 1940, before the
decision to form other divisions had been made. It was only later, and
overseas, that members of the four, and ultimately three, A.I.F. divisions came to see themselves as a distinct army. Until they went into
action, these men had little to distinguish them from the C.M.F. A
poem urging an A.I.F. battalion commander in Palestine to get his men
into battle touched on this irritating similarity in its metaphor for military inactivity: 'The boys . . . never gets no fighting in this darn Militia
Life.'[39]

The eventual involvement of these divisions in combat in 1941–2
added enormously to their confidence in asserting that the men of the
C.M.F. were inferior and cowardly. Captain Laybourne Smith contrasted his men with the militiamen at home thus: 'So much for the men
who are fighting and a few words about the yellow skunks who are not.'
He then referred to the promotion of a militia acquaintance:

He is I feel sure to be congratulated on this meritorious rise.
We do not forget that he told us at Woodside [camp in South

Australia] that 'any one joining the A.I.F. must be soft in the head'. Perhaps it was this lack of solidness up above that made me feel so very proud to be an Australian at Tobruch.[40]

The C.M.F. was regarded as representative of the selfishness and lukewarm effort of the people at home. A.I.F. men were delighted at the thought of the C.M.F. reaction to the possibility and then reality of Japan's entry into the war. A 6th Division infantryman wrote to his father: 'How are the Militia boys now that Japan is playing up a bit. I suppose shits would nearly be trumps in most cases.' Writing from Malaya, a sergeant commented: 'The calling up of the Militia for full time service was greeted with howls of delight.'[41] A 9th Division officer expressed similar feelings, but then cast some doubt on the depth of this conviction: 'Now is the time for Australia's Yellow Army (the Militia) to prove their worth. I expect before it's all over they will get away with all the glory, and the AIF will sneak home unsung and unheralded.'[42] Self-pity and bitterness were expressed by numerous A.I.F. men in the Middle East when they perceived that the threat of a Japanese invasion of Australia had raised the profile and status of the C.M.F. at home, largely at the A.I.F.'s expense.

An example of the way A.I.F. men in the Middle East came to regard the qualitative difference between their force and the C.M.F. appears in another of Laybourne Smith's letters: 'I knocked off to go and watch my troop work. The gundrill was being done with that snap and precision one expects from militia recruits so I stayed and raised Hell.'[43]

When the A.I.F. returned home, most of its members saw themselves as forming a unified entity, which should under no circumstances be tainted by association with the C.M.F. It was, therefore, to their horror that for the remainder of the war Australia's political and military leaders seemed to be trying to narrow the distinctions between the two forces and to spread throughout the army the benefits of the experience gained by A.I.F. soldiers overseas.

For instance, after graduating from officer cadet training units, lieutenants were sent to fill the first available army vacancy rather than being returned to their units. Fearnside explains that he and other newly commissioned A.I.F. lieutenants were anxious to be returned to original A.I.F. units, for 'many of them felt that if they were drafted to a Militia Unit the taint of conscription would touch them also'.[44]

When militia units were disbanded, many of the surplus volunteer officers and N.C.O.s were sent to A.I.F. units, and this was another reason for the cool reception often accorded reinforcement leaders. It became possible for A.I.F. recruits to serve in militia battalions, and thus A.I.F. volunteer reinforcements could be sent from a common pool to either A.I.F. or C.M.F. units, much to the initial disappointment of those sent to the latter.[45]

Large numbers of officers from A.I.F. units were sent to militia formations, often with promotions, so that by January 1945 only five of the 59 infantry battalions in the Australian army were not commanded by men with experience in the Middle East or the 8th Division. Although Fearnside suggests that these officer transfers lowered A.I.F. morale, they were moves to which the A.I.F. men concerned were not always averse, particularly as they could be stepping stones via which one returned, bearing more exalted rank, to an A.I.F. unit.[46]

A.I.F. men came to see many of these changes as part of a Labor party or army attack on the separate identity of the A.I.F. One group perceived a deliberate plot to belittle the achievements of the A.I.F. and magnify those of the C.M.F. There was talk, for instance, of the Salamaua campaign being stage-managed so that militiamen, rather than the A.I.F. who did the hard work, were the first to enter Salamaua; and that the army intentionally exaggerated the efforts of militiamen on New Britain in order to play down those of the A.I.F. at Aitape-Wewak. These fears contained little or no truth, but on the question of an attempt to attack the A.I.F.'s identity, even the official historian seems to agree that military and political leaders harboured a desire to 'erase the differences between the two [forces]'.[47]

However, it seems most unlikely that the authorities' serious plans went beyond raising the standard of the C.M.F. as far as possible towards that of the A.I.F. Indeed, as we shall see, it was the C.M.F. that underwent the greater changes. It is certainly difficult to perceive any official attempt to undermine the identity of the original A.I.F. units in Australia's final campaigns: in April 1945, the Commander-in-Chief told a 9th Division battalion that their forthcoming operations were 'the A.I.F. revived';[48] and, more generally, that year's extensive operations saw C.M.F. and A.I.F. units campaigning much more in their own separate spheres than previously in the S.W.P.A.

A strong indication of the depth of A.I.F. fears about a loss of identity is a controversy over the use of the term 'A.M.F.', which stood for 'Australian Military Forces', and included both the A.I.F. and the

C.M.F.[49] However, this abbreviation was commonly and erroneously used, for some time even in the highest official circles, to refer to the C.M.F. alone. For example, Lieutenant-General Rowell stated in New Guinea: 'After the experience of the 53rd Battalion I can have NO repeat NO confidence that any A.M.F. unit will stand.'[50]

Consequently, when in 1943 there were reports that 'A.I.F.' had been removed from crosses on New Guinea graves and replaced with 'A.M.F.', this 'sacrilege' raised a storm of protest. Government archives reveal that the decision to put 'A.M.F.' on graves was an army one, taken for security reasons, and that 'A.I.F.' was not at any time supposed to be carried on crosses in the South-West Pacific Area. Subsequently, a direction appeared that 'A.M.F.' was to be deleted and that, where applicable, 'A.I.F.' was to be inscribed on the crosses over the graves of dead members.[51] In this matter, the differences between the two forces remained highly visible.

Regardless of the intention behind their transfers, the A.I.F. officers and N.C.O.s posted to many militia battalions probably contributed, by reputation, performance and direct report, to greater tolerance being felt towards C.M.F. units. Most A.I.F. officers saw good in the militia battalions they led. Lieutenant-Colonel Dunkley, for instance, called the 7th Battalion 'a wonderful team of lads', while Brigadier Porter wrote of the Kokoda fighting: 'My choco's earned fame in the scrap over here.'[52]

On the other hand, these officers generally took opportunities to transfer back to A.I.F. units, for reasons partly expressed by Brigadier Porter on his posting to the A.I.F.'s 24th Brigade: '. . . it is marvellous to be back in the A.I.F. again with free men and voluntary fighters'.[53] Relinquishing the command of a militia battalion for that of an original A.I.F. one was considered tantamount to a promotion, and the alacrity with which commanders left did not go unnoticed amongst militiamen. Nevertheless, most of these officers returned to the A.I.F. with a belief, which presumably they spread within their circle, that beyond greater aggressiveness and initiative in A.I.F. units, there was little difference between Australian soldiers of the A.I.F. and C.M.F.

Policy decisions pushed some men of the two forces into each other's company, while A.I.F. and C.M.F. units also found themselves together on campaign in the S.W.P.A.[54] The disastrous efforts of certain militia units in these campaigns – some of which led directly to casualties in A.I.F. units – brought sharp criticism from A.I.F. men and leaders. For instance, a 6th Division infantryman wrote in New Guinea: 'The latest news is that the 58/59 BN ran out and left the 2/7 BN in the blue at K They have a very bad name around these parts that they will never live down.'[55] Such incidents undoubtedly bolstered the anti-militia feeling of many. So too did the belief that C.M.F. troops – front and base – stole from the packs and mail of A.I.F. men; a tendency that brought John Butler to quip: 'the Militia are capable of anything except fighting the enemy'.[56]

Some felt that the A.I.F. was carrying an unduly heavy burden of the fighting and dying: 'I think it is time the 6, 7 and 9 Divisions were left out and the other 'famous' AMF [sic] divs who gallantly served when we were in the M.E. had a go at the Japs.'[57] The stigma that remained attached to militia units is exemplified in the diary entry of a 6th Division veteran, written as he left New Guinea with other men of his brigade: 'A few chaps on the Warf called our boys Chocoe's. They finished up geting half the ship thrown at them.' Apparently this sensitivity was known to the Japanese, for men of the same A.I.F. brigade had earlier reported that at the height of battle, enemy soldiers had called out: 'Come and fight you conscript bastards', or 'Come out and fight, you Aussie conscripts'.[58]

A few A.I.F. men expressed strong resentment of any media praise given to militia units. For example, a signalman with the 7th Division on the Kokoda Trail wrote in September 1942: 'news service gives a lot of beloney about brave deeds of militia in N.G. – exceed deeds of Gallipoli or TOBRUK'.[59] However, at this time and later, many A.I.F. men were willing to acknowledge that nearly all militia units were performing adequately or well. A grimly amusing anecdote, which appears in the 39th Battalion history, tells of two 2/14th men, returning wounded after their battalion's hopes of a quick victory on the Kokoda Trail had been dashed. Their conversation reportedly ran:

> *1st 2/14th Digger*: 'How did you get yours?'
> *2nd 2/14th Digger*: 'I don't know. I didn't see any Japs but I got bayoneted'; adding: 'Who said those bastards couldn't fight?'
> *1st 2/14th Digger*: 'Who do you mean? The Japs or the "Chocos"?'; to which his mate replied "Both!"'[60]

The following year, a 9th Division veteran in New Guinea noted: 'We're awaiting an order to move – up the coast behind the 4th Militia

Brigade and therefore under its command. God help us!' Eleven days later his tone had changed, slightly but significantly: 'Have shifted to a possie just behind the 4th Militia Brigade, who are in contact with the Nip and are doing fairly well.'[61]

Many other A.I.F. men recognized the courage and achievements of the militia units that campaigned with them in 1943. Jack Craig, for instance, wrote: 'Heard the Chocko Unit (22 Bn) are pushing the Jap back but getting a few casualties a major told us they had plenty of guts but a lot of learning to do regards jungle training. It will come with experience.' This was not the only acknowledgement that, given experience, the militia battalions would progress, as had the A.I.F. battalions.[62]

Relations between the two forces were improved by formal and informal interchanges in the field. Militiamen appreciated advice from visiting A.I.F. 'combat teams', which in turn were generally impressed by the enthusiasm in militia units. At an unofficial level, too, good relations followed contact. One young militiaman wrote to his sister from New Guinea:

> The boys had a bit of a practical joke with me tonight by taking my bed and belongings down to a tent occupied by a couple of 9th Div. fellows. The reckon I live there which is not far wrong because I'm down there every night . . . I really go down there to hear some of their tales from the middle East By gee they are funny while some of the topics are quite interesting. Apart from that they are good blokes and turn on a brew which is always welcome.[63]

On the evening before going into its first full-scale action, at Lakona, the 22nd Battalion was camped near an A.I.F. battalion, the 2/28th. A militiaman tells of an inspiring incident, reportedly not unique, that occurred in his section when two veteran sergeants of the 2/28th came to visit that night:

> I haven't forgotten the way they talked. Quiet confidence are the only words to describe it, and a sort of 'professionalism', – the whole thing played down and made matter-of-fact. There wasn't any doubt about the effect on us. The coming action lost a good deal of its frightening mystery and we felt calmer and steadier, if only for a few hours . . . 12 Platoon, and particularly 9 Section, were to remember them and feel grateful.[64]

Even when relations were as warm as this, they were not equal, for almost invariably the men of the original A.I.F. units were older and more militarily experienced, and in any joint campaign they did the lion's share of the fighting.[65] Thus although relations between the two forces may have improved between 1942 and 1945, even friendly A.I.F. men tended to be patronizing rather than comradely towards militiamen.

A.I.F. and militia units had very little contact in the final campaigns of the war. Most of the latter were engaged on Bougainville and New Britain, unaccompanied by the original A.I.F. infantry. Ironically, it was in these campaigns that the militia were at their most impressive; in fact, the official historian states that the young militiaman typical of the forces on Bougainville was more eager than the average A.I.F. veteran in, say, the Aitape-Wewak region.[66]

This militiaman was probably an A.I.F. man himself, for most militia battalions had by then become entitled to the addendum '(A.I.F.)', their membership consisting of at least 75 per cent volunteers for overseas service. Mainly because of conversions within the C.M.F., by August 1945, 80 per cent of men in the army were A.I.F. volunteers, compared to 50 per cent in December 1942. This was the culmination of a trend that had been proceeding steadily since mid-1942. That the C.M.F. became increasingly like the original A.I.F. units in composition was a far more important development in the character of the Australian army than any spurious loss of identity in the A.I.F.[67]

Significantly, it seems that although from 1942 all militia battalions contained a mixture of A.I.F. and C.M.F. men, and despite the fact that officers transferred from A.I.F. units usually applied various degrees of pressure to make militiamen become A.I.F., there was within units very little friction between A.I.F. and C.M.F. other ranks. The contrast between these relations, on the one hand, and the antagonism between entire A.I.F. and C.M.F. units, on the other, further illustrates the antagonizing effects of the barriers created by *esprit de corps*.

Writing of the Wau-Salamaua fighting of 1943, war correspondent Allan Dawes said relations between A.I.F. and C.M.F. units had improved, principally because of the 'wholesale enlistment' of C.M.F. men into the A.I.F.[68] Yet his comment was wishful thinking. At that

time, only one of the six militia battalions engaged in the campaign had
75 per cent A.I.F. volunteer membership, and the others were well
short of that figure. More importantly, it seems that most men of the
original A.I.F. battalions simply did not know of the developments in
C.M.F. composition. Certainly no original A.I.F. soldier's writings
consulted in this study mention them, and the criticisms of 'chocos'
continued.[69]

Indeed, ignorance of the nature and performance of militia units
was a persistent feature of the A.I.F. soldier's war. The great eagerness
of tens of thousands of militiamen to join the A.I.F., and the age
restrictions that prevented many of them from doing so, were unknown
or unnoticed. Distortions and false rumours abounded.

None of these were more unjust than the ones surrounding the
fighting at Milne Bay. There the 7th Brigade's three militia battalions –
9th, 25th and 61st – played the key role in halting the Japanese attack,
which was then smashed by A.I.F. units. During the battle, an A.I.F.
soldier wrote: 'The 61st Militia Btn who are opposing the Japs are
supposed to have the position in hand, but had failed to take advantage
of it. Now the 2/10th have to go in and do the job.'[70] However, on the
same day Brigadier Field, in command of the 7th Brigade and a former
C.O. of one of the A.I.F. battalions present, wrote: '61 Bn. have fought
exceptionally well.'[71] In fact, at that point the 61st had, in this its first
action, checked the Japanese attack, which it had been opposing alone
for two nights and two days.

Four months after the battle, a member of an original A.I.F. supply
unit recently arrived in Milne Bay noted in his diary:

We hear stories of the fighting that took place around here . . .
it is said when the Japs landed here during heavy rain the
Militia were surprised and scattered all over the place. It was
through the efforts of the AIF that they were finally driven
back and pounded so much that they had to withdraw.[72]

That such distortions persisted is clear from a comment written by
an A.I.F. artilleryman early in 1944, concerning an Army 'Christmas
book': 'It isn't too bad but gives too much praise to the "Chocos". It
doesn't mention the 2/5 Regt. at Milne Bay or Buna – did a good job
there. But the 61st and 25th chocos – yellow curs too – receive praise.
Lord knows why!'[73]

The following statement, written by an A.I.F. battalion's historian concerning the unit's state of knowledge in 1944, illustrates well the ignorance and misrepresentation that were largely responsible for the hostility many in the original A.I.F. units bore towards those in the original C.M.F. units: 'Few members of the 2/28th had heard of 7th Brigade; but they had been told a great deal about the one militia battalion which had performed very badly on the Kokoda Trail.'[74]

C.M.F. PREJUDICES

Militiamen also had resentful prejudices. These derived in part from the knowledge that most Australians regarded the C.M.F. as inferior and largely ignored its achievements. In the 1942 campaign, men of the participating militia battalions also felt that Australia's military and political leadership considered them expendable.

Allied to these perceptions, which bred in militiamen an initial sense of inferiority, was a belief that even in the field the militia received less equipment and fewer reinforcements than were its entitlement. One C.M.F. battalion historian writes of the militia brigades of 1944 being 'the Cinderellas of the Australian Army'; another of 'resentment generated by the second class treatment accorded to the militia as compared with the AIF'.[75] Whereas the A.I.F. soldier regarded militiamen as sharing and representing civilian Australia's indifference towards the war, militiamen tended to perceive themselves as the chief victims of that public apathy.

It was against the A.I.F. that C.M.F. soldiers turned most of their anger. The malice and derision directed at them by men of the A.I.F. divisions inevitably provoked a reaction. So did the feeling that imported A.I.F. officers were taking jobs that should have been filled by militiamen, and the perceived arrogance of men of the 6th, 7th and 9th divisions – whom some militiamen dubbed the 'Middle East Mutual Admiration Society' (M.E.M.A.S.).

In 1945, men in militia units displayed indignation because their hard and dangerous work was being almost ignored by the press, while the efforts of the A.I.F. divisions, and particularly the 9th Division on Borneo, were receiving extensive coverage. The following, fairly typical, statement from a member of one of the militia battalions on Bougainville indicates that the complaint had considerable foundation:

> ... after six and a half months here we are allowed now to say we are on Bougainville. Seeing they announced the arrival of the ninth [division] on Tarakan in a few days and now they have given the sixth [division] headlines for their efforts in the Aitape-Wewak area, I suppose they have shamed themselves into at least letting our people know the third [division – composed mainly of battalions that were originally militia] has this campaign. Perhaps later on the boys in New Britain may be able to disclose what division is there. Of course we know and perhaps a lot in Australia do but it only goes to show how they push out the AIF shows and hide the good work the Militia is doing. We are of course AIF but like most of the Battalions on New Britain, ours are Militia. It is hardly fair to give the hardest and biggest campaigns without any civilian life for a break to the Militia shows and give all the raps to the AIF ...[76]

The resentment and anger of some militiamen led them to make vindictive claims in their letters that vastly exaggerated their own contribution and sacrifices compared to those of the original A.I.F. divisions. The following are representative examples from men on New Britain:

> I am proud to be a Choco, we are showing them we are not small time. In fact we make the big bronze Anzacs [an interesting acknowledgement of the Second A.I.F. as the true heirs of the First A.I.F. tradition], most of them with a pocketful of desert sand, look like rookies. We have now the longest service in the Islands of any fighting troops. What a difference from the 'conducted tour' of our Middle East, 'Womens Weekly heroes.'

> All this publicity all the time about the 'glorious' Ninth Div makes us sick, we are only waiting for them to hop in now and get the honour and glory after all the hard work has been done for them. Most people forget that shows like ours have been in actual fighting areas and under 100% worse conditions than ever the Ninth dreamed about – for two years and more.[77]

In reality, during the subsequent fighting on Tarakan the 9th Division's 2/24th and 2/48th battalions each suffered more battle casualties than the combined total of such casualties in the seven militia infantry battalions that took losses on New Britain.[78] The operations of the 9th Division in New Guinea in 1943–4 were no 'conducted tour', and the 6th and 7th divisions' New Guinea fighting was more demanding than that of any militia battalion other than the 39th. Little wonder that Brigadier Simpson, commander of a militia brigade and previously C.O. of two 9th Division battalions, wrote in 1945 of 'an unreasoning resentment of the reputation – hard won in battle over years of service in various theatres of war – of the 6, 7 and 9 Divisions.'[79]

If that resentment was unreasoning, it was also explicable. Perhaps even more important in its creation than A.I.F. malice and arrogance were the efforts of A.I.F. officers within C.M.F. battalions to persuade militiamen to apply for A.I.F. status.

These endeavours were often heavy-handed. In 1942, for instance, complaints were sent to the Minister for the Army that commanding officers were threatening to transfer non-volunteers to remote areas or undesirable units. Some of the best soldiers in the 39th Battalion, which had performed very well in the Papuan campaign, were transferred – or, in the words of their historian, 'banished' – in October 1942 for refusing to convert. In August 1942, a captain reportedly told N.C.O.s of the 3rd Battalion, which had not yet been committed to the increasingly desperate Kokoda campaign, that they 'would never see action as a militia battalion'. The lance-corporal who reported this incident noted that the N.C.O.s of his platoon stated their willingness to go forward, 'but only as "Choco's"'.[80]

That response is of symbolic importance, for the eventual dissolution of the 3rd, 39th and 49th battalions after their courageous performance in Papua was probably related to the refusal of many of their members to bow to pressure from A.I.F. officers within and outside their ranks. Only five other militia battalions had at the time seen action, and although manpower shortages made some disbandments necessary, there were some 14 brigades of militia in Australia from which to choose. It is possible that the three disbanded battalions were regarded as so demoralized by their recent experiences as to be unreliable, and some would suggest that the militiamen in these units refused to convert because of fear of overseas service. However, the lance-corporal's example casts doubt on this latter belief, and it seems at least equally likely that the chief reason for the dissolution was a determination not to be dictated to on this question of status. In declining, members sacrificed their battalions' chances of survival, but resentment against the unit leadership had in any case weakened the attachment of some.

However, these men and other militiamen felt stronger ties to the militia thereafter. The A.I.F.'s verbal and practical hostility was turned into the basis of a militia *esprit de corps*. 'Choco' became a term of which many were proud. For non-volunteers it was a symbol of defiance against the army. And as the mixed membership of militia battalions became increasingly confident of their martial ability, the word changed from a painful stigma into a mark of distinction.[81]

One example of a unit in which such attitudes were prevalent is the 19th Battalion, which in 1945 served on New Britain. In March 1945, a field censorship report stated that: 'A number of members of 19 Aust Inf Bn have been noted from time to time to state that they are proud to be CMF troops and feel that they can do just as good a job in that capacity.' The report also quoted a private, presumably an A.I.F. man, whose comments suggest that this spirit was very strong in the unit: 'I don't like this Bn, don't get along very well with the crowd in it, as they are nearly all militia and are a bit sour on the AIF.'[82] The battalion's antipathy to a majority of the Australian Army was apparently compatible with *esprit de corps*. That is the implication of remarks reportedly made by a 19th Battalion private one month later, and soon after a visit by General Blamey: 'General Blamey told us we have done a job unequalled in any New Guinea campaign. I am overwhelmed with pride for the good old 19th – they're soldiers from the Colonel down to the lowest pte – they sure keep the old tradition "Through mud and blood to the green fields beyond"'.[83]

The majority of Australian militiamen became A.I.F. volunteers sooner or later, but the initial treatment of those wanting to join was enough to anger the most insensitive. An official statement in May 1942 that men in militia units would soon be permitted to enlist in the A.I.F. was vague, and permitted the growth of a rumour that this enlistment might entail the break-up of C.M.F. units. According to senior militia commanders, *esprit de corps* within C.M.F. units was so strong that this suggestion threatened virtually to eradicate the widespread enthusiasm for A.I.F. enlistment.[84]

Although the problem was clarified, militiamen felt confused and insulted by the subsequent decision that the highly-valued 'X' numbers, which would be their due as A.I.F. volunteers, would not be calculated in the same way as those of men in the A.I.F. divisions.

Instead, in order to ease the administrative burden, a distinguishing feature would be added: at first it was the letter 'M', later the number 1 000 000. Dissatisfaction with these ideas was such that eventually numbers were allocated as if those converting were reinforcements to A.I.F. divisions.

Just as refusal to transfer was not necessarily a sign of timidity, neither was the decision to convert a sure sign of valour. A good illustration is this note from a militiaman in a fighting unit stationed in New Guinea: 'I havn't seen any Japs yet and have no desire to do so and as for shooting any, I am busy trying to dig down deeper in the trench when they come over to worry about shooting them . . . P.S. I have joined the A.I.F. at last.'[85] Many A.I.F. men were stationed in rear areas, many conscripts in forward areas, and it was not unknown for men to join the A.I.F. after transferring from a C.M.F. infantry battalion to a base unit.

The A.I.F. soldier's contempt for militiamen was sharpened by the fact that troops he encountered in rear areas on Australian territory, the 'base bludgers', were often in the C.M.F. In January 1943, for example, nearly two-thirds of all C.M.F. men were in base, line of communications and training units, while just over one-third of the A.I.F. men on Australian territory were in such units.

Thus, when A.I.F. units arrived at Port Moresby and heard defeatist talk, they could readily identify its source not just as base troops, but as 'militia' base troops; sick or wounded A.I.F. men in hospital might well meet rear area soldiers they could further characterize as 'whimpering A.M.F. types'; an 'X' list man waiting to return to his A.I.F. unit could refine his criticism thus: '. . . there were five cooks to feed eight men. How is that for making jobs for base wallards. Needless to say they were all Chocko's.'[86]

In the Middle East, Australian base troops were all A.I.F. men, and they increasingly came to be so in Australia too. However, the degree to which front-line soldiers in original A.I.F. units identified the C.M.F. with base troops was a major obstacle to one of the unique features of military comradeship. In other Allied armies there was among fighting soldiers a special solidarity that developed from the knowledge that they had shared an experience unknown to the troops who lived in relative comfort behind them.[87] If in the minds of men in the A.I.F. units there was a tendency not to regard or admit C.M.F. soldiers as fighting soldiers, clearly that army-wide front-line camaraderie could not grow. This is another example of mateship being stifled by the status distinctions associated with *esprit de corps*.

Direct evidence that such an attitude existed appears in the following two comments, written by a member of an original A.I.F. unit: 'The Yanks up this way are the fighting men of America as the AIF is of Australia . . .'; '[A relative] is in a fighting unit and not in the Militia'.[88] Further evidence of that opinion occurs in this note, from a member of an original C.M.F. unit: 'The 9 Div are hardly landed and its splashed all over the front page, but the militia Divs in the Solomons have been killing thousands of Japs but of course they're not considered <u>fighting</u> troops.'[89] At the very least, the existence of the C.M.F. complicated the front/base dichotomy amongst front-line soldiers in the original A.I.F. units.

One could argue that the comradeship of front-line soldiers is not something about which they philosophize in their letters, but is spontaneous. And indeed although men in A.I.F. and C.M.F. units probably saw little of each other during combat, there are some examples of individual soldiers from the two forces helping each other in the firing line: for example, 39th Battalion men on the Kokoda Trail providing covering fire for the retreating 2/16th Battalion, which in turn had earlier provided succour to 39th Battalion soldiers who had narrowly escaped encirclement. However, much of this assistance should be seen as adherence to the military principle of 'cooperation' rather than as an expression of fellow-feeling.

In his memoir of the Papuan campaign, Colin Kennedy writes of the pain he felt as a militia sergeant on the Kokoda Trail when men of an A.I.F. patrol told him they would do a job his unit had supposedly failed to do. This was only one incident in an early episode of a lengthy and possibly improving relationship between militia and A.I.F., but the elements of suspicion and hurt persisted. Thus in 1945, the story apparently still circulated in the 61st Battalion of how, three years earlier at Milne Bay, A.I.F. men of the 2/10th Battalion had arrogantly boasted that they would show the 'Chocos' how to fight.[90] The punch-line to the militiamen's story was that the 2/10th troops had failed, but its deeper import was that even the Australian soldiers in the front line could not reasonably be described as 'a band of brothers'.[91]

A neat illustration of the inadequacy of that metaphor is a wartime note in which an A.I.F. soldier writing from the Middle East scoffed at 'manly A.M.F. er – men' he had seen in a photograph.[92] His description denied the militiamen the masculinity that was a prerequisite for being an honourable, acceptable front-line soldier, and that was also a precondition of brotherhood.

Writing of the wounded he saw during his experiences with an A.I.F. battalion on the Kokoda Trail, Steward argues that 'nothing is closer than the brotherhood of pain'.[93] Yet the emotional pain caused to C.M.F. men by their A.I.F. compatriots off the battlefield created a gap that events on the battlefield did not and probably could not close. Mateship was the key to surviving the strains of the front line, but it was also dependent on appropriate membership.

The A.I.F.'s *esprit de corps* formed the basis of the mutual intolerance that marred relations between the two forces. To the extent that *esprit de corps* motivated men in battle, this rivalry may have improved the combat performance of A.I.F. and C.M.F. soldiers. However, one senses that for men in C.M.F. battalions, the enmity directed their way, combined with their secondary and unglamorous role, represented a most uncomfortable burden. The militiaman had a chip on his shoulder, but so did many A.I.F. combat soldiers, with their belief in government and army plots and civilian lack of interest or understanding. The sense of injury prevalent in each of the two forces brought a response of vehement and irrational antagonism towards the other.

Mateship functioned in the Australian Army like a double-edged sword. It helped soldiers to survive on the battlefield and to counter the frustrations and indignities of army service, but its exclusive, status-based nature also caused it to cut many combat troops who deserved better from their own colleagues.

CHAPTER ELEVEN

AFTERMATH AND CONCLUSIONS

*T*hroughout their service, whenever the strain and intense physical demands of the front were relaxed, soldiers reflected on the loss of dead friends. In New Guinea, for instance, a lieutenant wrote: 'I am suffering from reaction today, even tho' it is over three weeks since I have fired a shot in anger. The oppressive heat, our present inaction and restless nights, gives one too much time to think – of home, of those we knew so well and liked so much who copped it.'[1] Frank Rolleston recalls that only with the ending of the fighting at Buna did he have time to comprehend fully that two of his best friends had 'ended their life on this earth'.[2]

Whereas a laconic, masculine veneer covered relations between living mates, those whose friends were killed tended to drop their reticence when talking of the dead, and it is evident that many shared a Tobruk diarist's lament that 'it is the worst part of the war seeing your pals go down'. One soldier's struggle to cope with the deaths of close friends emerges in a note written from the Middle East: '. . . Don was a great pal of mine, now all the other pals are gone so I don't intend to make any more'.[3] Another touching effort to deal with death is recorded in Jack Craig's diary entry, written a week after El Alamein: 'Bought a case of beer and had a good session with Cobber. Yarning of our experiences and those that "bought" it an never came through the battle and finally singing our heads off to blot out the sorrow of loosing our mates.'[4]

193

That sorrow could only temporarily be blotted out. In the aftermath of battle, sometimes months later, men did find some way of
carrying on, some equanimity. Nevertheless, there is no reason to
doubt the conclusion reached by John Lovegrove when, two weeks
after the battle of El Alamein, he recalled the bloody first night of the
fighting:

> I am totally shattered and could weep as I look back now and
> feel just so strongly for my men . . . We had virtually all been
> together since enlistment 2½ years ago and entwined with a
> bond of respect and comradeship that mere words can't
> adequately describe – every bit as strong as a family 'blood'
> relationship and the horror of that night will live with those of
> us who survived for the remainder of our days . . .[5]

Just as relaxation of the stress of an individual battle or campaign
was followed by thoughts of the dead, so too was the end of the war. The
initial reaction to news of the Japanese surrender was usually relief: at
having survived the war, at being able to sleep at ease and to get out of
one's muddy hole in the ground – in short at no longer being under
threat of sudden, violent death. Various sources report that men's
thoughts soon turned to those who had not survived, and one can well
imagine that ruminations such as the following, reported by Allan
Jones to be a typical post-battle reflection, had doubled significance on
and after 15 August 1945: 'There seemed no logic in destiny, and what
survivor does not ponder the question of why he still lives, and others
do not?'[6] If this was a common reaction, it seems likely that Australian
front-line veterans, while being happy on leaving the army and the war,
usually emerged from the experience with a more serious outlook, and
for some, an improved ability to 'take' the knocks of civilian life.

In the postwar period, the attitude of the combat veteran towards
his war presumably developed in much the same way as those of his
counterparts in other armies. Time probably softened or erased many
bad memories, as it had done even during the war, and strengthened
recollections of the joy taken in the simple pleasures that had relieved
the monotony and strain of service.

Yet nostalgia probably has strict limits for most veterans. Even if
they do not remember their wartime anxiety to leave both front and
camp for ever, few would forget their own frightening brushes with

prospective death, and still fewer would forget the actual and often horrible deaths of friends. These would not be forgotten, because wartime friendship is what Australian ex-soldiers, like all veterans, remember most fondly. The efforts of organized veterans to glorify their dead mates in the name of the war's morally upright purpose suggest that those friends are still intimately associated with wartime memories, and thus that not all such memories are jolly and sanitized. One can also reasonably assume that after the war, as in it, Australian veterans saw in their mates' violent deaths ineradicable evidence of war's tragic nature. If so, it is ironic that while living mates have, inevitably, drifted from contact with each other since 1945, those killed in the war exert some influence from the grave.

A reading of Australian soldiers' wartime writings, and of the supplementary evidence, leaves impressions that can be summarized under five main headings.

AUSTRALIANS UNDER STRESS

Australian combat soldiers were under enormous strain both in and behind the front line. Each campaign brought participants to the limits of their physical endurance. It also brought to the fore a constant and heightened fear of death. Australians were not fearless, and some of them became unable to cope with their terror of artillery or aerial bombardment, the prospect of ambush or other chilling features of this war. The vast majority of Australian soldiers did not 'crack', largely because of the authorities' concern that units be relieved before most men reached breaking point. Few Australians in the line, however, were under any illusions that the conditions at the front had the potential to break them all.

Beyond the firing line, Australians were disquieted and angered by the inefficient organization of their lives. The boredom of army camps was so stressful that men soon became willing to exchange it for the front-line ordeal which they had recently been desperate to leave. They were also frustrated by callous or indifferent treatment from their seemingly all-powerful superiors. The privileges of those superiors rankled, as did the injustice of the supposed facts that the dishonest and cowardly soldiers behind the lines got the best of the military life, and that the best of the civilian life fell to the even more execrable villains who had not gone to war.

THE DISCIPLINED AUSTRALIAN

Australian soldiers entered the war with a reputation for indiscipline. The reputation lived on, but the reality did not justify its survival. For the Australian 'took' the ill-feeling and strain created by his life in and out of the line. Fear of punishment and a willingness to accept the extraordinary conditions of wartime were the main reasons. If on rare occasions the soldier defied authority, it was usually by overextending his precious leave, rather than misbehaving in camp, where his C.O. ruled with a firm hand. Statistical and anecdotal evidence does not support the myth that the typical Australian soldier was a larrikin, or that the minority of undisciplined men in the ranks made effective soldiers. The digger's anger and frustration were expressed not in disobedience, but in grumbling. However, he also tried to do something positive to overcome the terror of the front and the barrenness and monotony of life in camp and in transit.

MATESHIP: SALVATION AND DAMNATION

The Australian soldier maintained precious communications with the outside world, but these were tenuous. His chief source of comfort and enjoyment in the army lay in conversations and experiences shared with his friends.

The mateship found in Australian front-line units was a wonderful thing: it saved lives, it gave lives purpose, and it encouraged men to contribute to winning the war. Mateship and the associated considerations of self-esteem were the elements of a sense of honour, which ensured that most soldiers persevered in their ordeal to the very limits of their strength, patience and even sanity. However, the restricted scope of this mateship also hurt men who craved it and were prepared to risk death at the front: especially reinforcements and militiamen. Reinforcements who in their first campaign survived the enemy's attentions and their fellow soldiers' inattention were usually accepted as mates. However, A.I.F. fighting soldiers never considered their C.M.F. counterparts as equals, and thus never as true comrades or brothers-in-arms. Consequently, the comradeship unique to front-line soldiers, and known in every army, was peculiarly and sadly divided in the Australian Military Forces of World War II.

A few soldier-writers expressed the unrealistic hope that the troops' special mateship would play a role in peacetime Australia, and after the war veterans did try to recapture or maintain that feeling in unit associations or the R.S.S.A.I.L.A. (later R.S.L.).[7] Yet when they left the army, soldiers knew that they were returning to face society alone, as individuals.

THE PRIMACY OF MISERY

One postwar survey offers an alternative to the negative image of soldiering presented here. John Barrett suggests that the great majority of Australian soldiers (considered as a group undifferentiated by base or front-line status) either tolerated or enjoyed most features of the military life.[8] That most men in combat units tolerated the life, albeit with a large amount of complaining, is consistent with the wartime writings. However, one senses that in many cases the enjoyment has grown since the war, just as it has for the soldiers of other nations. During the war, positive remarks about Australian army life seem to have been unusual, and favourable comments about 'the army' still less common. Men expressed pride in the qualities and achievements of Australian soldiers and their units, and indeed of the A.I.F. and C.M.F., but not in those of the army itself.

Apart from the petty harassments, the frustrations and the callousness that Australian soldiers suffered like men of other armies, reasons for disliking their army existed within contemporary Australian life and traditions. There was, for instance, a traditional antipathy towards armed authority: Gammage considers 'an endemic dislike of the military' to have been chiefly responsible for Australian indiscipline in World War I.[9] This animosity was presumably greater in the army of 1939–45, which, unlike that of 1914–18, contained some unwilling conscripts.

There is also the Australian tradition, already mentioned, which allows one to talk of an ingrained 'impudence and science of bucking the system'. Added to a tendency for Australians of the 1930s and 1940s to distrust big organizations, these factors leave little wonder that where 'the army' was concerned, Australian front-line soldiers tended to say something unpleasant or nothing at all.[10]

For combat soldiers, especially, the redeeming features of the military life were considered insufficient compensation for its drawbacks. 'The great adventure' for which many had signed up soon palled, or proved itself illusory or horrible. In a sense the soldiers' experience was an adventure – 'We've starved and thirsted and have gone through experiences such as I thought existed only in fiction', wrote an exhausted survivor of a Malayan operation – but it was an adventure exciting and enjoyable only to non-participants, such as readers of fiction (or history).[11] Travel also proved to be less rewarding than Australians might have expected: most found little to admire in the places they visited, and could not wait to get home.

Numerous Australians did see some redeeming features in their service. They felt that they gained in maturity, and particularly in self-confidence and knowledge of human nature. Yet many of those who obtained such benefits were killed in the process.[12] The chief insight gained by Australian fighting soldiers was that war, far from benefiting those who waged it, was blindly destructive and wasteful.

The mateship, which mitigated that waste, was also at the heart of the 'maturing' process; men grew in their ability to relate to others. Yet inspiring and sustaining as it obviously was, wartime comradeship – the sharing of misery – was not enough. Even this powerful positive feeling was generally weaker than the negative emotions aroused by the 'unnatural life'. Nearly all who experienced service in a front-line unit had never regarded it as more than a temporary engagement, and once engaged, they soon wanted it to end. The passions aroused amongst soldiers by the matter of leave entitlements reflected dissatisfaction with army life. Even more telling evidence of the primacy of misery over mateship were the large discharge rates that applied throughout the war and the enthusiasm with which veterans embraced the possibility of early release in 1945.

One regimental historian makes an illuminating comment in his discussion of the end of the war: 'From the moment they had known that the fighting was indeed over, there had been one question on every man's lips. It was not, "When can we go home?" but "When can I go home?"'[13] Obviously many had asked that personal question long before the war's end, but this is a neat illustration of the fact that, as soon as their sense of propriety allowed it, Australians were keen to return to civilian individualism and to leave behind the herd existence that was army life.

THE HEROISM OF THE FRONT-LINE SOLDIER

The fact that Australian front-line troops were scared in battle does not detract from their military achievements. The magnitude of the Australian's effort in winning the respect of his opponents on every battle-field is actually enhanced by the fact that he succeeded despite his trepidation: with fear rather than without it. The willingness and determination of Australians to face and endure their ordeal – to 'take it' – were remarkable by any measure. This uplifting fact must not be forgotten in any discussion of the negative aspects of their service.

An appropriate conclusion on the Australian front-line soldier's experience is the following unforgettable tribute to his courage. It was written by a chaplain working among the sick and wounded during the fighting on the Papuan beachheads, which involved more Australian troops than any other campaign:

> Although I find this [work] a great strain I am grateful for the opportunity of serving these men. I do not believe there has ever been a campaign when men have suffered, hardship, privation and incredible difficulties as in this one. To see these men arrive here wounded and ill from terrible tropical diseases, absolutely exhausted, clothes in tatters and filthy, long matted hair and beards, without a wash for days, having lain in mud and slush, fighting a desperate cruel foe they could not see, emaciated through having been weeks in the jungle, wracked with malaria and prostrated by scrub typhus, has made me feel that nothing is too good for them. No description of their incredible sufferings could possibly be an exaggeration ... I have seen so much suffering and sorrow here that more than ever before I have realised the tragedy of war and the heroism of our men.[14]

APPENDIX A

WHO FOUGHT WHERE

IDENTIFYING THE FRONT-LINE SOLDIERS

The vast majority of Australians who entered the front line during World War II were volunteers. Men who volunteered for overseas service in the Australian Imperial Force (A.I.F.) did all the land fighting in Australia's name until 1942, and most of the fighting done thereafter.

Soldiers who were conscripted to serve on Australian territory, which included New Guinea, first came into action in 1942, as members of Citizen Military Forces (C.M.F.) – also known as Militia – battalions, which fought alongside A.I.F. units in Papua. From their earliest involvement, C.M.F. combat units also contained at least some volunteers: A.I.F. men sent as reinforcements and replacements; and also many soldiers who had offered to fight, provided it was only on Australian territory. By the end of the war, most members of C.M.F. units were volunteers who, like those in the original A.I.F. units, set no geographical boundaries to their service. This entitled them and their units to A.I.F. status. The original A.I.F. and C.M.F. units continued their separate existences within the A.M.F. (Australian Military Forces), but by 1945 some 80 per cent of all Australian soldiers were entitled to the coveted A.I.F. service number of the volunteer.

Each new recruit to the A.M.F. was allocated to a branch of the army, partly according to his personal preference and, more importantly, according to the army's assessment of his aptitudes and of its own requirements. The soldier's prospects of experiencing life at the front were inextricably linked to the army branch of which he was a member.

The Australian army, like the British, was divided into 'arms' and 'services'. There was little likelihood of combat for those assigned to the services, which included among many others the service corps, the ordnance corps, the medical corps, the amenities service and the provost corps. There were exceptions to this rule; notably, those members of the service corps who served in the front line for months during the siege of Tobruk. However, virtually all Australians at the front were members of the 'arms', namely: cavalry, armour, artillery, engineers, survey corps, signals corps and infantry.

Even within the arms, the role of many units virtually excluded the possibility of presence in the firing line. For example, thousands of artillerymen were members of anti-aircraft units, which generally served well behind the front. A high proportion of engineers worked in non-combatant capacities in workshops, construction companies and the like. Many members of the signals corps also never approached the front line, for it was not responsible for communications within the foremost infantry and artillery units.

Nevertheless, significant numbers of men in these three arms did play major roles at the front. Field artillery was a vital combat arm, and on at least one occasion, at Scarlet Beach (New Guinea), even anti-aircraft guns fought in ground combat. Engineers of the field companies were regularly in the vanguard of assaults, which could only proceed if wire was cut, paths in minefields cleared, entrenchments destroyed, or tracks checked for anti-tank mines. In advances and retreats, these 'ginger-beers' often took the position of maximum danger as they cleared or blocked the path between friend and foe. Members of the signals corps were also regularly conspicuous for their bravery, particularly during the defence of Singapore, at Alamein, and on the Finschhafen beachhead.

Mechanized cavalry and armoured units, which were organized entirely for battle, suffered frustrating shortages of equipment and opportunities to fight, culminating in the remodelling as infantry of all the former, and the disbandment of several of the latter.[1] Some militia infantry battalions also gained no front-line experience. However, almost all cavalry, armour or infantry units that went overseas saw service at the front. Some 45 per cent of Australians who served in the wartime army never left Australia. Of the 55 per cent who did serve overseas, it seems that 24 to 30 per cent served in base, line of communication and other non-combatant units. This suggests that about 40 per cent of all men who joined the Australian army had some experience of life at the front. A roughly equivalent proportion has been calculated for other Allied armies.[2]

THE STRUCTURES OF FRONT-LINE SOLDIERING

Every soldier was simultaneously a member of several units. The tankman or cavalryman, for instance, was usually part of a troop, a squadron and a regiment; the field engineer a squad, a section and a field company. Artillerymen were organized into sections, troops, batteries and regiments. Those artillerymen who saw action were generally members of field regiments – 614 to 700 strong, with 24 guns in their three batteries. Many in anti-tank artillery regiments also fought in combat. These units had a purpose in the Middle East, but in the Pacific, nearly all anti-tank gunners became either mortarmen or, like the cavalry, unofficial infantrymen.[3]

Jungle warfare brought modifications to the nature and organization of every combat arm, and even removed the rationale of some, but the infantry retained its position as the most important combatant branch. The 'poor bloody infantry' incurred the vast majority of A.M.F. casualties, and its battalions were the basic combat unit in the Australian army. The classic image of the Australian front-line soldier of World War II is, justifiably, one of a rifleman, Bren-gunner or sub-machine-gunner from such a battalion. He was also a member of battalion sub-units: section, platoon and company. The strengths of these units varied over time, and was supposed to be: 9 to 11 for the section; 30 to 37 for the platoon; and 120 to 130 for the company. For the battalion the figure varied between 780 and 850. However, it was a fact of army life that, even before they entered the firing line, these organizations were rarely at their 'establishment' strength.

The rifle section, nominally comprising five to nine riflemen, a Bren gunner and his No. 2, and from mid-1941 one or two submachine-gunners, was the most vital constituent of the principal arm of the A.M.F. However, the 'typical' rifleman and his officers and non-commissioned officers (N.C.O.s) were far from being the only infantrymen. The infantry battalion boasted not just four rifle companies and a headquarters, but also a 256–300-strong 'headquarters company'.

TABLE 3: Hierarchy of formations and units[4]

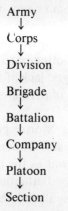

Army
↓
Corps
↓
Division
↓
Brigade
↓
Battalion
↓
Company
↓
Platoon
↓
Section

Note: In descending order

In Australia's early campaigns this company contained six platoons: signals, which linked battalion headquarters and the rifle companies by wireless or line communications; anti-aircraft; mortar, with six three-inch mortars; carriers, equipped when supplies permitted with 10 to 12 fast, lightly armoured vehicles armed with machine-guns or anti-tank rifles; pioneers, who did minor construction, repair and maintenance work, buried the dead, and were generally the work horse of the battalion; and transport and administrative, which was the largest platoon, and included the cooks, technical specialists, and also the drivers and mechanics for all the battalion's vehicles except the carriers.

Various changes were made to this structure. In the course of 1942 and 1943, battalions added an anti-tank platoon of two to eight two-pounder guns, and a medium machine-gun platoon of four Vickers guns.[5] These units often replaced the carrier and anti-aircraft platoons, which were abolished in the South-West Pacific. Transport platoons were also drastically reduced after units returned from the Middle East.

The headquarters company personnel were generally at less risk than riflemen, but all members of infantry battalions shared a high degree of danger. Furthermore, the work of some specialist platoons entailed special perils: signallers, for instance, often had to repair damaged lines under shelling or amidst the threat of ambush, and in action men with signals equipment were a high priority target for the enemy; mortarmen faced the hazards of retaliatory fire from enemy mortars and artillery, and of premature explosion of their own bombs; and even transport drivers faced threats from aircraft, mines, snipers and artillery. In addition, men from 'H.Q. Company' were often put into the line as riflemen, either because of manpower shortages, lack of specialist equipment, or because the need for their skills had permanently or temporarily disappeared.

Not all specialist platoons became superfluous. Mortar platoons and pioneer platoons, in particular, increased in size in some battalions. The pioneer role served from early in the war as the basis of four entire battalions. Members of these pioneer battalions were usually employed in engineering work identical to all but the most sophisticated tasks assigned to engineer units. However, they were also intended, and sometimes called upon, to perform limited infantry tasks: notable examples were the 2/1st Pioneer Battalion in Tobruk, the 2/2nd in Syria, and the 2/3rd at Alamein and Tarakan. They were not well-equipped or well-trained for this fighting role, and seem not to have been regarded entirely as equals by men in the infantry battalions. Thus, soon after its formation the 2/1st Pioneer Battalion made an appeal for a name change, claiming that 'pioneer' was a name 'repellent to the troops' and that they received a great deal of 'imbalanced vituperation' as a result of it.[6]

The Vickers machine-gun served as the organizational pivot for another type of infantry battalion. Many who joined these machine-gun battalions early in the war had expectations, based on the previous conflict, that they would see at least as much action as any other arm. In fact they were rarely able to use their tremendous firepower. Their role was especially limited in jungle warfare, so that for example the most significant work done by the three active machine-gun battalions in 1945 was in a role for which they were not fully trained or equipped: namely, as footsloggers in the Aitape-Wewak campaign.

Machine-gun and pioneer battalions were directly attached to the higher formations called corps, but other infantry battalions were grouped in threes, into infantry brigades. These, in turn, like most combat units of all arms, belonged to divisions.[7] The Australian army's divisions are the key strategic markers in its war. They started operations with a strength of between 16 000 and 18 800 men.

The Australian divisions which suffered most casualties and did

TABLE 4: The A.I.F. divisions and their infantry components[8]

Division	Brigade	Battalion	Original recruiting area
6th	16th	2/1st	Sydney/New South Wales
		2/2nd	Sydney/Northern Rivers, New South Wales
		2/3rd	West and South-west New South Wales
	17th	2/5th	Melbourne/Victoria
		2/6th	Melbourne/Victoria
		2/7th	Melbourne/Northern Victoria
	19th	2/4th	Sydney/New South Wales
		2/8th	Melbourne/Victoria
		2/11th	Perth/Western Australia
7th	18th	2/9th	Brisbane/Queensland
		2/10th	Adelaide/BrokenHill/Murray Bridge
		2/12th	Queensland and Tasmania
	21st	2/14th	Melbourne/North-east and Western Victoria
		2/16th	Kalgoorlie/South-east Western Australia/Perth
		2/27th	Adelaide/South Australia
	25th	2/25th	Brisbane/Darling Downs
		2/31st	All states. Formed in United Kingdom
		2/33rd	All states. Formed in United Kingdom
8th	22nd	2/18th	Newcastle/North-west New South Wales
		2/19th	Riverina/New South Wales
		2/20th	Sydney/Newcastle
	23rd	2/21st	Melbourne/Victoria
		2/22nd	Melbourne/Victoria
		2/40th	Tasmania
	27th	2/26th	Brisbane/Queensland
		2/29th	Melbourne/Victoria
		2/30th	Sydney/Northern New South Wales
9th	20th	2/13th	Sydney/New South Wales
		2/15th	Queensland
		2/17th	Sydney/North Shore
	24th	2/28th	Perth/Western Australia
		2/32nd	All states. Formed in the United Kingdom
		2/43rd	Adelaide/South Australia
	26th	2/23rd	Melbourne/North-east Victoria
		2/24th	Melbourne/Victoria
		2/48th	Adelaide/South Australia

most of the fighting were the four A.I.F. infantry divisions raised in
1939 and 1940: namely, the 6th, 7th, 8th and 9th divisions. The num-
bering of the divisions in the Second A.I.F. started with 6 because of the
desire to avoid confusion with the five existing C.M.F. divisions,
numbered 1 through 5. For the same reason, the A.I.F. brigades were
numbered from 16 to 27; the smaller units within these formations,
however, were numbered from 1 upwards, but given a prefix '2/' or
'Second' to distinguish them from their C.M.F. counterpart. Thus, for
example, there was a 2/1st Infantry Battalion in the A.I.F. and a 1st
Infantry Battalion in the C.M.F.[9] The main infantry components of the
four A.I.F. infantry divisions are listed in Table 4.

OUTLINE OF MAJOR EVENTS

The raising of the 6th Division began in the first month of the war, and
the formation sailed from Australia four months later, in January 1940.
In January the following year the 6th Division first went into action, in
Libya.

On 3 January 1941, the division attacked the Italian fortress of
Bardia in conjunction with British tanks and artillery. The assault was
a great success, capturing the town, together with 40 000 Italian troops,
400 artillery pieces and 130 tanks. The Australians and British pursued
the surviving Italians westwards to Tobruk, which fell to an assault on
21–22 January. The Italians continued their retreat, and by 7 February,
the Australians had occupied Benghazi. Since the assault on Bardia,
they had advanced nearly 600 kilometres.

In March the 6th Division was withdrawn from North Africa and
sent to Greece, which was under threat of German invasion. The Australians in Greece combined with the New Zealand division to form an
Anzac Corps, but the renewed association was shortlived. The Germans attacked Greece in overwhelming force in April 1941, and within
three weeks the Australians and other Commonwealth troops were
evacuated.

Most of the Australians who survived the Greek campaign were
evacuated to Egypt, but several thousand of them were landed on
Crete, where together with British, New Zealand and Greek troops they
participated in fierce fighting against a German invasion force –
including paratroops – in May 1941. The Australians inflicted heavy

casualties, but again were forced to retreat, and those not killed or captured joined the evacuation from a beach at Sfakia.

When the 6th Division had left the desert in March, their place had been taken by the 9th Division, which was short of combat readiness. To their misfortune Rommel, the commander of the newly arrived German Africa Korps, chose 31 March as the date to launch an offensive to recapture the lost Italian territories. The Australian and British forces were thrown back in confusion, and most were lucky to reach the temporary safety of Tobruk.

From 11 April, Tobruk was surrounded and unable to communicate with the British base in Egypt except by sea. The defenders consisted mostly of Australians: members of the 9th Division and of the 7th Division's 18th Brigade. Together with other Commonwealth forces, they worked to develop the old Italian perimeter defences and justify the title 'fortress'. This job was made very difficult in the western sector, where in May Rommel's forces captured a significant part of the perimeter. The defenders narrowly prevented a decisive breakthrough, but whereas elsewhere on the perimeter, they merely needed to supplement the existing deep and spacious Italian concrete posts, in this newly created salient they had to dig entirely new defences. Stints in the highly dangerous Tobruk Salient were dreaded, but everywhere in the fortress men had to contend with air attacks and shortages of food and water. It was not until September that the first of the nine Australian battalions in Tobruk were relieved. Most remained until October, and the 2/13th Battalion only left in December, when they were able to attack east to join relieving British land forces.

The part of the 7th Division that was not in Tobruk was first involved in action on 8 June 1941 when, together with several 6th Division units, they joined Commonwealth and Free French forces in the invasion of Syria. They encountered rugged terrain and unexpectedly stubborn resistance, but the Vichy French capitulated in mid-July.

The final campaign of Australian troops in the Middle East was fought by the 9th Division in 1942. The division was training in Syria when in June 1942 it was recalled to the desert to help against Rommel's advance into Egypt. After overrunning two Italian divisions on 10 July, the Australians bore the brunt of numerous attacks by German tanks and infantry. For two weeks they suffered enormous casualties, particularly around the Tel el Eisa ridge, but played a key part in halting

Rommel's invasion of Egypt. By October, the Commonwealth forces were ready to attack the Axis defences in strength. The 9th Division made a major contribution to the British 8th Army's victory in the Battle of El Alamein. Despite very high casualties, it captured and held ground on the crucial coastal flank, where it drew and 'crumbled' many of the enemy's best troops and tanks.

The 9th Division left the Middle East for Australia in February 1943, a year after the 6th and 7th divisions had done so. Those divisions had been moved as a response to the Japanese manoeuvres that eventually engulfed the 8th Division.

Two of the 8th Division's three brigades had been in Malaya at the time of the Japanese invasion of 8 December 1941. They first came into action against the Japanese on 14 January 1942 at Gemas, in southern Malaya. There the Japanese suffered one of their few reverses of the campaign, as they did again four days later at the hands of Australian anti-tank gunners, near Bakri. However, the Japanese eventually forced the Commonwealth forces back to the island of Singapore where, as had been the case in the earlier Australian defeats in Greece and Crete, the enemy enjoyed overwhelming air superiority. The Japanese invaded Singapore on 8 February. Most Australian troops were still holding their perimeter when the British command capitulated on 15 February 1942. More than 15 000 Australians were captured.

Catastrophe followed for the members of the 8th Division who had been sent to defend other islands in the region. The garrisons of Java, Timor, Ambon and New Britain were quickly overwhelmed by Japanese invasion forces in February and March.[10]

In July 1942, Japanese troops landed at Buna and Gona, on the Papuan north coast. They set out from Buna to cross the Owen Stanley mountains and capture Port Moresby. After initial successes against both C.M.F. and A.I.F. troops, they were halted at Ioribaiwa Ridge in September. Led by 7th and 6th division troops, the Australians now forced the Japanese back along the Kokoda Trail. The Japanese had set up formidable defences on the north coast at Buna, Gona and Sanananda, and organized Japanese resistance to the Australians and Americans in Papua only ended on 23 January 1943. This campaign was an extraordinarily demanding one, because of the environmental conditions and the skill and tenacity of the Japanese, who never again fought the Australians with quite the same determination.

The Japanese strategy for the conquest of Papua included the capture of Milne Bay, a natural harbour and air base on the island's eastern tip. In August 1942, a Japanese special naval landing force came ashore there, but in several days of vicious fighting with the 7th (militia) Brigade and the 18th (A.I.F.) Brigade it was defeated and forced to withdraw by sea. This was noteworthy as the first defeat the Japanese had suffered on land.

In February 1943, the 9th Division arrived in Australia from the Middle East, and from this point on all Australian land forces were engaged exclusively in the South-West Pacific Area (S.W.P.A.).

The Japanese had major bases in New Guinea at Lae and Salamaua. At the end of January 1943 they sent an overland expedition to capture the airfield at Wau. They were prevented by the 17th Brigade who blocked their path. Wau soon became the headquarters of the 3rd Division, which oversaw operations by A.I.F. and C.M.F. units to recapture Salamaua.[11] After months of fighting in mountainous terrain, Salamaua fell to the Australians on 11 September.

Five days later, Australian troops reconquered Lae, following an airborne transfer of the 7th Division to Nadzab, north-west of the town, and a major amphibious landing by the 9th Division to the east. Finschhafen fell to the 9th Division on 2 October 1943, after another amphibious landing, at 'Scarlet Beach'. A major Japanese counter-attack towards the beachhead was halted, and by November the Japanese had been cleared from Sattelberg and Wareo. C.M.F. troops took over as the Japanese went into full retreat.

The 7th Division had gone inland after the fall of Lae. They captured the airfield at Dumpu and cleared the enemy from the Finisterre ranges, before being relieved by C.M.F. units of the 11th and 5th Divisions. These captured the port of Madang in April 1944 and reached the mouth of the Sepik River in July.

In October and November 1944, Australian soldiers relieved the American garrisons on Bougainville, at Aitape in New Guinea and on New Britain. The Japanese garrisons of these areas were isolated from virtually all outside help, and their American opponents had been content to maintain a tacit truce. However, the Australian senior commanders were determined that their troops would take a more aggressive role in these areas.

On Bougainville, Australian troops had brought the centre of the island fully under their control by the end of the war, by which time

separate offensives in the north and south had also brought the
Japanese close to defeat. This campaign was carried on by original
C.M.F. units.

The 6th A.I.F. Division had responsibility for the Aitape region.
An offensive along the coast culminated in the capture of Wewak, the
main Japanese base, on 11 May 1945. Inland, a drive over the Torri-
celli Mountains took Maprik, but heavy fighting was still in progress
when the war ended.

On New Britain, the 5th Division advanced east along the north
and south coasts to the neck of the Gazelle Peninsula, where from
February 1945 they confined the Japanese, whose force far outnum-
bered their own.

The final Australian campaign of the war was fought on Borneo,
which was attacked by the 7th and 9th Divisions. The first phase of the
operation was an amphibious landing on the island of Tarakan, off the
east coast, on 1 May 1945. The 26th Brigade conquered the island, but
only after nearly two months of vicious fighting. The remainder of the
9th Division landed in North Borneo on 10 June, and on 1 July, the 7th
Division landed in the Balikpapan region, on the island's east coast.
Both of these landings were successful.

The war ended on 15 August 1945. The Australian army had in the
course of the conflict lost 10 694 men who had died in battle or of
wounds, or who were missing, presumed dead. A further 8019 Australian soldiers died while prisoners of war, and 1165 died from other
causes in operational areas.[12]

APPENDIX B

STATISTICAL COMPARISONS: RELIGION, OCCUPATION, RESIDENCE

Presented here are some comparisons between the soldiers whose writings were consulted for this study, and the Australian population and army from which they came. All background information on the soldier-writers comes from the Central Army Records Office or the biographical footnotes of the official history volumes.

TABLE 5: Religion

Category	Males aged 5–54 in Australia at Census 30 June 1933* %	Soldier-writers %
Church of England	38.7	53.6
Roman Catholic	19.1**	13.6
Presbyterian	10.5	13.6
Methodist	10.0	10.7
Other Christian	6.8	5.8
Non-Christian	0.4	0.3
Indefinite and no religion	0.5	1.0
Unknown	14.0	1.3
Numerical total	2 606 463	308

Notes: *These ages have been chosen as best reflecting the group who became soldiers in 1939–45.
**Includes those listed as 'Catholic, Undefined'.
Source: Census of the Commonwealth of Australia 1933.

211

TABLE 6: Occupation

Category	Males in Australian army 1942–3 %	Soldier-writers %
Fishing and trapping	0.3	1.0
Rural	18.2	12.9
Forestry	1.0	1.3
Mining and quarrying	2.1	0.7
Industrial	24.8	17.8
Building	6.2	3.9
Transport, et cetera	9.5	10.4
Commerce and finance	15.5	21.0
Public administration, professional, clerical, et cetera	14.9	26.2
Entertainment, et cetera	1.0	0.3
Personal and domestic	2.7	0.3
Ill-defined and other	3.2	1.9
Not gainfully occupied	0.6	2.3
Numerical total	42 350	309

Notes: The 'Army Census 1942–3' covered about 90 per cent of the army. The figures given here are taken from a 10 per cent sample tabulation. The figures for soldier-writers could have been compared with those for males in the 1933 census, but this would seem to be pointless given that the wartime army had a different occupational composition to that group: for example, only 4.7 per cent of working males were in the 'Public Administration' category in 1933.

The categories of occupation, or 'industry', used here are those of the army census and the 'Occupation Survey of the Commonwealth of Australia, 1945'. The categories are very broad: butchers and storemen both come under 'Commerce and Finance', soldiers and medical practitioners under 'Public Administration'.

Sources: A.A.V.: MP729/6, File No. 58/401/485, 'Army Census 1942–3'; Australian Bureau of Statistics: Census of the Commonwealth of Australia 1933; and Occupation Survey of the Commonwealth of Australia 1945.

TABLE 7: Residence

Category	Males in Australia at census 30 June 1933 %	Soldier-writers %
Capital city	44	56
Non-metropolitan	56	40
Unknown	0	4
Numerical total	3 367 111	310

Source: Census of the Commonwealth of Australia 1933.

Notes

INTRODUCTION

1 Pte A. Wallin, 2/5 Bn, D2?/1/45.
2 Gammage, *The Broken Years*, p. xvi.
3 Pte T. Kennedy, 2/43 Bn, D16/7/42.
4 Bdr H. Adeney, 2/2 Fd Regt, LW26/1/41.
5 Anonymous N.C.O., 2/3 Bn, LU–/–/41.
6 Kennett, *G.I.*, pp. 73–4.
7 Sgt C. Greenwood, 2/17 Bn, D25/10/42.
8 Lt G. Gill, 2/48 Bn, LP12/6/41.
9 Calculated from Field Censorship Report for Month Ending 31/3/45. These figures saw an overall decline from 2.47 to 1.46 per cent treated and 0.39 to 0.24 per cent stopped, so the figures may have been higher earlier in the war. 12 to 14 per cent of the letters included in these totals were written by civilians, not soldiers. It is not clear how much of this mail had already been franked by unit officers.
10 Letter from O.C. 1 Fd Censorship Coy to Det. 1 Fd Censorship Coy, Lae Base Sub-Area, 16 Feb 1945.
11 In Shelton Smith (ed.), *Boys Write Home*, p. 92.

CHAPTER ONE: THE UNNATURAL LIFE AT THE FRONT

1 Tpr B. Love, 2/7 Cav. Regt, D16/12/42.
2 Sgt C. Edwards, 2/27 Bn, LP1/1/44.
3 Lt E. Wilmoth, 2/8 Bn, LM7/3/41.
4 Sigmn T. Neeman, 17 Bde Sigs, LF10/2/41.
5 LW–/7?/41.
6 Department of Information, *Jungle Trail*, p. 5.

7 L/Cpl H. Spindler, 3 Bn, D5/9/42; W.O.II G.W. Mowat, 39 Bn, D25, 27, 28/7/42.
8 Capt. F. Piggin, 3 Bn, LB10/12/42.
9 Pte R. Robertson, 2/2 Bn, LM15/12/42.
10 LW4/6/43, 30/7/43.
11 Lt A. Robertson, 2/7 Bn, LW20/5/43.
12 A/Sgt Edwards, D1/9/42.
13 Dexter, *New Guinea Offensives*, p. 51; Hay, *Nothing Over Us*, pp. 297–300.
14 Legg, *War Correspondent*, pp. 56–7.
15 Hay, *Nothing Over Us*, pp. 424, 429.
16 A.A.V.: MP729/6, File No. 33/401/368.
17 Pte S. Clarke, 2/14 Bn, D17–20/8/42.
18 Cpl. J. Craig, 2/13 Bn, DR31/10/43.
19 Pte C.P. Keys, 2/15 Bn, LS22/10/43.
20 Craig, DR1/12/43.
21 Pte C. O'Dea, 2/28 Bn, D4/9/42.
22 Capt. G. Laybourne Smith, 2/3 Fd Regt, LW3/2/41.
23 Wallin, D23/1/45.
24 Cpl Edwards, D16/6/41.
25 Craig, DR1/11/43.
26 Dexter, *New Guinea*, p. 675.
27 Mowat, D10/8/42.
28 Walker, *Island Campaigns*, p. 233; A.A.V.: MP742/1, File No. 211/10/64; Walker, *Clinical Problems*, pp. 92, 96.
29 LW9/6/41.
30 Lt-Col W. Cremor, 2/2 Fd Regt, LF16/6/41.
31 Long, *Greece, Crete, Syria* p. 304.
32 Walker, *Island Campaigns*, p. 69; Edwards, (A/Sgt), D12,17/9/42, (Lt), LP27/5/45.
33 Pte T. Murphy, 2/23 Bn, D18/9/43. Pte A. Armstrong, 2/13 Bn, D10 or 11/43.
34 Kokoda: Walker, *Island Campaigns*, p. 36. Tobruk: Pte G. Nowland, A.A.S.C. attached to 2/15 Bn, D24/5/41.
35 A/Sgt Edwards, D22–23/9/42.
36 Cpl G. Perazzo, H.Q. 21 Bde, LM late 1942 or early 1943.
37 McCarthy, *South-West Pacific*, p. 143.
38 Singapore: Wigmore, *Japanese Thrust*, p. 321. Malaya: Capt. V. Brand, 2/29 Bn, D22/1/42, in Christie, *History of the 2/29*, p. 80. Kokoda: McCarthy, *South-West Pacific*, p. 127.
39 Wallin, D3/1/45.
40 Haywood, *Six Years in Support*, pp. 89–90.
41 Maj. H. Thomas, 2/7 Bn, D26/5/41.
42 F. Hole, 'Record of Events, East Coast, Johore, December 1941/January 1942 as remembered by a private soldier in a rifle company of an infantry battalion', p. 17.

43 Laybourne Smith, LW25/1/41. However, the captain did more work that day.
44 Cpl R. Eaton, 2/28 Bn, LP20/7/41.
45 'Done'; Sgt F. Legg, 2/48 Bn, D1/11/42. Greece: Lt W. Dexter, 2/6 Bn, D20/4/41. Predisposing: Holmes, *Firing Line*, p. 115; Walker, *Middle East*, p. 514.

CHAPTER TWO: EXPERIENCES OF FEAR AND DEATH

1 Cpl M. Hopson, 2/18 Bn, P.O.W. diary.
2 Gill, LP19/1/41.
3 Pte A. Hackshaw, 2/11 Bn, D5/1/41. Pte E. MacLeod, 2/11 Bn, LF6/4/41.
4 D9–10/10/42. Capt. M. Lewis, 2/7 Cav. Cdo Regt, account of Balikpapan experiences, p. 7.
5 Wilmoth, LM7/3/41.
6 D10/1/43.
7 Australians must have dreaded wounds as well as death. Nevertheless, whereas the latter is frequently mentioned, references to fear of wounds are very rare. Thus it is reasonable to regard general references to fear as primarily or exclusively concerned with death.
8 O'Brien, 'Rat of Tobruk', p. 24. Sgt J. Lovegrove, 2/43 Bn, DR12/9/42.
9 Pte T. Derrick, 2/48 Bn, D30/4/41, Memorandum. 'SX' was the prefix to South Australian A.I.F. numbers. Derrick was SX7964.
10 D18/5/41, (Cpl) 10/7/42, (Sgt) 24/12/43.
11 2/48th: Farquhar, *Derrick V.C.*, pp. 106, 113–14. Continual fear: Wick, *Purple Over Green*, p. 286.
12 Ellis, Sharp End, pp. 102–3; Hay, *Nothing Over Us*, p. 305; Barrett, *We Were There*, p. 302.
13 Pte R. Zuckur, 2/24 Bn, LS – /10?/41. He commented that this stage had now passed.
14 Pte A. Wright, 2/16 Bn, LM – /7?/41; L/Cpl J. Craig, D17/9/42. There were, of course, other physical symptoms of fear, including chattering teeth, trembling and sweating.
15 Clarke, D29/8/42; Cpl C. White, 2/1 M.G. Bn, LW30/1[sic–4?]/41.
16 W.O.II C. Craig, 2/13 Bn, LP–/12/42; Pte R. Anson, 2/17 Bn, DR7, 9/11/42.
17 'Rat of Tobruk', p. 23.
18 Pte J. Butler, 2/23 Bn, D7/6/41.
19 C. Craig, LP–/12/42; Love, D15/12/42, 1/1/43.
20 In Combe, 'My Three-Score Years and Ten', p. 332.
21 Sgt R. Robertson, H.Q. 1 Corps, LM19/5/41.
22 LW21/6/43.
23 LP18/6/41.
24 LS–/5?/41.
25 Bennett, *Rough Infantry*, p. 167.

26 L/Cpl C. Scudds, 2/1 Pnr Bn, LF23/4/41.
27 Pte E. Lambert, 2/15 Bn, D28/10/42.
28 Gnr H. Sunley, 2/1 Fd Regt, D21/12/42.
29 Pte A. Jones, 2/43 Bn, LP–/42/42.
30 Gullett, *Not as a Duty Only*, p. 130. Pte R. Aldridge, 2/13 Bn, LF20/8/41.
31 Fearnside, *Half to Remember*, pp. 102–3.
32 Nowland, D14/6/41.
33 Masel, *Second 28th*, p. 51; Medcalf, *War in the Shadows*, p. 92.
34 Sgt A. Hill, 2/6 Bn, D17/7/43; Lambert, D31/10/42.
35 LF5/7/42.
36 A.A.V: MP742/1, File No. 193/1/657.
37 Fussell, *Wartime*, pp. 281–2.
38 Figures in Table 2 are taken from or calculated from: Wick, *Purple Over Green*, pp. 369, 378; Clift, *War Dance*, pp. 435–49; Hay, *Nothing Over Us*, p. x; Binks, *The 2/11th (City of Perth) Australian Infantry Battalion*, p. 2; Graeme-Evans, *Storms and Rainbows*, p. 249; Uren, *1,000 Men at War*, pp. 247–55, 276–90; Crooks, *Footsoldiers*, pp. 487–8; Penfold, Bayliss, Crispin, *Galleghan's Greyhounds*, p. 405; Fearnside, *Bayonets Abroad*, p. 419; Combe, *Second 43rd*, pp. 243, 245; Share, *Mud and Blood*, pp. 438–47; Share, *Roll Call*, p. 114; Serle, *Second Twenty-Fourth*, pp. 3, 364–5; Austin, *To Kokoda*, pp. 237–48, 255.
39 Cpl R. Hoffmann, H.Q. 16 Bde, LM27/1/41.
40 Steward, *Recollections*, p. 134.
41 Maj. H. Dunkley, H.Q. 17 Bde, LS11/6/43.
42 White, LW30/1(4?)/41.
43 Maughan, *Tobruk and El Alamein*, p. 292.

CHAPTER THREE: MAJOR SOURCES OF FRONT-LINE STRESS

 1 Cpl J. Stoner, 2/30 Bn, LB23/1/42.
 2 Cpl K. MacArthur, 2/15 Bn, D29/4/41, 1/5/41.
 3 White, LW30/1/41.
 4 'Hell': Neeman, LF1/6/41. S/– Nurse B. Duval, 2/2 A.G.H. D4/6/41.
 5 Pte C. D. Keys, 2/7 Indep. Coy, LS9/7/43.
 6 Enemy artillery appeared on a much smaller scale in the S.W.P.A. Generally, the Japanese employed only individual pieces, especially small mountain guns, which were nevertheless often frighteningly effective. Larger artillery was encountered on Bougainville and Borneo.
 7 L/Cpl J. Craig, D8/9/42; Capt. C. Chrystal, 2/4 Bn, LW2/11/41.
 8 'Hardest': White, LW30/1/41. Volume: Maughan, *Tobruk*, p.336 and Wilmot, *Tobruk*, p. 170. There seem to be no statistics concerning the first two months.
 9 Cpl Greenwood, D10/7/41.
10 Pte F. Paget, 2/28 Bn, D14–15/9/41.

11 Crooks, *Footsoldiers*, pp. 102, 115, 119; Cpl Derrick, D16/7/42; Pike, *What We Have . . . We Hold!*, pp.128–9.
12 D–/12/41.
13 LW8/5/11.
14 Matthews, 2/10 Bn, D28/8/42.
15 Murphy, D28/7/42.
16 A.W.M. 54, Item No. 519/7/26, 'Lessons of Second Libyan Campaign, 9 Aust Div Tng Instn No. 5', 1941, p. 5.
17 D2/12/42.
18 Cpl J. Craig, DR17/10/43.
19 Walker, *Island Campaigns*, p. 68.
20 D10/1/45.
21 Sinclair, 'Psychiatric Casualties', *Medical Journal of Australia* (hereafter *M.J.A.*), 1943; 2: p. 456.
22 Dunkley, LS29/4/43.
23 D24/12/42.
24 D20/7/45.
25 Pte C. Johnson, 2/3 M.G. Bn, LF21/6/45.
26 Pte V. Tommasi, 57/60 Bn, D1/7/45.
27 Wall, *Singapore and Beyond*, p. 34.
28 'Toothy': Steward, *Recollections*, p. 107.
29 'Operations Milne Bay 24 Aug. – 8 Sep. 42. Lessons from Operations – No. 2', conclusion by Cdr, 7 Aus. Inf. Bde.
30 Sunley, D20/12/42.
31 Jones, 'Volunteer's Story', p. 227.
32 Reassurance: A.W.M.: Canungra Instructions, Serial No. 62, 'Jungle Fighting'. Battle death ratio: Robertson, *Australia Goes to War*, p. 217.
33 It seems that only five Australian soldiers – all part of the 2/14th Battalion headquarters – were taken into imprisonment by the Japanese after that date. Apparently all five died in captivity. Russell, *Second Fourteenth*, p. 148; McCarthy, *South-West Pacific*, p. 595.
34 Diarist: Pte R. Dove, 2/4 Bn, D–/12?/44. Postwar inquiry: A.A.V.: MP742/1, File No. 336/1/285. Testimony given to a board of inquiry into Japanese war crimes, held at Wewak in late 1945 and early 1946.
35 Milne Bay: Reported in Pte R. Berry, 2/9 Bn, D18/9/42. Crooks, *Footsoldiers*, pp. 145–6.
36 Brig. J. Field, 7 Bde, D2/9/42. Rolleston says that at Milne Bay 'we were instructed not to take prisoners', *Not a Conquering Hero*, p. 82.
37 Pte R. Robertson, 2/2 Bn, LM15/12/42.
38 Brigg, *The 36th*, p. 136, Brigg's paraphrase. Colin Kennedy quotes Herring, possibly in a different setting, as saying: 'The Japanese have eaten our soldiers and they'll eat you too.' 'Campaigning in Papua', p. 3.
39 D31/12/43.
40 Butler, D21/9/43.
41 In Austin, *To Kokoda*, p. 104.
42 Religion: Barrett, *We Were There*, pp. 72–3. Heat: Haywood, *Six Years*,

pp. 152–3; Chapman, *Iven G. Mackay*, p. 198. World War I hatred: Gammage, *Broken Years*, p. 222. Anxiety: Nowland, D19/5/41; Wilmot, *Tobruk 1941*, p. 24.

43 Pte W. Phillips, 42 Bn, DR6/8/45, Pte C. Mears, 2/17 Bn, D18/3/41; L/Cpl J. Craig, D5/9/42.
44 Nowland, D10/6/41.
45 Long, *Greece, Crete, Syria*, p. 460; Gallipoli: Pte D. Hughes, 2/4 Fd Amb. D20/7/41.
46 D18/6/41.
47 Pte J. Armstrong, 2/21 Bn, DR, p. 2.
48 Allchin, *Purple and Blue*, p. 298.
49 Pte J. Ewen, 61 Bn, D21/2/45, 22/2/45. The Japanese did attack later that morning.
50 Anson, DR24–26/10/42.
51 D30/5/41.
52 Nightmare: Shaw, *Brother Digger*, p. 55.
53 Ewen, D1/4/45.
54 Gill, LP17/9/41.
55 Capt. Chrystal, LP2/9/41.
56 Pte B. Sawford, 2/29 Bn, LW26/1/42.
57 Walshe, *Splinter's Story*, p. 13.
58 A/Sgt Edwards, D8/9/42.

CHAPTER FOUR: WHEN FEAR BECAME UNBEARABLE

1 Neeman, LF1/5/41.
2 'Bomb happy': Braithwaite, 'The Regimental Medical Officer', *M.J.A.*, 1943; 1: p. 141. Re officially preferred terminology, see Walker, *Clinical Problems*, pp. 676–7, 680.
3 Sister E. G. Allen, 7 A.G.H., LP21/11/42; Sinclair, 'Psychiatric Aspects of the Present War', *M.J.A.*, 1944; 1: pp. 511, 512.
4 Sinclair, 'The Psychological Reactions of Soldiers', Lecture II, *M.J.A.*, 1945; 2: pp. 264–5.
5 DR5/10/43.
6 DR12/9/42.
7 Duval, D4/6/41.
8 Cooper and Sinclair, 'War Neuroses in Tobruk', *M.J.A.*, 1942; 2: p. 74; Love, 'Neurotic Casualties in the Field', *M.J.A.*, 1942; 2: p. 138.
9 Curtis, 'Pages from a Military Psychiatric Notebook', *M.J.A.*, 1946; 2: p. 78. Curtis suggested that this figure was lower than comparative American and British ones, but the figures in Ellis, *Sharp End*, p. 367 suggest that it was slightly higher.
10 Sinclair, ' Psychological Reactions', p. 264.
11 Youngman, 'The Psychiatric Examination of Recruits', *M.J.A.*, 1942; 1: p. 287; Troup, 'The Medical Examination of Army Recruits', *M.J.A.*, 1941; 2: p. 111.

12 Borneo: Curtis, 'Pages', pp. 76–7. New Guinea: Walker, *Clinical Problems*, p. 704. Cooper and Sinclair, 'War Neuroses', p. 74. Cooper and Sinclair also stated that 58 per cent of the patients seen in Tobruk had an 'inferior' personality; 23 per cent had a history of previous nervous breakdown and 17 per cent of serious head injury, p. 74.

13 Walker, *Middle East*, pp. 228, 345; Sinclair, 'Psychiatric Aspects', p. 504.

14 Official: Walker, *Clinical Problems*, p. 688. Dressing station: A.A.V.: Report on Medical Service 7 Div, Appendix VII. Crooks, *Footsoldiers*, p. 189.

15 Curtis, 'Pages', p. 78. Holmes, *Firing Line*, pp. 259–60.

16 Walker, *Clinical Problems*, p. 687.

17 Walker, *Clinical Problems*, pp. 681, 689; *Island Campaigns*, p. 69.

18 Lt-Col G. Matthews, 9 Bn, D29/1/45.

19 Walker, *Clinical Problems*, p. 680. The article was the original version of Cooper and Sinclair, 'War Neuroses in Tobruk'. The staff's reservations reportedly also related to security matters.

20 Gill, LP19/11/41.

21 DR5/10/43.

22 Recollection: Jones, 'Volunteer's Story', p. 149. LP4/5/42.

23 *War in the Shadows*, p. 86.

24 Sinclair, 'Psychological Reactions', p. 264. Also Walker, *Middle East*, p. 391.

25 Nowland, D22/6/41.

26 Spindler, D4/12/42.

27 Cpl J. Craig, D9/11/42.

28 Walker, *Clinical Problems*, p. 688.

29 Holmes, *Firing Line*, p. 215.

30 Contact days: my calculations using the official history volumes. Remaining originals: for example, Barter, *Far Above Battle*, p. xxi (44 by end of war); Crooks, *Footsoldiers*, p. 425 (41); Givney, *First at War*, p. 395 (19 by February 1945); Serle, *Second Twenty-Fourth*, p. 312 (70). The 2.6 per cent figure calculated from Long, *Final Campaigns*, p. 391n. Wartime battalion numbers: for example, Graeme-Evans, *Storms and Rainbows*, p. 249 (3491); Masel, *Second 28th*, p. i (more than 4000); Uren, *1,000 Men*, pp. 276–90 (3275).

31 1941 figure calculated from A.A.V.: MP508/1, File No. 304/750/17. Later figures in A.A.T.: CRS P617 527/1/126, 'Recruiting for A.M.F. History 1939/45', pp. 69, 104.

32 The arguments in this paragraph owe much of their conviction to a discussion with Tony Roe, of the Central Army Records Office, Melbourne, in August 1990.

33 Battalion experiences: Crooks, *Footsoldiers*, pp. 136–7, 444; Hay, *Nothing Over Us*, pp. 236, 382, 488–9; Griffiths-Marsh, *Sixpenny Soldier*, p. 231. Desertion rates: calculated using A.A.V.: MP742/1, File No. 85/1/706, 'Illegal Absentees', and Ellis, *Sharp End*, p. 244, and taking a British

definition of 'deserters' as men more than 21 days absent. The official Australian term for these men was 'illegal absentees'. MP742/1, File No. 85/1/706.

34 Long, *Final Campaigns*, p. 80n. Long's formulation is quoted because it is not clear whether he means absent while the units were fighting or at any time.

35 Refusal: Bougainville examples discussed later in this chapter, and in Cpl P. Casey, 3 Div. Pro. Coy, D14/5/45, 15/6/45, 3/7/45. Incidents reported elsewhere: Sgt Edwards, D12/10/43; Share, *Mud and Blood*, pp. 188–9. Dermatitis and self-inflicted wonds: Steward, *Recollections*, pp. 26, 155. Timing malaria relapse: name withheld, LP25/3/45.

36 Casualty registers: A.A.V.: MP917/2 (the total of deaths is not available for Papua, and nor are the names of individuals with self-inflicted wounds). Official history: Walker, *Middle East*, pp. 203, 228–9. Unofficial cases reported in: Capt. J. Cumpston, 2/23 Bn, D29/9/42; Cpl Lovegrove, DR15/4/41; Matthews, D29/1/45; Paget, D21/10/42; Sgt C. Symington, 2/17 Bn, D30/6/41 and 1/7/41 (two cases). There are other cases in published literature. See especially Barter, *Far Above Battle*, pp. 54, 198–9.

37 Walker, *Island Campaigns*, p. 35.

38 Share, *Mud and Blood*, p. 212.

39 Butler, D24/1/42.

40 Jones, *Volunteer's Story*, p. 55. Capt J. May, 2/10 Fd Amb, DR29/1/43.

41 Matthews, D23, 29/11/44 (re this action, see Long, *Final Campaigns*, p. 108), 4/12/44.

42 D18, 19, 24, 28/12/44.

43 Quotation from Long, *Final Campaigns*, p. 148.

44 Matthews, D29, 30/1/45.

45 D31/1/45.

46 D1/2/45.

47 D3, 16, 21/2/45. On 24/2/45 he mentioned that the troops were 'very happy' about killing some Japanese.

48 Ewen, D20/2/45.

49 D25/2/45.

50 Matthews, D25, 27/2/45.

51 Ewen, D9/3/45.

52 Matthews, D19, 20/3/45.

53 D21/3/45.

54 Ewen, D9/4/45.

55 Matthews, D26–27/3/45.

56 D17, 20, 22, 30/4/45, 1/5/45.

57 Matthews, D2/5/45. Ewen, D28/4/45, 7/5/45.

58 D7/1/46.

59 D9/3/45.

60 Matthews, D7/5/45, 8/6/45. The high-ranking officer is described only as the G.O.C. This could have been General Bridgeford (G.O.C. 3 Div), Savige (G.O.C. II Corps) or Sturdee (G.O.C. First Army).

61 Long, *Final Campaigns*, pp.77, 147–8, 327. Long refers briefly on p. 148 to the strain of the Bougainville campaign.

CHAPTER FIVE: TAKING THE STRAINS OF THE FRONT LINE

1 Outpost: Mears, D11/10/41. Distribution: A.A.V.: MP742/1, File No. 264/16/416. Addiction: Walker, *Clinical Problems*, p. 292.
2 Pte L. Williams, 2/11 Bn, LF3/11/41.
3 Pte F. Rolleston, 2/9 Bn, LP–/2/43.
4 D17/5/41.
5 Long, *To Benghazi*, p. 164n. Barter, *Far Above Battle*, pp. 66–7. Combe, *Second 43rd*, p. 48.
6 Chrystal, LP2/11/41. Cumpston, D4/10/42.
7 In Masel, *Second 28th*, p. 115.
8 'Scrounged' bottles: J. Craig, D24/7/42. Anson recollection: Letter to author, 10/10/90. 'Shot': L/Cpl Mears, D22(23)/10/42. Scotch: In Pike, *What We Have*, p. 160.
9 In the Libyan campaign, most of the drinking of Italian wine was done in the immediate aftermath of the victories at Bardia and Tobruk, but some was done in the course of those battles.
10 Serle, *Second Twenty-Fourth*, p. 316.
11 LW26/1/42.
12 Spr J. Cannam, 2/8 Fd Coy, LF23/3/41.
13 Neeman, LW4/6/43.
14 DR18/10/41.
15 Lt L. Heffron, 2/48 Bn, LP24/7/41; Jones, LP24/10/41; Laybourne Smith, LW1/2/41.
16 Long, *Final Campaigns*, p. 73.
17 Lt Chrystal, D26/6/41.
18 Maughan, *Tobruk and El Alamein*, p. 292.
19 Zuckur, LS-/5?/41.
20 L/Cpl Jones, LP27/7/41. Wilmot notes that the commander of the Tobruk fortress, Major-General Morshead, objected to the use of the phrase on the grounds that the defenders' role was to 'give it', not 'take it'. Wilmot, *Tobruk 1941*, p. 111.
21 A/Cpl J. Roxburgh, Rfts G.B.D., D14/2/42.
22 Pte A. Collins, 2/20 Bn, D12/2/42.
23 Casey, D22/5/45.
24 In the S.W.P.A., the ratio of officers to men set down for infantry battalions was approximately 1:22, Dexter, p. 46n. The ratio of officers to men killed in action or died of wounds in that region to March 1945 was 1:10.5, calculated from A.A.V.: MP742/1, File No. 51/1/198. Adding wounded in action, the rate was 1:13.4, ibid. Casualties in the subsequent months would have widened the ratio fractionally. Similar casualty ratios appear to have pertained in the Middle East; among the infantry battalions at the

capture of Bardia and Tobruk it was 1:11.2, in Syria 1:12 (including field regiments), Long, *To Benghazi*, pp. 203n, 238n; Long, *Greece, Crete, Syria*, p. 526n. The 9th Division's battalions suffered very heavy officer casualties at Alamein, Maughan, *Tobruk and El Alamein*, pp. 582, 584n, 703, 716. It seems likely that officer casualty rates were higher in World War II than I, see figures in C.E.W. Bean, *The A.I.F. in France: May 1918–The Armistice*, p. 1099.

25 LB23/1/42.
26 Capt. W. Travers, 2/1 Bn, LP19/3/41.
27 D21/7/42.
28 Officers' beliefs notwithstanding. American study: see Ellis, *Sharp End*, p. 229.
29 Barrett, *We Were There*, pp. 135, 154.
30 Cremor, LF16/6/41. Spindler, DR13/12/42. Capt. S. Graham, 24 Bn, LF – /4 or – /5/45.
31 Pte H. Russell, 2/30 Bn, LM6/2/42.
32 Johnston, *War Diary 1942*, p. 127. Written on 5/11/42.
33 Participants: Clift, *Saga*, p. 161 . Maj.-Gen. P. Cullen, Foreword to Givney, *First at War*, p. ix. Historians: McQueen, *Gallipoli to Petrov*, p. 4. McLachlan, *Waiting for the Revolution*, p. 259. On a well-publicized visit to Kokoda in 1992, Prime Minister Paul Keating emphasized the patriotism of the Australians who had fought there. The Melbourne *Age* on 27 April 1992 carried the headline 'PM honors the blood spilled at Kokoda'.
34 R. Robertson, LM15/12/42.
35 Clive Edwards, letter to the author, 10/12/90.
36 Robinson, *Record of Service*, p. 75.
37 Fancke, *Mud and Blood in the Field*, p. 128 (8 July 1941). My emphasis.
38 *War in the Shadows*, p. iii.
39 Stouffer and others, *The American Soldier: Combat and its Aftermath*, p. 151. The study depicts patriotism as a factor of minor importance in battle. pp. 149–55.
40 Gnr S. Hough in Shelton Smith, *Boys Write Home*, p. 12.
41 Hetherington, *The Australian Soldier*, pp. 24–5.
42 Poem: 'Fort Regima Pass 2/13th Bn' in Anson DR. Also re other divisions' rites of passage or consciousness of tradition to uphold: Long, *Greece, Crete, Syria*, p. 345; Beaumont, *Gull Force*, p. 17; Crooks, *Footsoldiers*, p. 21; Serle, *Second Twenty-Fourth*, p. 2.
43 The poem, written by 'SX 6726' appears on the diary pages for 27–29/8/41.
44 Pte L. Carroll in Shelton Smith, *Boys Write Home*, p. 11. Dawes, *'Soldier Superb'*, p. 44.
45 Reported comments to that effect appear in: Butler, D14/9/41; Cpl N. Campbell, 2/5 Bn, LP2/5/41; Hughes, D20/7/41; Gnr W. J. Mearns, 2/15 Fd Regt, LC3/2/42.

46 *Tanks in the East*, p. 32.

47 Lt Edwards, 1 A.A.R.D., LP18/8/45.

48 Long, *Greece, Crete, Syria*, p. 562; Bean, *Anzac to Amiens*, p. 488. The relationship between the World War II units and those of 1914–18 is problematic. The Second A.I.F. battalions shared colour patches and state affiliations with their numerical counterparts in the First A.I.F., but beyond this there was little continuity, for the Second A.I.F. units had strictly speaking been raised from scratch. The militia battalions had a much more direct link to their First A.I.F. numerical namesakes. One should not simply dismiss the claims of continuity made in various Second A.I.F. battalion histories, but it seems that those soldiers interested in the old A.I.F. were chiefly concerned with the entire force rather than their respective units' earlier equivalent. Although organizationally the C.M.F. units had a more direct link to the First A.I.F., men conscripted to their ranks for front-line service probably found it difficult to muster enthusiasm for the need to emulate the First A.I.F. – especially considering the criticism many received from members of the Second A.I.F.

49 Russell, *Second Fourteenth*, p. 13.

50 Share, *Mud and Blood*, p. 342.

51 D28/10/41. See also Barter, *Far Above Battle*, p. 32.

52 Sinclair, 'The Psychological Reactions of Soldiers', *M.J.A.*, 1945; 2: p. 233.

53 Arneil, *One Man's War*, pp. 8–9.

54 D8/7/42.

55 Serle, *Second Twenty-Fourth*, p. 164; Combe, *Second 43rd*, p. 129.

56 *South-West Pacific*, p. 448.

57 ibid., p. xi. A. Robertson, LW2/3/43.

58 Sinclair, 'Psychological Reactions', I, p. 233.

59 McCarthy, *South-West Pacific*, p. 207. Honner quoted in Austin, *To Kokoda*, p. 159.

60 The continuation of prewar friendships within the army is not a strong feature of the literature. Soldiers' army friends seem usually to have been new mates.

61 In Hay, *Nothing Over Us*, p. 314.

62 *War in the Shadows*, p. iii.

63 Perazzo, LM late 1942 or early 1943.

64 Survey: Barrett, *We Were There*, p. 298. 'Support and comfort': Gullett, *Not as a Duty*, pp. 134, 140. 'Mother, father, God': in Austin, *To Kokoda*, p. 109.

65 S/Sgt J. Mitchell, 2/30 Bn, LM28/1/42.

66 O'Brien, 'Rat of Tobruk', p. 19; Bdr Armstrong, LM late 1942?, in Shelton Smith, *Boys Write Home*, p. 47; Fancke, *Mud and Blood in the Field*, p. 213.

67 Bean, *The Story of Anzac*, p. 7; Bean, *May 1918–The Armistice,* p. 1084; Inglis Moore, 'The Meanings of Mateship', *Meanjin Quarterly*, 24, 1965, p. 52; Ward, *Australian Legend*, pp. 2, 214.

68 Pte J. Craig, D21/12/41.
69 LW–/8/45, in 'My Three Score', p. 333.
70 Mackay quoted in Chapman, *Iven G. Mackay*, p. 237. The exact date of
   these remarks is not given. See also Darter, *Far Above Battle*, pp. 153–
   4.
71 Marshall, *Men Against Fire*, p. 50. He later gave higher figures for the
   Korean and Vietnam wars, and his World War II figure should certainly
   not be taken to apply unequivocally to the Australian army. Re Korea and
   Vietnam, see Watson, *War on the Mind*, p. 44; Holmes, *Firing Line*, p.
   325.
72 *Men Against Fire*, pp. 42, 65.
73 Chapman, *Mackay*, p. 237.
74 LM27/1/41.
75 'Rat of Tobruk', p. 23.
76 ibid., pp. 23–4.
77 *Story of Anzac*, p. 607.
78 In Russell, *Second Fourteenth*, p. 138.

CHAPTER SIX: CALLOUS BIGWIGS AND BOREDOM

1 Severe: Long, *Final Campaigns*, p. 73. Prison: Pte J. Young, 2/28 Bn,
  LP16/5/44. Denigration: Jones, 'Volunteer's Story', p. 297.
2 Pte A. Currie, 2/23 Bn, LP30/6/40.
3 Pte A. Grady, 2/21 Bn, DR–/6/40. Young, LP30/4/43.
4 Neeman, LF1/5/41; J. Craig, D27/6/42.
5 A/Cpl L. Clothier, 2/13 Bn, D3/12/43 in Gillan, *We Had Some Bother*, p.
  111.
6 Pte R. Holt, 2/31 Bn, D21/11/42.
7 Mathews, *Militia Battalion*, p. 39.
8 J. Armstrong, P.O.W. diary.
9 O'Dea, D18/9/42; Cpl J. Craig, D29/10/42.
10 Sgt Edwards, 2/27 Bn, D18/12/43.
11 D30/12/42.
12 In Dexter, *New Guinea*, p. 387.
13 D22/4/41.
14 Letter to the author, 10/12/90.
15 Sunley, D21/9/42.
16 Unnamed N.C.O. in A.W.M.: Middle East Field Censorship, Weekly Summary for 17–23/6/42.
17 Cpl A. Mogg, 2/12 Bn, LP10/1/44.
18 D17/3/45.
19 Last man: Dexter, *New Guinea*, pp. 304, 525, 540, 749. Serle, *Second
   Twenty-Fourth*, p. 58. A.W.M.: Canungra Instructions, Serial No. 35
   'Defence in the Jungle'. L. Williams, LF –/10/41.
20 D30/8/42.

21 A. Armstrong, D–/7?/45. The availability of shipping was not entirely in Australian hands.
22 Hackshaw, D8/4/42.
23 LW10/2/41.
24 Pte D. Wall, 2/4 Bn, LP /12/39?
25 Speaking to Australian troops at Morotai, on Anzac Day 1945. In Legg, *War Correspondent,* p. 167.
26 Paget, D27/3/42, 11/5/42.
27 LW17/3/41.
28 A.W.M.: Middle East Field Censorship, Weekly Summary for 12–18/11/41.
29 Letter from sergeant in 2/1 M.G. Bn, quoted in A.W.M.: 1 Field Censorship Coy Report for Month Ending 31/1/45.
30 AAV: MP742/1, File No. 193/1/657.
31 Letter from N.C.O. of 29/46 Bn quoted in A.W.M.: Field Censorship Coy Report for Month Ending 28/2/45.
32 A.W.M.: Field Censorship Report for Month Ending 31/3/45.
33 Dunkley, LS29/3/43.

CHAPTER SEVEN: ARMY MUCK-UPS

1 Lt F. Coffill, 7 Div Amn Sub Park, D5/6/40.
2 Maj. S. Porter, 2/5 Bn, LM2/2/40.
3 Pte W. Richardson, 2/1 M.G. Bn, LP9/1/41.
4 J. Ackland, R. Ackland (eds), *Word From John,* p. 211.
5 Gill, LP17/3/42. Cpl Edwards, D20/10/40.
6 Quoted in Irving, *The Trail of the Fox,* p. 113.
7 DR24/7/41.
8 Wigmore, *Japanese Thrust,* p. 290.
9 ibid., p. 96.
10 *Tobruk and El Alamein,* p. 304.
11 'Volunteer's Story', p. 297.
12 Sigmn S. Cook, 1 Aus. Corps Sigs, D2/7/40.
13 Masel, *Second 28th,* p. 24.
14 Hole, 'Record of Events', pp. 3–6.
15 Austin, *To Kokoda,* p. 66.
16 *Greece, Crete, Syria,* pp. 36, 548.
17 Cook, D–/7/41.
18 A.A.V.: MP508/1, File No. 17/715/120.
19 Maughan, *Tobruk and El Alamein,* pp. 525n, 544. Butler, D22/7/42.
20 Shortages: AAV: MP508/1, File No. 15/718/87, 'Statement of Weapon Position in Australia at 1/3/42'. The requirements for Bren and submachine-guns include 1080 and 3200 respectively, for the Volunteer Defence Corps, or 'Home Guard'. Totals based on comparison of stocks on hand in Australia and deficiencies in 'Initial Equipment'. If required reserves were taken into account, the deficiencies were even higher. Invasion: Ross,

Armed and Ready, p. 415. Kokoda: Cpl H. Marshall, R.A.A.F., D11/10/42.

21 D7/1/43.
22 'Volunteer's Story', p. 6.
23 A staff sergeant of 2/28 Bn and a 7th Div. artillery officer, quoted in A.W.M.: Field Censorship Report for Month Ending 30/6/45.
24 Wallin, D21/6/45.
25 Participant quoted in Hay, *Nothing Over Us*, p. 448.
26 On inefficiencies in army ordering of equipment up to 1943, see Ross, *Armed and Ready*, pp. 350–7, 398.
27 A.A.V.: MP508/1, File No. 17/715/120.
28 Jones, 'Volunteer's Story', pp. 272–3.
29 A.A.V.: MP508/1, File No. 17/702/608.
30 Butler, D21/4/41.
31 Maughan, *Tobruk and El Alamein*, p. 210.
32 A.A.V.: MP742/1, File No. 94/1/450.
33 A.A.V.: MP742/1, File No. 61/1/172.
34 L/Bdr J. Hack, 2/5 Fd Regt, LS2/11/44.
35 A member of 2/3 Fd Regt and a gunner of 2/2 Fd Regt, quoted in A.W.M.: Field Censorship Report for Month Ending 30/4/45.
36 A.W.M.: Canungra Training Instructions, Serial No. 33.
37 A.A.V.: MP742/1, File No. 61/3/316.
38 Chaplain of 57/60 Bn, quoted in A.W.M.: Field Censorship Report for Month Ending 31/5/45.
39 Walker, *Clinical Problems*, p. 91.
40 Calculated from Long, *Final Campaigns*, p. 636, and excluding those who died of wounds while prisoners of war. If these were included the respective figures would be 7.89 per cent and 9.08 per cent.
41 Mathews, *Militia Battalion*, p. 100.
42 Calculated from Long, *Final Campaigns*, pp. 633, 634.
43 Kennett, *G.I.*, p. 178. Ellis gives an American figure of 4.5 per cent. Unfortunately, British army figures do not seem to have been compiled in such a way as to differentiate 'died of wounds' from 'killed in action' cases.
44 Kyle, 'The Treatment of Wounded in Forward Areas', *M.J.A.*, 1942; 2: p. 462.
45 Walker, *Middle East*, pp. 154–5.
46 Gnr J. Birney, 2/1 Svy Regt, D5/3/42.
47 Campbell, LP2/5/41.
48 Mearns, LS3/2/42.
49 Wall, *Singapore and Beyond*, p. 103.
50 Laybourne Smith, LW8/5/41.
51 A.A.V.: MP729/7, File No. 29/421/27.
52 Russell, LM6/2/42.
53 Criticism: Barter, *Far Above Battle*, pp. 118–19. Praise: Anon, 2/3 Bn, LU–/–/41; Bellair, *Amateur Soldier*, pp. 54–5.
54 Shaw, *Brother Digger*, pp. 54, 56.

55 D18/9/43.
56 Gnr A. Cobb, 2/1 A-Tk Regt, D27/4/41.

CHAPTER EIGHT: RESENTMENT OF INEQUALITY

1 Gill, LP25/10/41.
2 A.A.T.: Recruiting for A.M.F. History, p. 78.
3 Laybourne Smith, LW4/2/41.
4 In L/Sgt Adeney, LW24/7/41. This is one of several versions. Various authors who wrote about it suggested that it was written by an artilleryman who was subsequently killed early in 1941, or that it was written in World War I.
5 Spindler, DR13/12/42; Graham, LF–/4 or –/5/45.
6 A.W.M.: Middle East Field Censorship, Weekly Summary 18–25/2/42, and summaries throughout May 1942.
7 Fancke, *Mud and Blood in the Field*, pp. 55–6; Sawford, LW2/11/41; Wigmore, *Japanese Thrust*, p. 71.
8 Lt E. Lecky, 9 Div. Sigs, LP13/5/41.
9 Lecky, LP26/6/41; A.W.M.: Middle East Field Censorship, Weekly Summary for 19–25/11/41.
10 Quoted in A.W.M.: Field Censorship Report for Month Ending 31/5/45.
11 'Volunteer's Story', p. 219.
12 *Final Campaigns*, p. 79.
13 ibid.
14 Barrett, *We Were There*, pp. 322–3.
15 D10/4/43.
16 'Tail Sitters': Capt. Dunkley, 2/7 Bn, LS29/8/41. 'Senile': In Long, *Final Campaigns*, p. 239.
17 Nowland, D late June or early July 1941.
18 LF–/7/41.
19 Sunley, D20/9/42.
20 Gill, LP15/7/41.
21 Jones, LP5/5/41.
22 C. P. Keys, LS11/9/41, 12/10/43.
23 Laybourne Smith, LW30/1/41.
24 Walker, *Clinical Problems*, p. 320. A.W.M.: Field Censorship Report for Month Ending 31/12/44. Ryan, *Fear Drive My Feet*, p. 133.
25 Sgt E. Little, H.Q. 76 Base Sub-area, D13/7/41, 15/8/41.
26 Calculated from A.A.V.: MP742/1, Files No. 96/2/224, 251/1/1612.
27 Baker, *Australian Language*, p. 179. Casey, D30/7/45.
28 Name withheld, D30/7/42.
29 Pte? K. Bishop, 1st Ord. Fd Park, LF15/6/41. In 1945, Bishop died of wounds accidentally received.
30 A.A.V.: MP742/1, Files No. 96/2/224, 275/1/43.
31 Jones, 'Volunteer's Story', p. 279.
32 Casey, D22/7/45.

33 'Conscience': Wallin, No. 2 Aust. Rlwy Constr. Coy, D14/7/41. 'Bludger': in Long, *To Benghazi*, p. 186.
34 Pte N. Bennett, A.A.M.C. Training Wing, LM12/11/41.
35 A.A.V.: MP742/1, File No. 264/16/133.
36 ibid.
37 *Firing Line*, pp. 78–9.
38 D26/7/43, in Gillan, *Bother*, p. 105.
39 D27/3/42.
40 D21/2/42.
41 Sgt R. Bourke, 2/1 Bn, LP–/7?/41.
42 *War in the Shadows*, pp. 35–6.
43 Long, *Final Campaigns*, p. 588.
44 'Team spirit': ibid.
45 'Helpers': Bean, *The A.I.F. in France: May 1918–The Armistice*, p. 6. 'Servants': Symington, D18/4/41.
46 Names withheld.
47 Combe, *Second 43rd*, p. 191.
48 Beaumont, *Gull Force*, p. 27; Barrett, *We Were There*, p. 85; Long, *Final Campaigns*, p. 79.
49 A.A.V.: MP742/1, Files No. 85/1/706, 251/1/1612.
50 *Anzac to Amiens*, pp. 536–7.
51 Edwards, D5/1/44.

CHAPTER NINE: DISCIPLINE AND MAKING THE MOST OF ARMY LIFE

1 'Hooliganism': Bean, *Anzac to Amiens*, p. 538.
2 Grandstand: Bentley, *Second Eighth*, p. 5. Pte A. Ulrick, 2/2 Bn, LP24/10/40.
3 Overcoats: Cumpston, D18/9/42. L/Cpl J. Craig, D1/8/42.
4 Ulrick, LP25/8/40.
5 D15,16/9/41.
6 Sgt Lovegrove, DR24/12/42.
7 Sawford, LW5/5/41. He reported a similar incident on 24/10/40.
8 Long, *To Benghazi*, p. 75.
9 A.A.V.: MP742/1, File No. 193/1/474.
10 A.A.V.: MP742/1, File No. 193/1/643. Masel, *Second 28th*, pp. 154–5.
11 Australian tradition: Ward, *Australian Legend*, pp. 2, 144–5. Sawford, LW13/4/41.
12 Clothier, D21/5/44 in Gillan, p. 114.
13 *Rough Infantry*, p. 123.
14 LW–/7/42 in 'My Three-Score', p. 187.
15 LP–/12/42.
16 LP12/11/41.
17 LP–/12/42.

18 Lt-Col (later Maj.-Gen.) N. W. Simpson in Pike, *What We Have*, p. 192.

19 Gnr E. Glover, 'About Officers', in various authors, *Jungle Warfare*, p. 142. No other individual was as important as the C.O., but there were other disciplinarians, notably sergeant-majors.

20 *Nothing Over Us*, p. 20.

21 A.A.V.: MP742/1, File No. 85/1/612. This file contains material prepared by the Australian army's Director of Legal Services in March 1945, and comparing English and Australian military law concerning disciplinary powers on active service.

22 *War in the Shadows*, p. 31.

23 Remarks: Butler, D11/7/44; Wall, *Singapore and Beyond*, p. 7. Smoke bomb: Bentley, *Second Eighth*, p. 297. Muddy car: Sgt E. Weaver, 2/1 Fd Coy, LS10/6/41.

24 C. P. Keys, LS26/4/41.

25 Lecky, LP10/5/41. See also Barter, *Far Above Battle*, p. 31.

26 Maj. Dunkley, 17 Bde H.Q., LS29/6/43.

27 In Allchin, *Purple and Blue*, p. 275.

28 Safety valve: John Laffin uses this metaphor concerning swearing. *Digger*, p. 219. 'Soldier's privilege': Hay, *Nothing Over Us*, p. 135. 'Soldier's right': Allchin, *Purple and Blue*, pp. 3–4.

29 Provost Marshal's report: A.A.V.: MP742/1, File No. 133/1/158. Middle East: Long, *To Benghazi*, p. 125; Long, *Greece, Crete, Syria*, pp. 546–7.

30 These practices in other World War II armies: Ellis, *Sharp End*, pp. 233–4.

31 January 1943 figures: A.A.V.: MP729/6, File No. 19/401/406. Deserters: calculated from A.A.V.: MP742/1, Files No. 85/1/706, 251/1/1612. For example, in December 1943 there were 443 390 personnel in the Australian army. In that month, there were 7402 outstanding illegal absentees. For official purposes, 'illegal absentees' were not counted on the strength of the army, but my general point about proportions of illegal absentees is valid. Short-term absentees: A.A.V.: MP508/1, File No. 85/701/295; A.A.T.: CRS P617, File No. 527/1/126. Recruiting for A.M.F. History 1939/45, p. 76.

32 Middle East: A.A.V.: MP729/6, File No. 43/401/45. Percentage: at the end of August 1943, there were 462 725 men in the Australian army. Dexter, *New Guinea*, p. 227n. In Australia: A.A.V.: MP742/1, File No. 85/1/706. Personnel in civil gaols were not counted on the official strength of the army. In September 1943, they numbered 1066. A.A.V.: MP742/1, File No. 85/1/706. Most A.W.L.: A.A.V.: MP742/1, File No. 85/1/836.

33 Adeney, LW8/12/41.

34 A.A.V.: MP508/1, File No. 84/751/3. A.A.V.: MP729/7, File No. 50/421/10.

35 *Half to Remember*, p. 164. British charges: Long, *To Benghazi*, p. 238; Long, *Greece, Crete, Syria*, p. 545; Maughan, *Tobruk and El Alamein*, pp. 43–45.

36 'Volunteer's Story', p. 121.
37 AAV: MP508/1, File No. 101/750/123.
38 Long, *Final Campaigns*, p.77n. The majority of these men were almost certainly conscripts, but I have found no direct evidence to that effect.
39 In Long, *Final Campaigns*, p. 79. This notion of a sizeable minority is as approximate as it sounds, and is based on the knowledge that in October 1944, 20 of the 33 militia infantry battalions contained at least 75 per cent volunteers. Long, *Final Campaigns*, p. 20.
40 Mant, *You'll Be Sorry*, p. 26.
41 Long, *To Benghazi*, p. 105.
42 T. Kennedy, D21/9/42; Lt-Col Dunkley, 7 Bn, LS12/5/45.
43 Kennedy, *Campaigning in Papua*, p. 27. L/Cpl R. Cattley, 2/25 Bn, LP22/10/42.
44 Fancke, *Mud and Blood in the Field*, p. 94. Paget, 2/13 Fd Coy, D5/5/45.
45 D6/9/43.
46 Pte J. Jones, 2/13 Bn, LS13/5/41. Aldridge, LF15/10/41. Jones, 'Volunteer's Story', p. 78. Steward, *Recollections*, p. 129.
47 Capt. R. Shillaker, 2/48 Bn, letter to family of Lt Gill, 2/9/42.
48 D27/10/42.
49 LP23/10/43.
50 Nowland, D10/6/41. Spr R. Beilby, 2/1 Fd Coy, D27/12/40. A. Jones, LP27/7/41.
51 Love, D9/1/43.
52 Butler, D18/9/41.

CHAPTER TEN: A BAND OF BROTHERS?

1 *Amateur Soldier*, p. 6.
2 Name withheld, D25/9/41.
3 Nerves: name withheld, D5/5/45. LP2/5/41.
4 Pte L. Ayling, 2/18 Bn, P.O.W. diary re 26/9/41.
5 In Wick, *Purple over Green*, p. 428.
6 D5/7/41.
7 Berry, D26/12/42.
8 In R. W. Christie, R. Christie (eds), *History of the 2/29 Battalion*, p. 93.
9 The poem appears in the diary of Cpl F. Quinn, 2/6 Bn. In Hay, *Nothing Over Us*, p. 390.
10 A.A.V.: MP729/6, File No. 58/403/40. This practice may have continued in some cases into 1943.
11 D24/1/42.
12 Cpl J. Craig, DR22/11/43.
13 Wigmore, *Japanese Thrust*, p. 323.
14 Sgt W. Taylor, 24 I.T.B., D25/9/41. 'X man': soldier temporarily away from his unit, often after wounds or illness. Taylor had recently been evacuated from Tobruk with pneumonia.

15 A/Sgt J. Craig, DR20/12/43.
16 Serle, *Second Twenty-Fourth*, p. 300.
17 Capt. Chrystal, D20/3/42,
18 *Sixpenny Soldier*, p. 223.
19 Adency, LW26/8/41.
20 Lt-Col Field, 2/12 Bn, D8/8/41.
21 The state identities became diluted because reinforcements were sent to units regardless of their state of origin. Long, *Final Campaigns*, p. 78.
22 D1/11/41.
23 A.W.M.: Field Censorship Report for Month Ending 31/5/45.
24 Name withheld, LP7/7/41.
25 Name withheld, LP22/5/41.
26 6 Div. officer: Laybourne Smith, LW3/2/41. His emphasis. Further adverse: A.W.M.: Middle East Field Censorship, Weekly Summary for 5–11/3/42.
27 A.W.M.: Middle East Field Censorship, Weekly Summary for 20–26/5/42.
28 Ewen, D17/4/45.
29 D22/1/42.
30 Share, *Mud and Blood*, p. 212.
31 Uren, *1,000 Men*, p. 22.
32 A.W.M.: Middle East Field Censorship, Weekly Summary for 6–12/5/42 and 3–9/6/42.
33 One distinction which gave rise to very little acrimony was that between the various combat arms. Infantrymen perhaps felt and showed a sense of superiority over artillerymen, whom they sometimes criticized, but generally there was mutual respect between the two groups.
34 Long, *To Benghazi*, p. 52. On the other hand, one can argue that the distinct, volunteer status of men in the A.I.F. was partly responsible for their success.
35 Long, *To Benghazi*, pp. 61–2. A.A.V.: MP508/1, File No. 275/750/127.
36 The C.M.F. more than doubled in size, to 80 000, in the year prior to the beginning of the war. *Official Yearbook of the Commonwealth of Australia*, 36, 1944–5, p. 1016.
37 Long, *To Benghazi*, pp. 61–2, 204, *Final Campaigns*, pp. 73–5. McCarthy, *South-West Pacific*, p. 13. Serle, *Second Twenty-Fourth*, p. 4. A.A.V.: MP742/1, File No. 275/1/286.
38 Charlton, *Thirty-Niners*, p. 45.
39 Anonymous, 2/11 Bn, 'A Plea in Verse (To Lt-Col T. S. Louch M.C.)'.
40 LP13/3/41. His emphasis.
41 6 Div.: Ulrick, LP2/3/41. Malaya: Sgt J. Lloyd, H.Q. 27 Bde, LU21/12/41.
42 Gill, LP24/1/42.
43 LW1/2/41.
44 Fearnside, *Half to Remember*, p. 176.
45 Although by 1944 the shortage of reinforcements was such that nearly all

A.I.F. reinforcements were being sent to the original A.I.F. units. A.A.V.: MP742/1, File No. 251/3/190.

16 *Half to Remember*, p. 167.
47 Attack: A.W.M.: Field Censorship Report for Month Ending 28/2/45; F. Legg, *War Correspondent*, p. 55. Salamaua: Butler, D13/11/43. New Britain: Legg, p. 150. Long, *Final Campaigns*, p. 77.
48 Legg, *War Correspondent*, p. 167.
49 The A.M.F. included the permanent and citizen forces. The A.I.F. was part of the Permanent Military Forces. A.A.V.: MP508/1, File No. 275/701/631. A.A.V.: MP508/1, File No. 240/701/433.
50 McCarthy, *South-West Pacific*, p. 226. Another example is A.A.V.: MP508/1, File No. 61/701/813 (including a reference, by the adjutant-general, to the error). The situation was clarified in October 1942 by a general routine order on nomenclature, but some continued to use 'A.M.F.' incorrectly. Some postwar historians have persisted in this error. For example, Charlton, *Thirty-Niners*, p. 243; Robertson, *Australia Goes to War*, p. 101.
51 Sacrilege: Sgt L. Jenkins, 2/2 M.G. Bn, LP 13/11/43, in A.A.V.: MP742/1, File No. 132/1/97. Storm of protest: A.A.V.: MP742/1, File No. 132/1/147. Security decision: A.A.V.: MP742/1, File No. 132/1/147. A.M.F. deletion: A.A.V.: MP742/1, Files No. 132/1/170, 132/1/179.
52 Dunkley, LS28/8/45; Porter, 30 Bde, LM3/10/42.
53 LM2/11/43.
54 In 1942, A.I.F. and C.M.F. units served together in the campaign on New Britain, where relations seem to have been good. Selby, *Hell and High Fever*, pp. 6–7.
55 Hill, D19/8/43.
56 D28/10/43.
57 Hack, LS26/8/44.
58 Veteran at wharf: Hill, D27/9/43. Dexter, *New Guinea*, pp. 79, 149. The Japanese concerned were probably conscripts themselves.
59 Sigmn L. Locke, 7 Div. Sigs, D28/9/42.
60 Austin, *To Kokoda*, p. 155.
61 Clothier, D3,14/12/43, in Gillan, *Bother*, pp. 111–12.
62 Cpl Craig, DR7/12/43. Dexter, *New Guinea*, p. 721.
63 Pte C. Purss, 29/46 Bn, LS6/11/43.
64 In Macfarlan, *Etched in Green*, pp. 128, 130.
65 See the respective casualty totals in McCarthy, *South-West Pacific*, pp. 171, 185, 334; Dexter, *New Guinea*, p. 324n; Long, *Final Campaigns*, p. 385n. C.M.F. units played a valuable role in all of the joint fighting, and particularly at Milne Bay, where it might be unfair to describe the A.I.F.'s fighting as the lion's share. See page 185.
66 Long, *Final Campaigns*, pp. 77, 327.
67 On statistics in this paragraph, see: A.A.V.: MP508/1, File No. 240/701/421; MP729/6, File No. 19/401/406; MP742/1, File No. 96/2/28 and 96/2/224.

68 Dawes, *'Soldier Superb'*, pp. 83, 84.
69 Statistics: Dexter, *New Guinea*, p. 295n. Where terms such as 'A.I.F. soldier' or 'A.I.F. artilleryman' appear in this chapter they refer only to members of the original Second A.I.F. units, unless otherwise noted. This is done for convenience – being preferable to formulations such as 'a member of an original Second A.I.F. unit' – and is not intended to imply that A.I.F. men in original C.M.F. units were less entitled to the 'A.I.F.' adjective.
70 Berry, D27/8/42.
71 D27/8/42.
72 Wallin, 6 Div. A.A.S.C., D16/12/42.
73 Name withheld, LS15/3/44. The book was *Khaki and Green*.
74 Masel, *Second 28th*, p. 153n.
75 Cinderellas: Mathews, *Militia Battalion*, p. 118. Second class: Austin, *To Kokoda*, p. 231.
76 A.W.M.: Field Censorship Report for Month Ending 31/5/45.
77 Both quoted in A.W.M.: Field Censorship Report for Month Ending 28/2/45.
78 Long, *Final Campaigns*, pp. 269n, 451.
79 ibid, p. 239.
80 Complaints: A.A.V.: MP508/1, File No. 275/701/631. Banished: Austin, *To Kokoda*, pp. 182–3. Spindler, D20/8/42.
81 Pride: A.W.M. Middle East Field Censorship, Weekly Summary for 17– 23/6/42 (quoting an Australian magazine); Kennedy, 'Campaigning in Papua', p. 76. Symbol of defiance: Long, *Final Campaigns*, p. 79; Budden, *That Mob*, pp. 73, 118–19.
82 A.W.M.: Field Censorship Report for Month Ending 28/2/45. This is an exception to the earlier generalization about good A.I.F./C.M.F. relations within original C.M.F. units.
83 A.W.M.: Field Censorship Report for Month Ending 31/3/45.
84 A.A.V.: MP508/1, File No. 275/701/631.
85 Name withheld, LP7/8/42.
86 Crooks, *Footsoldiers*, p. 148; Clift, *Saga of a Sig*, p. 167; Birney, 2/6 Svy Bty, D16/5/43.
87 Ellis, *Sharp End*, pp. 335, 342.
88 C. P. Keys, LS4/10/43, 22/12/43.
89 A.W.M.: Field Censorship Report for Month Ending 31/5/45. Emphasis in original.
90 Kennedy, 'Campaigning in Papua', p. 49. 61 Bn: Ewen, D9/3/45, 27/4/45. Ewen had joined the 61st Bn in 1944, and was presumably repeating battalion folklore. Like the A.I.F. account of the battle, this one reflected a one-sided viewpoint.
91 The Australian quoted earlier as referring to 'a band of brothers' was describing the A.I.F. in Malaya. Other uses of that Shakespearean phrase by Australian soldiers: Masel, *Second 28th*, p. 193; Gullett, *Not as a Duty*, p. 93. In his history of the most criticized C.M.F. unit, Budden refers to militia units' 'more experienced "brother" units' in *That Mob*, p. 35. The

inverted commas are noteworthy. Griffiths-Marsh writes of A.I.F. units campaigning in the Pacific with their militia 'brothers' in *Sixpenny Soldier*, p. 2. This is exceptional.
92 A.W.M Middle East Field Censorship, Weekly Summary for 17 23/6/42 The fact that the militia is meant by 'A.M.F.' here is unequivocally clear in the remainder of the passage.
93 *Recollections*, p. 115.

CHAPTER ELEVEN: AFTERMATH AND CONCLUSIONS

1 Lt A. Crawford, 2/3 Indep. Coy, LM17/3/43.
2 *Not a Conquering Hero*, p. 137.
3 Tobruk: Pte Mears, D28/5/41. Don: Cpl G. Puplin, 2/4 Bn, LF23/6/41.
4 D11/11/42.
5 DR14/11/42.
6 'Volunteer's Story', p. 271.
7 R.S.S.A.I.L.A.: Returned Sailors', Soldiers' and Airmen's Imperial League of Australia. From 1965, the Returned Services League of Australia.
8 *We Were There*, p. 177.
9 *Broken Years*, p. 236.
10 Distrust: Long, *Final Campaigns*, p. 586.
11 Malayan survivor: Stoner, LB23/1/42.
12 Including Gill, Hoffmann, and Scudds, each of whom referred to these gains before their deaths.
13 Haywood, *Six Years in Support*, p. 204.
14 Chaplain R. Smith, 2/9 A.G.H., LF10/1/43.

APPENDIX A: WHO FOUGHT WHERE

1 The cavalry regiments essentially became headquarters for the units previously known as independent companies. The latter were conceived as guerrilla forces, but also did some conventional work as infantry against the Japanese.
2 Australian figures calculated from: Long, *Final Campaigns*, pp. 217, 633, 636; Dexter, *New Guinea Offensives*, p. 15; Long, *Greece, Crete and Syria*, p. 550; Maughan, *Tobruk and El Alamein*, p. 600; A.A.V.: MP729/6, File No. 19/401/406. Other armies: Ellis, *Sharp End of War*, pp. 156, 158, although Ellis also mentions a figure of 20–25 per cent (p. 158).
3 In Libya in 1941, most anti-tank gunners were in anti-tank companies rather than regiments.
4 Of course this table does not show how many of these units were at each level: for instance, that there were three battalions in a brigade.
5 Some battalions started the war with one to three medium machine-gun platoons.
6 Osborn, *The Pioneers*, p. 6.

7 In army terminology, brigades, divisions, corps and armies were 'formations', and smaller organizations were 'units'. Infantry brigades consisted of four battalions each until early 1940.

8 Information supplied by Australian War Memorial, Canberra.

9 A.A.V.: MP508/1, File No. 96/750/2, 'Formation, Designation and Organization of the Special Force'.

10 Some of the troops lost at Java were reinforcements from the Middle East. Australians participated in a guerrilla campaign on Timor until January 1943.

11 Later the 5th Division took responsibility for this area. The divisions and brigades to which smaller units were attached changed quite frequently in this campaign.

12 Long, *Final Campaigns*, p. 634.

Bibliography

The bibliography is divided into four sections: personal wartime testimonies and their authors; government and army documents; unpublished postwar reminiscences; published works.

PERSONAL WARTIME TESTIMONIES AND THEIR AUTHORS

Only those soldiers and other wartime writers whose names are referred to in the notes above are listed here. The writings of nearly 200 additional servicemen were consulted for the thesis on which this book is based, and are described in the Bibliography of that work. This can be found in the Baillieu Library at the University of Melbourne under the title 'We Can Take It: The Experience and Outlook of Australian Front-line Soldiers in The Second World War'.

The biographical and bibliographical entries below are organized as follows, with examples in brackets:

Name (X. Y. Smith), *decorations* gained for wartime service (V.C., D.C.M.), *rank(s)* referred to in this book – not necessarily in chronological order (Pte to Capt), *unit(s)* of which individual was a member in period covered by documents referred to here (2/1 Bn and 2/1 Fd Regt). *Pre-enlistment occupation* (Orchardist); *pre-enlistment residence* (of Hay, New South Wales); *year of birth* (b. 1910). *Wartime death*, if applicable (Killed in action 1/2/43). *Description of collection*, including campaigns covered (Diary 1941, including Tob.). *Source of collection* (A.W.M. PR85/abc) or *donor* (Mrs A. B. Smith).

Pre-enlistment details were obtained from Central Army Records Office files, almost invariably from attestation forms.

For key to abbreviations of ranks, units and archival holdings, see 'Conventions and Abbreviations' at the beginning of the book.

237

Abbreviations of campaigns:

A.W.	Aitape-Wewak
Balik.	Balikpapan
N.B.	New Britain
Boug.	Bougainville
Cte	Crete
E.A.	The Battle of El Alamein, 23 October–5 November 1942
Gce	Greece
Kok.	Kokoda Trail
Lae-Finsch.	Lae-Finschhafen
Lib.	Libya, Jan–Feb 1941
M.B.	Milne Bay
Mlya	Malaya
N.G.	New Guinea
Ramu	Ramu and Markham Valleys
Sing.	Singapore
Snda	Sanananda
Tarak.	Tarakan
T.E.	Tel el Eisa: Alamein front July–22 October 1942
Tob.	Siege of Tobruk
W.S.	Wau-Salamaua

H. W. Adeney, Bdr to Sgt, 2/2 Fd Regt. Wool classer; of Camberwell, Victoria; b. 1913. Letters to wife 1939–42, including Lib., Gce, Cte. MS10868.

R. Aldridge, Pte, 2/13 Bn. Labourer; of Sydney; b. 1917. Letters to donor 1941–2, including Tob., T.E. Donor: Mrs D. Woodlock.

E. G. Allen, Sister, 2/7 A.G.H. Biographical details unavailable. Letters to parents 1942, including E.A., and copied diary extracts 1941–2. Donor: Mrs E. G. Hawke.

Anonymous, 2/11 Bn. Two wartime poems addressed to C.O., Lt-Col T. S. Louch. A.W.M. 3DRL 6045.

Anonymous, N.C.O., 2/3 Bn. Letter re Greece 1941. A.W.M. PR85/429.

R. J. Anson, Pte, 2/17 Bn. Drover; of Canterbury, New South Wales; b. 1916. Letter to mother 1942, including T.E. Diary containing original 1941 entries (including Tob.); also 1940 entries made in 1956 from wartime letters, and July–November 1942 (including T.E., E.A.) entries copied from wartime diary and notes. Donor: R. J. Anson.

A. Armstrong, Pte, 2/13 Bn. Postal assistant; of Crookwell, New South Wales; b. 1914. Diary with entries for 1941 (including Tob.), 1943 (including Lae-Finsch.), 1945 (including Borneo). A.W.M. PR85/165.

J. F. Armstrong, Pte, 2/21 Bn. Farm labourer; of Noorinbee North, Victoria; b. 1919. Killed on Hainan Is. 8/4/44. Typed copy of P.O.W. diary, including Ambon service. A.W.M. PR89/165.

L. Ayling, Pte, 2/18 Bn. Orchard hand; of Batton, New South Wales; b. 1903. Died as P.O.W. Typed P.O.W. diary, including Mlya, Sing. Donors: J. Ayling, H. Hetherington.

R. C. Beilby, Spr, 2/1 Fd Coy. Soldier; of Perth, Western Australia; b. 1918. Diary 1940-1, including Lib. MS10019.

N. Bennett, Pte, 2/2 M.G. Bn and A,A.M.C. Fitter's labourer; of Sydney; b. 1908. Letters to mate 1941 Donor: Mrs R. S. Munro.

R. M. Berry, Pte, 2/9 Bn. Labourer; of Mossman, Qld; b. 1919. Diary 1941, 1942, including Tob., N.G. (M.B., Buna). A.W.M. PR84/21.

J. Birney, Gnr, 2/1 Svy Regt and 2/6 Svy Bty. Textile foreman; of Lithgow, New South Wales; b. 1909. Typed copy of diaries 1942-3. Donor: J. Birney.

K. W. Bishop, Pte?, 1 Ord. Fd Park. Salesman; of Mosman, New South Wales; b. 1917. Died of wounds accidentally received 1945. Letter 1941 to donor. Donor: Miss T. Hopkins via Barrett collection.

R. H. Bourke, Sgt, 2/1 Bn. Sales manager; of Potts Point, New South Wales; b. 1915. Died of disease 1942. Letters to parents and friends 1940-2, including Lib., Cte. A.W.M. PR88/125.

J. M. Butler, Pte to Cpl, 2/23 Bn. Accountant; of Red Cliffs, Victoria; b. 1900. Typed copies of diaries 1940-45, including Tob., T.E., E.A., N.G. (Lae-Finsch.). Originals of several New Guinea reflections. A.W.M. 3DRL 3825 and donor: Mrs G. Butler (1940 diary).

N. B. Campbell, Cpl, 2/5 Bn. Soldier; of Toorak, Victoria; b. 1915. Died of wounds 12/7/41. Letter to family 1941, including Gce. A.W.M. 3DRL 505.

J. G. Cannam, Spr, 2/8 Fd Coy. Orchard hand; of Lavington, New South Wales; b. 1905. Letter to friend 1941, including Lib. MS9800.

P. J. Casey, Pte to Cpl, 58/59 Bn and 3 Div. Pro. Coy. Accountant; of Newcastle, New South Wales; b. 1917. Diary 1944-5, including Boug. Donor: Mrs E. Pattison.

R. W. Cattley, L/Cpl, 2/25 Bn. Departmental Manager (unemployed); of Sydney; b. 1905. Letter to mother 1942, including N.G. (Kok.). A.W.M. 3DRL 6105.

C. Chrystal, Lt to Capt., 2/4 Bn. Bank officer; of Liverpool, New South Wales; b. 1917. Diaries 1940-2, including Lib. Gce, Cte. Letter 1941, including Gce. Donor: Mrs P. Chrystal.

S. J. Clarke, Pte, 2/14 Bn. Farm hand; of Glenormiston South, Victoria; b. 1907. Diary 1942, including N.G. (Kok.). MS10894.

A. S. Cobb, Gnr, 2/1 A-Tk Regt. Builder's labourer; of Elwood, Victoria; b. 1918. Diary 1941, including Gce, Cte. MS10131.

F. S Coffill, Lt to Capt., 7 Div. Amn Sub Park. Bank officer; of Strathfield, New South Wales; b. 1916. Diaries 1940-5, including Lib. E.A., N.G. (A.W.). Donor: F. S. Coffill, M.B.E.

A. Collins, Pte, 2/20 Bn. Occupational details unavailable; of Lake Macquarie, New South Wales; b. 1921. Diary 1942, including Mlya, Sing. Donor: P. Bronger.

S. H. Cook, Sigmn, 1 Corps Sigs. General carrier; of Orange, New South Wales; b. 1904. Diary 1940-3, including Lib., Gce, N.G. (Kok.). Donor: Mrs J. Williamson.

C. L. Craig, W.O.II, 2/13 Bn. Calibrator; of Newtown, New South Wales; b.

1917. Typed copy of letter to mother, 1942, including E.A. Donor: J. Craig.

J. Craig, Pte to A/Sgt, 2/13 Bn. Farmer; of Ashfield, New South Wales; b. 1915. Postwar copy of 1942 diary, including T.E., F.A., and of 1943 diary, including N.G. (Lae-Finsch.). Latter copy contains postwar interpolations, but both are so detailed and contain so much material of a transient nature that the existence of originals is certain. I have called the 1943-4 diary a 'DR' in footnotes. Donor: J. Craig.

A. W. Crawford, Lt, 2/3 Indep Coy. Salesman; of Camberwell, Victoria; b. 1917. Typed copy of 1943 letter to friend, including N.G. (W.S.). Donor: A. R. J. Causon.

W. Cremor, Lt-Col, 2/2 Fd Regt. Secretary; of Malvern, Victoria; b. 1897. Letter to wife of former C.O. of regiment 1941, including Gce, Cte. Donor: R. L. Newbold, via Barrett collection.

J. S. Cumpston, Capt, 2/23 Bn. Public servant; of Canberra; b. 1909. Diaries 1940-2, including Tob., T.E., E.A. A.W.M. PR87/147.

A. E. Currie, Pte, 2/23 Bn. Insurance agent; of Hamilton, Victoria; b. 1904. Letters to mother and wife 1940-2, including Tob., T.E. Donor: Mrs E. Currie.

T. C. Derrick, V.C., D.C.M., Pte to Sgt, 2/48 Bn. Orchardist; of Berri, South Australia; b. 1914. Killed in action 24/5/45. Diaries 1941-5, including Tob., T.E., N.G. (Lae-Finsch.), Tarak. A.W.M. PR82/190.

W. R. Dexter, D.S.O., Lt, 2/6 Bn. Student; of Melbourne; b. 1917. Diary 1940-2, including Gce. A.W.M. PR85/218.

R. R. Dove, Pte, 2/4 Bn. Milkman; of Arncliffe, New South Wales; b. 1924. Diary 1944-5, including N.G. (A.-W.). Donor: R. R. Dove.

H. L. E. Dunkley, D.S.O., M.C., Capt to Lt-Col, 2/7 Bn, 17 Bde and 7 Bn. Schoolmaster; of Geelong, Victoria; b. 1911. Letters to sister 1941-5, including Lib., N.G. (W.S.), Boug. A.W.M. PR84/35 and donor: Mrs L. Jones.

B. Duval, S/Nurse, 2/9 A.G.H. Biographical details unavailable. Copied diary 1941-2, including Gce, Tob. Donor: Mrs B. Cornford.

R. F. Eaton, Cpl, 2/28 Bn. Clerk; of Perth, Western Australia; b. 1914. Letters to mother 1941, including Tob. Donor: R. F. Eaton.

C. E. Edwards, Cpl to Lt, 2/27 Bn, O.C.T.U., 1 A.A.R.D. Salesman; of Guildford, South Australia; b. 1917. Diaries 1940-4, including Syria, N.G. (Kok., Ramu), letters to family 1940-5, including Syria, N.G. (Kok., Gona, Ramu). Donor: C. E. Edwards.

J. H. Ewen, Pte, 61 Bn. Mailman; of Cootamundra, New South Wales; b. 1915. Diaries 1945, including Boug. A.W.M. PR89/190.

J. Field, C.B.E., D.S.O., E.D., Lt-Col to Brig, 2/12 Bn and 7 Bde. Mechanical engineer and university lecturer; of Hobart; b. 1899. Diaries 1941-2, including Tob., M.B. A.W.M. 3DRL 6937.

G. T. Gill, Lt, 2/48 Bn. Soldier; of Prospect, South Australia; b. 1915. Killed in action 23/7/42. Letters to mother 1940-2, including Tob., T.E. A.W.M. 3DRL 7945.

A. Grady, Pte, 2/21 Bn. Labourer; of Metcalfe, Victoria; b. 1913. Diary reminiscence re 1940–2. A.W.M. PR88/92.

S. C. Graham, O.B.E., M.C., Capt, 24 Bn. Soldier; of Canberra; b. 1920. Letter to sister of dead soldier 1945, including Boug. Donor. Mrs M. E. Parks

C. F. Greenwood, Cpl to A/Sgt, 2/17 Bn. Car spray painter; of Mudgee, New South Wales; b. 1920. Diaries 1940–2, including Tob., T.E., E.A. Donor: C. F. Greenwood.

J. M. Hack, L/Bdr, 2/5 Fd Regt. School teacher; of Tenterfield, New South Wales; b. 1914. Letters to sister and mother 1941–5, including N.G. (Finsch.), Balik. Donor: Miss G. Hack.

A. Hackshaw, Pte, 2/11 Bn. Truck driver; of Bencubbin, Western Australia; b. 1912. Typed copy of diaries 1940–5, including Lib., Gce, Cte, Borneo. A.W.M. 3DRL 6398.

L. H. Heffron, Lt, 2/48 Bn. Tailor's cutter; of Goodwood Park, South Australia; b. 1915. Killed in action 22/7/42. Letters to family 1941–2, including Tob. Donor: Mrs E. Schodde.

A. J. Hill, Sgt, 2/6 Bn. Farm labourer; of Terang, Victoria; b. 1916. Diary 1943, including N.G. (W.S.). A.W.M. PR85/221.

R. L. Hoffmann, Cpl, 16 Bde. Journalist; of Sydney; b. 1907; d. 3/8/45. Letters to friend 1941, including Lib. This spelling of the surname differs from that given in the official history, but is the one used by Hoffmann himself. M.L. Document 703.

R. H. Holt, Pte, 2/31 Bn. Clothing salesman; of Neutral Bay, New South Wales; b. 1908. Diary 1942–3. A.W.M. PR84/192.

M. W. Hopson, Cpl, 2/18 Bn. Steward; of Collaroy, New South Wales; b. 1916. P.O.W. diary, including Mlya, Sing. A.W.M. PR82/13.

D. Hughes, Pte, 2/4 Fd Amb. Tramway employee; of Coogee, New South Wales; b. 1902. Diary 1941 and letters home 1941, including Syria. Donor: Ms J. Holdup.

L. F. Jenkins, Sgt, 2/2 M.G. Bn. Bus driver-conductor; of Woollahra, New South Wales; b. 1908. Letter to mother 1943. A.A.V.: MP742/1, File No. 132/1/197.

C. R. Johnson, Pte, 2/3 MG Bn. Farm worker; of Parilla, South Australia; b. 1918. Letter to fiancee 1945, including N.G. (A.W.). Donor: C. R. Johnson.

A. A. Jones, Pte to L/Cpl, 2/43 Bn. Motor painter; of Renmark, South Australia; b. 1918. Letters to family 1940 to 1944, including Tob., T.E., E.A., N.G. (Lae-Finsch.). Donor: A. A. Jones.

J. C. Jones, Pte, 2/13 Bn. Dairy farmer; of Enfield, New South Wales; b. 1919. Letters to sister 1940–1, including Tob. Donor: Mrs E. Crocker.

T. J. Kennedy, Pte, 2/43 Bn. Labourer; of Albany, Western Australia; b. 1921 (actually 1925 or 1926). Diary 1942, including T.E., E.A. Donor: Mrs F. Mangini.

C. D. Keys, Pte, 2/7 Indep Coy. Clerk; of Dalby, Qld; b. 1918. Letter to sister 1943, including N.G. (W.S.). Donor: Miss W. J. Keys.

C. P. Keys, Pte, 2/15 Bn. Linotype operator; of Dalby, Qld; b. 1907. Letters to sister 1940–4, including Tob., T.E., E.A., N.G. (Lae-Finsch.). Donor: Miss W. J. Keys.

E. Lambert, Pte (to L/Cpl?), 2/2 MG Bn and 2/15 Bn. Student radio [sic]; of Bulgowlah, New South Wales; b. 1918. Diaries 1941–2, including E.A. MS10049.

G. Laybourne Smith, M.C., Capt, 2/3 Fd Regt. Architect; of Millswood, South Australia; b. 1908. Letters to wife 1939–41, including Lib., Gce. Diary of Cretan campaign. Donor: Mrs H. Laybourne Smith.

E. Lecky, M.B.E., Lt, 9 Div Sigs. Public servant (clerk); of Coolah, New South Wales; b. 1920. Letters to parents 1941–3, including Tob., T.E., E.A., N.G. (Lae-Finsch.). A.W.M. 3DRL 7816.

F. H. Legg, Sgt, 2/48 Bn. Journalist and broadcaster; of Adelaide; b. 1906. Diary 1942, including E.A. PRG 466.

M. T. Lewis, Capt, 2/7 Cav Cdo Regt. Clerk; of Kensington, New South Wales; b. 1918. Account of Balik. experiences, written on Borneo, September 1945. A.W.M. 3DRL 3848.

E. J. Little, Sgt, H.Q. 76 Base Sub-Area. Clerk; of Ivanhoe, Victoria; b. 1903. Diary 1941, including Tob. MS9643.

J. Lloyd, Sgt, H.Q. 27 Bde. Agriculture officer; of Burnie, Tas; b. 1903. Died at Japanese hands. Letter home 1941. A.W.M. 3DRL 7913.

L. L. Locke, Sigmn, 7 Div. Sigs. Customs official; of Brisbane; b. 1906. Diary 1942, including N.G. (Kok.). A.W.M. 3DRL 6780.

B. Love, Tpr, 2/7 Cav Regt. Tailor; of Naremburn, New South Wales; b. 1908. Diary 1942–3, including N.G. (Snda). A.W.M. 3DRL 7211.

J. H. Lovegrove, Cpl to Sgt, 2/43 Bn. Clerk; of Orroroo, South Australia; b. 1918. Typed, expanded versions of wartime diaries for 1940–4, including Tob., T.E., E.A., N.G. (Lae-Finsch.). Donor: J. H. Lovegrove.

K. B. MacArthur, Cpl, 2/15 Bn. Salesman; of Mackay, Qld; b. 1902. Diary 1940–3, including Tob., T.E., E.A. A.W.M. PR86/121.

E. MacLeod, Pte, 2/11 Bn. Miner; of Coolgardie, Western Australia; b. 1905. Letter to acquaintance 1941, including Lib. Donor: Mr. E. MacLeod, M.B.E.

H. J. R. Marshall, Cpl, R.A.A.F. Biographical details unavailable. Diary 1942. Donor: Mrs C. Jarred.

G. R. Matthews, D.S.O., E.D., Maj to Lt-Col, 2/10 Bn and 9 Bn. Public servant; of Hazelwood Park, South Australia; b. 1910. Diaries 1942–5, including N.G. (M.B., Gona), Boug. A.W.M. PR87/79.

J. J. May, Capt, 2/10 Fd Amb. Dentist; of Condobolin, New South Wales; b. 1910. Expanded diary of Wau campaign. A.W.M. PR87/135 and donor: J. J. May.

W. J. Mearns, Gnr, 2/15 Fd Regt. Storekeeper; of Condobolin, New South Wales; b. 1906. Killed in action 11/2/42. Letters to family 1941–2, including Mlya. A.W.M. PR87/45 and donor: D. C. Mearns.

C. W. Mears, Pte to L/Cpl, 2/17 Bn. Shop assistant; of Queanbeyan, New South Wales; b. 1919. Diary 1940–3, including Tob., T.E., E.A. A.W.M. PR84/379.

J. Mitchell, S/Sgt, 2/30 Bn. Assistant clerk of Petty Sessions; of Lithgow, New South Wales; b. 1906. Died as P.O.W. Letters to friend 1941–2, including Mlya. A.W.M. 3DRL 6451.

A. G. R. Mogg, Cpl, 2/12 Bn. Labourer; of Toowoomba, Qld, b. 1920. Killed in action 24/1/44. Letters to mother 1943–4, including N.G. (Ramu). A.W.M. PR84/189.

G. W. Mowat, M.M., W.O.II, 39 Bn. Grocer; of Geelong, Victoria; b. 1895. Killed in action 30/12/42. Diary 1942, including N.G. (Kok.). A.W.M. 3DRL 7137 and donor: Mrs V. Fry.

T. L. Murphy, Pte, 2/23 Bn. Fisherman; of Yarraville, Victoria; b. 1921. Diaries 1941–4, including T.E., E.A., N.G. (Lae-Finsch.). Donor: T. L. Murphy.

T. R. Neeman, M.M., Sigmn, 17 Bde Sigs. Gardener; of North Brighton, Victoria; b. 1917. Letters to fiancee (later wife) 1940–3, including Lib., Gce, Syria, N.G. (W.S.). Donor: T. R. Neeman, M.M.

G. T. Nowland, Pte, 9 Div AASC, including attached to 2/15 Bn. Bank clerk; of Ryde, New South Wales; b. 1909. Typed copy of diary 1941, including Tob. With postwar comments, clearly differentiated from wartime remarks. Donor: G. T. Nowland, via Barrett collection.

C. J. O'Dea, Pte, 2/28 Bn. Clerk; of Rockdale, New South Wales; b. 1920. Diary 1942–3, including T.E. Donor: C. J. O'Dea.

F. M. Paget, Pte, Reinft draft and 2/28 Bn and 2/13 Fd Coy. Farm hand; of Harvey, Western Australia; b. 1920. Diaries 1941–5, including Tob., T.E., E.A., N.G. (Lae-Finsch.), Tarak. Donor: F. M. Paget, via Barrett collection.

G. V. Perazzo, Cpl, H.Q. 21 Bde. Stenographer and typist; of Port Melbourne; b. 1906. Letter to friend late 1942 or early 1943, including N.G. (Kok.). MS10622.

W. H. J. Phillips, Pte, 42 Bn. Storeman; of Bexley, New South Wales; b. 1924. Copy of 1945 diary and expanded version of 1944–5 diary, both including Boug. Donor: W. H. J. Phillips.

F. Piggin, Capt, 3 Bn. Survey draftsman; of Drummoyne, New South Wales; b. 1917. Letter to headmaster of Canberra High School 1942, including N.G. (Kok.). A.W.M. 3DRL 626.

S. H. W. C. Porter, C.B.E., D.S.O., Maj to Brig, 2/5 Bn, 30 Bde and 24 Bde. Bank official; of Wangaratta, Victoria; b. 1905. Letters to friend 1939–43, including Lib., Syria, N.G. (Kok., Lae-Finsch.). MS11477.

G. W. Puplin, Cpl, 2/4 Bn. Carpenter; of Young, New South Wales; b. 1919. Letter to dead mate's girlfriend 1941, including Lib., Gce. Donor: D. W. Pedler.

C. H. Purss, Pte, 29/46 Bn. Labourer; of Lidcombe, New South Wales; b. 1923. Letters to family 1943. Donor: C. H. Purss.

F. J. Quinn, Cpl, 2/6 Bn. Truck driver; of W. Brunswick, Victoria; b. 1918. Diaries, possibly reconstructed, 1941, 1943, 1945, including Lib., N.G. (W.S., A.W.). Also a collection of wartime poems. A.W.M. PR85/209.

W. Richardson, Pte, 2/1 M.G. Bn. Unemployed (estate agent); of East Malvern, Victoria; b. 1917. Letters to family 1940–1. Donor: W. Richardson.

A. H. Robertson, Lt, 2/7 Bn. School teacher; of Bacchus Marsh, Victoria; b. 1907. Letters to wife 1941–3, including N.G. (W.S.). Donor: Mrs H. Lind.

R. G. Robertson, Pte to Sgt, H.Q. 1 Aust Corps and 2/2 Bn. Civil servant; of East Melbourne; b. 1915. Letters to friend 1941 and 1942, including Gce, N.G. (Kok., Snda). A.W.M. 2DRL 1304.

F. Rolleston, Pte, 2/9 Bn. Farm labourer; of Mackay, Qld; b. 1915. Letter to family 1943, including N.G. (Buna). A.W.M. 3DRL 3876.

J. A. Roxburgh, A/Cpl, Rfts G.B.D. Tram conductor; of North Sydney; b. 1909. Diary 1941–2, including Sing. A.W.M. PR84/117.

H. E. Russell, Pte, 2/30 Bn. Warehouse employee; of Canterbury, New South Wales; b. 1918. Died as P.O.W. 20/6/43. Letter to friend 1942, including Mlya, Sing. MS10918.

B. G. Sawford, Pte, Reinft draft and 2/29 Bn. Timber cutter; of Melbourne; b. 1914. Died as P.O.W. 11/4/45. Letters to girlfriend (later wife) 1940–2, including Mlya. MS11709.

C. E. W. Scudds, L/Cpl, 2/1 Pnr Bn. Labourer; of Inverell, New South Wales; b. 1918. Died of wounds 2/5/41. Letters to girlfriend 1941, including Tob. A.W.M. PR87/60.

R. S. Shillaker, M.C., Capt, 2/48 Bn. Cadet engineer; of St Peters, South Australia; b. 1919. Letter of sympathy re death of Lt G. T. Gill 1942, including Tob., T.E. A.W.M. 3DRL 7945.

R. Smith, Chaplain, 2/9 A.G.H. Salvation Army officer; of East Brunswick, Victoria; b. 1921. Letter to friend 1943, including N.G. (Kok., Buna, Gona, Snda). MS10142.

H. P. Spindler, L/Cpl, 3 Bn. Farm labourer; of Central Tilba, New South Wales; b. 1911. Diary 1942–3, letter to mother 1942, including N.G. (Kok., Gona). There is also an expanded version of the diary, referred to in footnotes as a 'DR'. A.W.M. PR83/171.

J. R. Stoner, Cpl, 2/30 Bn. Bank officer; of Grafton, New South Wales; b. 1906. Letters to bank 1942, including Mlya. Donor: J. R. Stoner, O.A.M., via Barrett collection.

H. C. Sunley, Gnr, 2/1 Fd Regt. Dairy hand; of Merrylands, New South Wales; b. 1911. Diaries, some typed copies 1940–5, including Lib., N.G. (Buna, A.W.). Donors: H. C. Sunley and R. Sunley.

C. G. Symington, Sgt, 2/17 Bn (attached to A.A.M.C.). Fruiterer; of Orange; b. 1907. Typed copy of diary 1941, including Tob. Donor: Mrs H. Maguire.

W. D. Taylor, Sgt, 2/43 Bn and 24 I.T.B. Salesman; of Parkside, Western Australia; b. 1903. Diary 1941, including Tob. Donor: Mrs A. J. Taylor.

H. W. Thomas, Maj, 2/7 Bn. Hosiery mechanic; of Armadale, Victoria; b. 1916. Diary 1941, including Lib., Gce, Cte. A.W.M. 54, Item No. 253/1/10.

V. C. Tommasi, Pte, 57/60 Bn. Occupation and residence unavailable; b. 1910. Diary 1944–5, including Boug. A.W.M. PR86/83.

W. H. Travers, Capt, 2/1 Bn. Salesman; of Sydney; b. 1915. Letter to father 1941, including Lib. A.W.M. PR88/125.

A. J. Ulrick, Pte, 2/2 Bn. Telephonist; of Ulmarra, New South Wales; b. 1918. Letters to family 1939–41, including Lib., Gce. A.W.M. PR82/177.

D. Wall, Pte, 2/4 Bn. Market gardener; of Coffs Harbour, New South Wales; b. 1909. Killed in action 26/1/41. Letter to family late 1939 or early 1940. Donor: D. W. Pedler.

A. E. Wallin, Pte, No. 2 Rlwy Constr. Coy, 6 Div AASC and 2/5 Bn. Railway employee; of Richmond, Victoria; b. 1913. Diaries 1940–5, including N.G. (W.S., A.W.). MS10172.

E. A. Weaver, Sgt, 2/1 Fd Coy. Carpenter and joiner; of Gilgandra, New South Wales; b. 1905. Letter to sister 1941, including Lib., Gce, Cte. Donor: Mrs A. J. Smithers.

C. G. White, Cpl, 2/1 MG Bn. Labourer; of Renmark, South Australia; b. 1904. Letter to wife 1941, including Gce. Donor: Mrs M. E. White.

L. F. Williams, Pte, 2/11 Bn. Coffin maker; of Fremantle, Western Australia; b. 1916. Typed copies of letters to friend 1941, including Gce, Cte. Donor: M. Barr.

E. R. Wilmoth, Lt, 2/8 Bn. Law student and radio announcer; of Horsham, Victoria; b. 1917. Letter to friend 1941, including Lib. A.W.M. PR86/370.

A. K. Wright, Pte, 2/16 Bn. Motor driver; of Joondanna, Western Australia; b. 1908. Letter to friend 1941, including Syria. Donor: Mrs E. Wright.

J. A. Young, Pte, Reinft draft and 2/28 Bn. Clerk; of Canberra; b. 1925. Letters to mother 1943–5, including Borneo. A.W.M. PR87/9.

R. L. Zuckur, Pte, 2/24 Bn. Station hand; of Moulamein, New South Wales; b. 1905. Died of illness 30/6/42. Letters to sister and brother-in-law 1941, including Tob. Donor: Mrs L. Beaumont.

GOVERNMENT AND ARMY DOCUMENTS
Only documents mentioned in the notes are listed here.

Australian Archives (Tasmania): CRS P617 Correspondence files, multiple numbers series 1924–51; 527/1/126, 'Recruiting for A.M.F. History 1939/45', 1947.

Australian Archives (Victoria): Central Army Records Office; MP917/2, 'Casualty Registers of Australian Servicemen in the War of 1939–45'.

—— Department of the Army; MP508/1, General correspondence 1939–42.

—— Department of the Army; MP729/7, Classified correspondence files, multiple number series, 1940–42.

—— Department of Defence (II) and Department of Army; MP729/6, Secret correspondence files, multiple number series (Class 401), 1936–45.

—— Department of Defence (III). Army Headquarters. MP742/1, Correspondence files, multiple number series, 1943–51.

Australian War Memorial: A.W.M. 3DRL 6599, 'Aus. Trg. Centre Jungle

Warfare Canungra Training Syllabus Precis & Instructions', as at February
1945. In collection donated to the A.W.M. by Lt-Col P. D. S. Starr, E.D.
—— A.W.M. 54, Item No. 175/3/4, Field Censorship Reports by 1 Aust. Fd
Censorship Coy (A.I.F.), December 1944–July 1945.
—— A.W.M. 54, Item No. 519/7/26, 'Lessons of Second Libyan Cam-
paign – 9th Division Training Instruction'.
—— A.W.M. 54, Item No. 883/2/97, 'Middle East Field Censorship: Part 1,
Summary of British Troops in Egypt and Libya 1941; Part 2: Weekly Sum-
mary, British Troops in Egypt and Libya – January to June 1942'. Each of
these weekly summaries includes a separate section on the A.I.F.

UNPUBLISHED POSTWAR REMINISCENCES
Only writings referred to specifically in the notes are listed here.
Combe, G. D., 'My Three-Score Years and Ten', Part I, 1987. Contains repro-
ductions of and extended extracts from Combe's wartime writings. Donor:
G. D. Combe, C.M.G., M.C.
Hole, F., 'Record of Events, East Coast, Johore, December 1941/January 1942
as remembered by a private soldier in a rifle company of an infantry
battalion', n.d. A.W.M. 3DRL 6922.
Jones, A. A., 'A Volunteer's Story', 1988. Donor: A. A. Jones.
Kennedy, C., 'World War 2: Campaigning in Papua', n.d. A.W.M.
PR85/305.
O'Brien, M., 'A Rat of Tobruk', n.d. Donor: M. O'Malley.

PUBLISHED WORKS
This list refers only to those books mentioned in the notes. A broader range was
consulted in the research for the thesis on which the book is based, and can be
found in the bibliography of the thesis.
    Note: Asterisks denote works which contain extended extracts from, or
complete reproductions of, wartime letters or diaries.
*Ackland, John and Richard (eds), Word From John: An Australian Soldier's
Letters to his Friends, Cassell, Sydney, 1944.
Allchin, Frank, Purple and Blue: The History of the 2/10th Battalion, A.I.F.,
Griffin Press, Adelaide, 1958.
*Arneil, Stan, One Man's War, Alternative Publishing Co-Operative, Sydney,
1981.
Austin, Victor, To Kokoda and Beyond: The Story of the 39th Battalion 1941–
1943, Melbourne University Press, Carlton, 1988.
Baker, Sidney J., The Australian Language, Currawong Publishing Co., Syd-
ney, 1966.
Barrett, John, We Were There: Australian Soldiers of World War II Tell Their
Stories, Viking, Ringwood, 1987.

Barter, Margaret, *Far Above Battle: The Experience and Memory of Australian Soldiers in War 1939–1945*, Allen and Unwin, Sydney, 1994.

Bean, C. E. W., *Anzac to Amiens: A Shorter History of the Australian Fighting Services in the First World War*, Australian War Memorial, Canberra, 1968.

—— *The A.I.F. in France: May 1918–The Armistice*, Angus and Robertson, Sydney, 1942.

—— *The Story of Anzac*, Angus and Robertson, Sydney, 1938.

Beaumont, Joan, *Gull Force: Survival and Leadership in Captivity 1941–1945*, Allen and Unwin, Sydney, 1988.

Bellair, John, *Amateur Soldier: An Australian Machine Gunner's Memories of World War II*, Spectrum Publications, Melbourne, 1984.

Bennett, Cam, *Rough Infantry: Tales of World War II*, Warrnambool Institute Press, Brunswick, 1985.

Bentley, A., *The Second Eighth*, 2/8 Battalion Association, Melbourne, 1984.

Binks, H. M., *The 2/11th (City of Perth) Australian Infantry Battalion*, H. M. Binks, Perth, 1984.

Braithwaite, P., 'The Regimental Medical Officer', *Medical Journal of Australia*, 1943; 1: pp. 137–42.

Brigg, Stan and Brigg, Les, *The 36th Australian Infantry Battalion*, The 36th Battalion, Sydney, 1967.

Budden, F. M., *That Mob: The Story of the 55/53rd Australian Infantry Battalion, A.I.F.*, F. M. Budden, Ashfield, 1973.

*Camarsh, F., Diaries 1941–4, reprinted in *2/17 Bn A.I.F. Newsletter*, April 1983–December 1987.

Chapman, Ivan D., *Iven G. Mackay: Citizen and Soldier,* Melway Publishing, Melbourne, 1975.

Charlton, Peter, *The Thirty-Niners*, Macmillan, Melbourne, 1981.

*Christie, R. W. and Christie, R. (eds), *A History of the 2/29 Battalion — 8th Australian Division AIF*, Enterprise Press, Sale, 1983.

Clift, Ken, *The Saga of a Sig*, KCD Publications, Randwick, 1972.

——, *War Dance: A story of the 2/3 Australian Infantry Battalion A.I.F.*, P. M. Fowler, 2/3rd Battalion Association, Kingsgrove, New South Wales, 1980.

Combe, Gordon, Ligertwood, Frank and Gilchrist, Tom, *The Second 43rd*, Second 43rd Battalion A.I.F. Club, Adelaide, 1972.

Cooper, E. L. and Sinclair, A. J. M., 'War Neuroses in Tobruk: A Report on 207 Patients from the Australian Imperial Force Units in Tobruk', *Medical Journal of Australia*, 1942; 2: pp. 73–77.

Crooks, William, *The Footsoldiers: The Story of the 2/33rd Australian Infantry Battalion, A.I.F. in the War of 1939–45*, Printcraft Press, Brookvale, 1971.

Curtis, W. D., 'Pages From a Military Psychiatric Notebook', *Medical Journal of Australia*, 1946; 2: pp. 76–80.

Dawes, Allan, *'Soldier Superb': The Australian Fights in New Guinea*, F. H. Johnston Publishing Co., Sydney, 1944.

Dexter, David, *The New Guinea Offensives*, Australian War Memorial, Canberra, 1961.

Department of Information, *Jungle Trail* in 'The Australian Army at War' series, Sydney, 1944.

Ellis, John, *The Sharp End of War: The Fighting Man in World War II*, David and Charles, Newton Abbot, 1980.

Fancke, Dick (ed.), *Mud and Blood in the Field*, John Sissons, Hughesdale, 1984. (A collection of the 2/23rd Battalion's wartime newsletters.)

Farquhar, Murray, *Derrick V.C.*, Rigby, Adelaide, 1982.

Fearnside, G. H., *Half to Remember: The reminiscences of an Australian infantry soldier in World War II*, Haldane Publishing Co., Sydney, 1975.

Fearnside, G. H. (ed.), *Bayonets Abroad, A History of the 2/13th Battalion A.I.F. in The Second World War*, Waite and Bull, Sydney, 1953.

Fussell, Paul, *Wartime: Understanding and Behavior in the Second World War*, Oxford University Press, New York, 1989.

Gammage, Bill, *The Broken Years: Australian Soldiers in the Great War*, Penguin, Harmondsworth, 1975.

*Gillan, H. (ed.), *We Had Some Bother: 'Tales from the Infantry'*, 2/13 Battalion Assocation, Sydney, 1985.

Givney, E. C. (ed.), *The First at War: The Story of the 2/1st Australian Infantry Battalion 1939–45*, Association of First Infantry Battalions, Earlwood, 1987.

Graeme-Evans, A. L., *Of Storms and Rainbows: The Story of the Men of the 2/12th Battalion*, Volume 1, Southern Holdings, Hobart, 1989.

Griffiths-Marsh, Roland, *The Sixpenny Soldier*, Angus and Robertson, North Ryde, 1990.

Gullett, Henry ('Jo'), *Not as a Duty Only: An infantryman's war*, Melbourne University Press, Carlton, 1984.

Hay, David, *Nothing Over Us: The Story of the 2/6th Australian Infantry Battalion*, Australian War Memorial, Canberra, 1984.

Haywood, E. V., *Six Years in Support: Official History of the 2/1st Australian Field Regiment*, Angus and Robertson, Sydney, 1959.

Hetherington, John, *The Australian Soldier: A Portrait*, F. H. Johnston Publishing Co., Sydney, 1943.

Holmes, Richard, *Firing Line*, Penguin, Harmondsworth, 1987.

Inglis Moore, T., 'The Meanings of Mateship', *Meanjin Quarterly*, 1965; 24: pp. 45–54.

Irving, David, *The Trail of the Fox: The Life of Field-Marshal Erwin Rommel*, Futura, London, 1978.

*Johnston, G., *War Diary 1942*, Collins, Sydney, 1984.

Kennett, Lee, *G. I. : The American Soldier in World War II*, Charles Scribner's Sons, New York, 1987.

Kerr, Colin, *Tanks in the East: The Story of an Australian Cavalry Regiment*, Oxford University Press, Melbourne, 1945.

Kyle, C. W., 'The Treatment of Wounded in Forward Areas', *Medical Journal of Australia*, 1942; 2: pp. 459–63.

Laffin, John, *Digger: The Legend of the Australian Soldier*, Sun Books, Melbourne, 1990.

Legg, Frank, *War Correspondent*, Rigby, Adelaide, 1964.

Long, Gavin, *Greece, Crete and Syria*, Collins/Australian War Memorial, Sydney, 1986.

—— *The Final Campaigns*, Australian War Memorial, Canberra, 1963.

—— *The Six Years War*, Australian War Memorial, Canberra, 1973.

—— *To Benghazi*, Collins/Australian War Memorial, Sydney, 1986.

Love, H. R., 'Neurotic Casualties in the Field', *Medical Journal of Australia*, 1942; 2: pp. 137–43.

Macfarlan, Graeme, *Etched in Green: The History of the 22nd Australian Infantry Battalion 1939–1946*, 22nd Australian Infantry Battalion Association, Melbourne, 1961.

Mant, Gilbert, *You'll Be Sorry*, Frank Johnson, Sydney, 1944.

Marshall, S. L. A., *Men Against Fire*, William Morrow, New York, 1947.

Masel, Philip, *The Second 28th*, 2/28th Battalion and 24th Anti-Tank Coy, Perth, 1961.

Mathews, Russell, *Militia Battalion at War: The History of the 58/59th Australian Infantry Battalion in the Second World War*, 58/59th Battalion Association, Sydney, 1961.

Maughan, Barton, *Tobruk and El Alamein*, Australian War Memorial, Canberra, 1966.

McCarthy, Dudley, *South-West Pacific Area – First Year: Kokoda to Wau*, Australian War Memorial, Canberra, 1959.

McLachlan, Noel, *Waiting for the Revolution: A History of Australian Nationalism*, Penguin, Ringwood, 1989.

McQueen, Humphrey, *Gallipoli to Petrov: Arguing with Australian History*, Allen and Unwin, Sydney, 1984.

Medcalf, Peter, *War in the Shadows: Bougainville 1944–5*, Australian War Memorial, Canberra, 1986.

Official Yearbook of the Commonwealth of Australia, 36, 1944–5 and 37, 1946–7.

Osborn, G., *The Pioneers: The Story of 2/1st Australian Pioneer Battalion*, M. D. Herron, Beverly Hills, 1988.

Penfold, A.W., Bayliss, W. C. and Crispin, K. E., *Gallaghan's Greyhounds, The Story of the 2/30th Infantry Battalion*, 2/30th Infantry Battalion A.I.F. Association, Sydney, 1979.

Pike, P. and others, *'What We Have ... We Hold!': A History of the 2/17 Australian Infantry Battalion*, 2/17 Battalion History Committee, Balgowlah, 1990.

Robertson, John, *Australia Goes to War*, Doubleday, Sydney, 1984.

Robinson, Bruce, *Record of Service: An Australian Medical Officer in the New Guinea Campaign*, Macmillan, Melbourne, 1944.

Rolleston, Frank, *Not a Conquering Hero, Frank Rolleston, Eton, 1984.*

Ross, A. T., *Armed and Ready: The Industrial Development and Defence of Australia 1900–1945*, Turton and Armstrong, Sydney, 1995.

Russell, W. B., *The Second Fourteenth Battalion*, Angus and Robertson, Sydney, 1949.

Ryan, Peter, *Fear Drive My Feet*, Angus and Robertson, Sydney, 1959.

Selby, D. M., *Hell and High Fever*, Currawong Publishing Co., Sydney, 1956.

Serle, R. P. (ed.), *The Second Twenty-Fourth*, The Jacaranda Press, Brisbane, 1963.

Share, Pat (ed.), *Mud and Blood: 'Albury's Own' Second Twenty-third Australian Infantry Battalion*, Heritage Book Publications, Frankston, 1978.

Share, Pat and Keating, Allan (eds), *Roll Call of the Second Twenty-Third Australian Infantry Battalion*, Acacia Press, Blackburn, 1994.

Shaw, Patricia, *Brother Digger*, Greenhouse Publications, Richmond, 1984.

*Shelton Smith, Adele, *The Boys Write Home*, Consolidated Press, Sydney, 1944. (A collection of extracts from servicemen's letters that were passed to the *Women's Weekly*. It contains some surprisingly frank references to fear and to the reverses in Malaya and Papua.)

Sinclair, A. J. M., 'Psychiatric Aspects of the Present War', *Medical Journal of Australia*, 1944; 1: pp. 501–14.

——— 'Psychiatric Casualties in an Operational Zone in New Guinea', *Medical Journal of Australia*, 1943; 2: pp. 453–60.

——— 'The Psychological Reactions of Soldiers', Lecture I, *Medical Journal of Australia*, 1945; 2: pp. 229–34.

——— The Psychological Reactions of Soldiers', Lecture II, *Medical Journal of Australia*, 1945; 2: pp. 261–9.

Steward, H. D., *Recollections of a Regimental Medical Officer*, Melbourne University Press, Melbourne, 1983.

Stouffer, S. A. and others, *The American Soldier: Combat and its Aftermath*, Princeton University Press, Princeton, 1949.

Troup, G. R., 'The Medical Examination of Army Recruits', *Medical Journal of Australia*, 1941; 2: pp. 110–11.

Uren, Malcolm, *1,000 Men at War: The Story of the 2/16th Battalion, A.I.F.*, John Burridge, Swanbourne, 1988.

Various authors, *Jungle Warfare: With the Australian Army in the South-West Pacific*, Australian War Memorial, Canberra, 1944.

Walker, Allan S., *Clinical Problems of War*, Australian War Memorial, Canberra, 1956.

——— *Middle East and Far East*, Australian War Memorial, Canberra, 1956.

——— *The Island Campaigns*, Australian War Memorial, Canberra, 1957.

Wall, Don, *Singapore and Beyond: The Story of the Men of the 2/20 Battalion*, 2/20 Battalion Association, Netley, 1985.

Walshe, J. P., *Splinter's Story: '... and we were young'*, Literary Productions, Sydney, 1989

Ward, Russel, *The Australian Legend*, Oxford University Press, Melbourne, 1965.

Watson, Peter, *War on the Mind: The Military Uses and Abuses of Psychology*, Penguin, Harmondsworth, 1980.

Wick, S., *Purple Over Green: The History of the 2/2 Australian Infantry Battalion*, Printcraft Press, Brookvale, 1977.

Wigmore, Lionel, *The Japanese Thrust*, Australian War Memorial, Canberra, 1957.

Wilmot, Chester, *Tobruk 1941*, Angus and Robertson, Sydney, 1945.

Yeates, J. D. and Loh, W. G. (eds.), *Red Platypus: A Record of the Achievements of the 24th Australian Infantry Brigade Ninth Australian Division 1940–45*, Imperial Printing, Perth, 1946.

Youngman, N. V., 'The Psychiatric Examination of Recruits', *Medical Journal of Australia*, 1942; 1: pp. 283–7.

Index

absence without leave, 144, 148–9, 151, 154–5, 158, *see also* desertion
accommodation, front-line, 12, 66, 172–3, 194
adapting to danger, 66–9
Adeney, H. W., 12, 214 n4, 230 n33, 232 n19
A.I.F., *see* Australian Imperial Force
aircraft
    enemy, 20, 29–30, 33, 64, 68, 136, *see also* Crete; Greece; Malaya; Tobruk
    friendly, 30, 113, 122
Aitape-Wewak, 15, 20, 53, 113, 174, 204, 209, 210
    attitudes to campaign, 62, 184
    publicity, lack of, 174, 180, 187
alcohol, 64–6, 133, 161, 162, 193, 222 n9
    officers and, 138, 139
Aldridge, R., 24, 25
Allen, A. S., 123
Allen, E. G., 219 n3
Ambon, 93, 94, 208
ambush, 35, 136
American forces, 86, 114, 128, 135, 191, 208
    contrasting late war approach, 94, 209
    desertion, 55
    died of wounds rate, 120, 227 n43
    leadership in battle, 72
    patriotism, 75
    psychiatric casualties, 51, 54, 219 n9

shipping shortages and, 113
superior equipment, 114, 116
unit loyalty, 80, 82
'A.M.F.', *see* 'Australian Military Forces'
animal metaphors, 8, 39, 92–3
Anson, R. J., 65, 216 n16, 219 n50
anti-aircraft units, 201, 203
anti-tank rifles, 8, 115, 203
anti-tank units, 33, 202, 203, 208, 235 n3
Anzac tradition, 75–8, 187, 206
armoured units, 201, *see also* tanks
arms and services, 201, 232 n33
Armstrong, A., 33, 98, 215 n33
Armstrong, J. F., 219 n47, 225 n8
artillery, 232 n33
    25-pounder guns, 111, 115–6
    dangers to, 33
    enemy fire, 20, 26, 30–3, 58, 217 n6
    friendly fire, 33
    organization, 201, 202
atrocities, 39
attacking, 42, 93–4
    in the desert, 34
Australia, 113, 124–30, 145, 159, 176, 197
    threat to, 39, 72–5, 111, 177–8, 179
    see also patriotism; civilians and civilian life
Australian army, 57, 101–3, 105, 197–8
    infantry battalions, 81, 180, 235 n4, (2/1st) 7, 14, 172, 205, (2/2nd) 14, 27,

252

Sepik River, 209
sex, 158
Sfakia, 13
'shell shock', 31, 52, *see also* 'fear state'
Shillaker, R. S., 231 n47
signallers, 45, 201, 203–4
Simpson, N. W., 188
Singapore, 11, 13, 14, 37, 69, 73, 80, 121, 122, 123, 174, 201, 208
    reinforcements to, 107, 169, 171
Slater's Knoll, 44
sleep, 11–12, 14, 66
Smith, R., 235 n14
smoking, 63–4, 123, 136–7, 161, 169
Spindler, H. P., 18, 34, 72, 215 n7, 220 n26, 228 n5, 234 n80
sport, 125
Steward, H. D., 56, 161, 192
Stoner, J. R., 29, 71, 235 n11
stretcher bearers, 120
strikes, 61, 127, 147
submachine guns, 110, 111, 113–14, 116, 202, 226 n20, *see also* Owen gun
Sunley, H. C., 24, 218 n30, 225 n15, 228 n19
supplying the front, 137
surrender, 11, 38, 208
Syria, 4, 10, 11, 20, 23, 32, 42, 100, 110, 131, 156, 173, 174, 204, 207, 223 n24

tactics, 93–4
tanks, 33–4, 44, 115, 206, 208, *see also* armoured units
Tarakan, 159, 187, 204, 210
tax evasion, 133
Taylor, W. D., 171
tea, 66
Tel el Eisa, 71, 207
theft, 132–3, 145–6, 148, 154, 182
Thomas, H., 215 n41
Timor, 93, 208, 236 n10
tobacco, *see* smoking
Tobruk, 9, 12, 15, 23, 24, 28, 53, 56, 64, 74, 81, 93, 96, 101, 106, 109, 110, 115, 120, 125, 127, 132, 133, 140, 150, 173, 174, 175, 182, 193, 201, 204, 207
    Australian assault, 3, 42, 65, 206, 222 n9, 223 n24

enemy air attacks, 24, 29, 30, 68, 153
enemy artillery, 31–2
fear at, 19, 30, 50
food in, 13, 132
patrolling, 42, 110
psychiatric casualties in, 49, 50, 51, 52, 53, 220 n12
reinforcements to, 107, 168–9
relationships within garrison, 131, 173
relaxation in, 159, 161, 162
relief from, 21–2, 67, 85
Salient, 32, 53, 69, 207
stressful waiting, 43, 63
'Tobruk happy', 168
Tommasi, V. C., 36
Torricellis, 9, 113, 210
training, 34, 91–2, 169
    boredom and, 68, 99, 100
    discipline and, 147, 151, 155
    equipment for, 108, 109, 110
    'hard', 67–8, 78
    of officers, 141, 142
    see also jungle warfare
transport, 138, 203, 204
    shortages, 98, 110, 113, 226 n21
travel, 198
Travers, W. H., 223 n26

Ulrick, A. J., 229 n2, 229 n4, 232 n41
unfriendliness
    individual, 167–8
    other units, 172–6
    to reinforcements, 168–70, 172, 180
    Australian Imperial Force *vs* Citizen Military Forces, 177–92
    see also Australian Imperial Force; Citizen Military Forces
units, 80, 170
    formations and, 236 n
    good relations between, 175–7
    loyalty to, 78–82, 88, 172–6, *see also* esprit de corps
    organization of, 78, 86, 202–6
    rivalry, 81, 172–7
    tradition, 76, 223 n42, 224 n48, 234 n90
    see also families
U.R.T.I., 105
U.S.S.R., 139